Universal UX Design

Universal UX Design

Building Multicultural User Experience

Alberto Ferreira

AMSTERDAM • BOSTON • HEIDELBERG • LONDON
NEW YORK • OXFORD • PARIS • SAN DIEGO
SAN FRANCISCO • SINGAPORE • SYDNEY • TOKYO

Morgan Kaufmann is an imprint of Elsevier

Morgan Kaufmann is an imprint of Elsevier
50 Hampshire Street, 5th Floor, Cambridge, MA 02139, United States

British Library Cataloguing-in-Publication Data
A catalogue record for this book is available from the British Library

Library of Congress Cataloging-in-Publication Data
A catalog record for this book is available from the Library of Congress

ISBN: 978-0-12-802407-2

For Information on all Morgan Kaufmann publications
visit our website at https://www.elsevier.com

Working together
to grow libraries in
developing countries

www.elsevier.com • www.bookaid.org

Publisher: Todd Green
Acquisition Editor: Todd Green
Editorial Project Manager: Anna Valutkevich
Production Project Manager: Priya Kumaraguruparan
Designer: Mark Rogers

Typeset by MPS Limited, Chennai, India

Dedicated to those who make every day bearable and are living role models to me.

To Lucy, for showing me what love is.

To my father, for showing me the limits of (im)possibility.

To my brother, for personifying passion and resilience.

And to my mother, for the deepest devotion and compassion.

Contents

PART I • Grey Matter

PART II • Magnum Impulse

PART III • About Face

About the Author

Alberto Ferreira is an UX researcher and consultant with a past background in linguistics, localization, and communication technology. He has a degree in Modern Languages and Literatures, an M.A. in Cultural Studies. He worked for both public institutions like the European Commission and before turning his attention to web design, customer experience, and service design. He has developed internationalization strategies, usability testing frameworks, and process optimization techniques in some of the biggest companies in the world. He is finishing his PhD on interdisciplinary research at the University of Bristol and is a regular speaker and coach at UX and localization conferences.

Introduction

Design is the language of contemporary sustainable problem-solving. While we are able to solve the challenges that the natural world poses to us by creating ways to subvert or eliminate aspects that may be inconvenient to our rise as the dominant species on this planet. We managed it through the wiles of our intellect, and with it we stuck with what worked. Steel and swords, pen and paper, gears and machines: all of them are predicated on the eternal cycle of finding the best possible solution, applying it, improving it, and abandoning it once the next best thing comes up. Within the realm of human experience, thought and engagement, depend on the specificity of interaction and interpretation. Culture, as a socially enforced system of signs and meanings, inevitably conditions us to specific practices that shape our interpretation of the world, as well as the way we design solutions for others. In particular, the technological mediation offered by human–computer interaction prompts the specialization of interaction models determined by specific user interaction models, as well as the culturally informed expectations[1] that follow these. The conceptual categories used in Western media and communication are transferrable onto other cultural contexts, but the way that these are used and interpreted differs.

The role of culture in interactionhas been debated and discussed in different quadrants and largely has been relegated to a secondary role in HCI research in recent years, after a swell of interest in the late 1990s and early 2000s. This is partly due to the haziness of the monolithic and hard-to-grasp concept of culture, which is hard to quantify and standardize in a world with so many streams of communication and contamination between nations. This book treats cross-cultural research and design as an inclusive practice, and rather than defining culture, I will be focusing much more on the differing practices and preferences of local groups rather than adopting a prescriptive approach to design. This is more akin to a practice of universal design where rather than designing for all at once, design should address the needs of the few, delivering solutions and optimizations that match the actual requirements of these groups. In literature regarding human–computer interaction, it is often

---

[1] Cultural differences need to be accounted for when refactoring graphics and, most especially, when adapting text. For instance, while headings are often the primary focus of interest for most European countries and the USA, an element's context and background perception are much more important for Japanese. Several eye-tracking studies have shown that the typical user follows an 'F' path while browsing pages for information.

assumed that universal design and cognitive perception factors are culturally neutral, and therefore can be successfully replicated between different cultures. A design which may appear visually appealing or even desirable in Germany can be applied and used appealingly by Arabic users. Apart from the issues pertaining to web acculturation, discourse dominance, and colonialist voices that effectively condition the perception of *good* aesthetics in the target cultures, the impact of culture on web interpretation and navigation is wider than simply providing a functional canvas for the user to exercise its tasks. Rather than mere design templates, a user interface with the right semantic content can produce a measurable impact on the user in both task performance and emotional perception, depending on its background and context.

This area of user experience does not have a fixed name, with some baptizing it as "cultural UX" or "localized UX". The reason for the "universal UX" present in this book's title is to point out the need for personalization. When there is a single theme of "user experience for all", the need to bring the area closer to the more remote audiences and designers at the outer rim of Western influence is more essential than ever. Ignoring these groups implies missing on an audience of billions, and the rich diversity that is at the heart of each of these groups. Globalizing user experience implies user research and deep market knowledge in order to inform design accurately. Localization is the additional process of achieving a proper local version of a website, is understood as the process of adapting and transcreating primarily linguistic content into a target language and culture. In the localization industry, the process is often understood as the simpler product of translation, which aims at producing a text equivalent of the original source. Often, this source is in English, and as any language, it already carries its own set of cultural markers and linguistic expectations. Content submitted to a process of adaptation already carries a semiotic weight that cannot be easily shrugged off. Analyzing the specificities of the human perception and intellect in a cultural framework in the context of digital interaction is the main purpose of this book, and the importance of the case studies and techniques showcased within is connected to the awareness of the need to include diversity and variability, both individual and social.

I would like to thank all of the contributors and collaborators that made this book possible: Paige Williams* at Microsoft, Aurélien Rigart and the good folks at IT Consultis in Shanghai, Dr Masaaki Kurosu, Tetsuzo Nakamura, Sergio Nouvel of Continuum, Alvaro Susena, Stefanie Kegel and Jennifer Moss at The Geekettez, Giovanni Moraja, Saravjit Rihal, Paulette Comrie, Radu Marcoci, Stefan Bittner, Lindsay Jernigan, Jacob Creech, Juan Pablo Manson, Pablo @ Celerative, Santiago Bustelo, Tommaso Martucci, Lorenzo Franchini, Melina Alves, everybody at MING Labs, and Denny Huang and the user researchers at Tang Consulting. Special thanks to the Moyse family for being who they are. Apologies to any who are not included, and rest assured your contribution is valued beyond words.

PART I
Grey Matter

CHAPTER 1

Are You Experienced?

ABSTRACT

Is technology universal? This is the question at the core of this book, and the reason behind its inception is mainly related to our perception of technological artifacts and the way our lives have become symbiotic with these. In a world where McDonalds is readily found in any major African city, and iPhones are available in China without any major design changes, does it make sense to talk about cultural specialization and the context in which it occurs?
Can technology be designed in a way that usability and appeal are universally appealing?

Keywords: Technology; user experience; user interface; market; audience; design; research

1.1 DIGITAL TO HUMAN EXPERIENCE

Is technology universal? This is the question at the core of this book, and the reason behind its inception is mainly related to our perception of technological artifacts. In a world where McDonalds is readily found in any major African city, and iPhones are available in China without any major design changes, does it make sense to talk about cultural specialization and the context in which it occurs?

Design, in all of its forms, is at the core of human experience. It drives our advancements as a species. We would not have contemporary mobile phones without the technology behind televisions, and we would not have television without the invention of the antenna. We are on a multithreaded path of complexity, paving it as we move forward technologically and socially (Fig. 1.1.1).

FIGURE 1.1.1
Technology is ubiquitous, cross-cultural, and cross-generational.

As a civilization, we are more interdependent and self-aware than ever before. The complexities of the world economy and the realities of a globalized market ensure that almost every single one of our products and artefacts is part of a value chain that can span dozens of countries worldwide. Although a MacBook may be primarily designed in California, it is assembled in China, with parts sourced from all over the world. Most products are inherently international and this renders them as much a product of full-blown globalization in terms of supply chain and production requirements as a result of the commercial and cultural crossroads that date back to our own inception as a species.

It is important that we consider technology as a "fully cultural process, soaked through with social meaning that only makes sense in the context of familiar kinds of behavior" (Ross, 1991, p. 3). In other words, the only way to consider the variability and variety of design is to study and analyze it according to the variety of individual contexts where technology is used and designed.

The day of the steam-powered, ash-spewing, gear-cranking machine is long gone. Ever since the dawn of the digital age, equipment has progressively become networked, embedded, and miniaturized. Technology is literally everywhere. And it can deliver us any information from any point in the world in a heartbeat.

Yet there are commonalities in human experience that surpass the technological upheaval. We experience the world around us using largely similar cognitive structures. Our brains make use of similar sub-structures when acquiring and processing information, including what we see and feel. The shirt we wear, the air temperature, the subtle pressure of a seat against the body, a television blaring in the background, the screaming neighbors next door: these are all simultaneous peripheral stimuli that may be taking place at the moment, but we are seldom mindful of them, as our selective attention steers away from it (James, 1890). But one vibration from our mobile phone, in our pocket, and our awareness is immediately redirected.

The concept of experience is hotly debated amongst philosophers and cognitive scientists (Combs and Snygg, 1959; McDowell, 1994), and deals with complex issues of subjectivity and interaction with reality. It has passed into popular wisdom that experience differs between people. For example, two people can look at the same beer ad and focus on very different things: its mixed message, perhaps, or the famous actor employed. And both would be right. There is no right or wrong about a sensation or perception, and no prescriptive way to judge it but intrinsically. Anybody can describe what a color or smell means for him or her, but this is not held as a scientific account of the stimuli itself. For instance, the perception of colors is inherently different between individuals (Hardin, 1989), and deeply linked to cultural practice and perception (Gage, 1993). We are unable to describe red other than with analogies, and it has a completely different meaning depending on your upbringing and personal experiences. Red is a "quale": a figment of personal experience that can be likened to a "raw feel," or something that is indescribable yet immediately perceived by our senses. Our reality is a compounded mix of qualia, making the way we experience the world deeply personal, yet rooted in the same stimuli. As such, what we see and feel is processed by our own flawed and unique systems in an intrinsically individual and subjective way, making experience a state, transient and immaterial, perennial and inconstant. The impact that a digital designer may have on it is usually of short duration. The world of interaction is one of details and nuances, where the success of the outcome is reflected in a split second when the user makes a decision on whether to install an app, or click on a subscription button.

However, apart from converting website visitors to clients, user experience design is meant to promote an *engaging and usable* experience, and for that it must be *relevant* for the user.

In this complex web of globalization and intertwining economics, technology plays a key role in aligning our experiences. We use similar devices across the globe, from tablets to smartphones, produced by only a handful of international companies, with very similar interaction guidelines and modes. The biggest difference lies in how we experience and use mobile and interactive technology, whether it is for work, entertainment, or even for immediate survival.

A Kenyan user may use his phone to receive SMSs with information on weather changes through the iCow service, while an Indian gamer may be absorbed by the latest edition of the Monster Strike Android game. Both can be using modest devices on a low bandwidth threshold and share their devices with their families on a shared data plan, with each member individually having a preference for different apps and services once online (Fig. 1.1.2).

FIGURE 1.1.2

iCow is a service designed in Africa providing agricultural information to Kenyan farmers. *Source: iCow. Webpage screenshot from http://www.icow.co.ke/*

Local and individual habits and assumptions constitute the basis for cross-cultural design as only understanding these will allow to appropriately design apps and services that respond to the needs and requirements of these users. International user research, as well as the qualitative outlook it provides on the preferences, activities, and goals, is the best means to understand a growing and ever more complex plethora of technology users.

Despite the interest and investment of recent years, that does not imply that all international and minority communities are equally represented in or able to access digital technology. Although the borders are dwindling, the digital divide is still ubiquitous, even in Western economies. In the United Kingdom, one of the most European countries with the highest proportion of adult usage, almost 6 million people reported never having used the Internet in 2015. According to a report by the Office for National Statistics, adults aged 16–24 years consistently show the highest rates of Internet use.

FIGURE 1.1.3

Accessibility is just another component of universal design: inclusive design that allows all to use a service or product.

The situation is much more extreme in Africa, where the average Internet penetration rate is 28.1%, with troubled Eritrea holding the record at 1% and Congo and Niger under 2% (on the other hand, over 60% of the Kenya, Mauritius, and Morocco populations are able to access the Internet, with several other countries boasting access rates of over 50%).

The situation is no different elsewhere in the globe, with over 55 countries in the lowest echelon of the Digital Access Index, which measures the infrastructure, affordability, knowledge and quality, and actual usage of information technology.

This is the actual context of a divided world, and one where technology is ubiquitous, but not universal. Digital services and products are produced on a global scale, but used in contexts that may not always have the best bandwidth, equipment, or technical literacy. This is where universal design, and specifically in the context of user experience, can respond to usability and utilization of web technology.

The definition of "universal design," which lends this book its title, has been most popularized as a field mainly concerned with accessibility issues in buildings and facilities (Goldsmith, 2000; Staines, 2012) (Fig. 1.1.3).

However, it is an intrinsic part of the very concept of "universal design" that it is inclusive and available to all, regardless of their background, age, or ability, and its applicability extends far beyond architecture. It constitutes a social need, one that has alluded to in the academic and political world. One of the most emphatic examples has been proposed by the Council of Europe in a resolution passed in 2001 and again in 2007:

> Universal Design is a strategy which aims to make the design and composition of different environments, products, communication, information technology and services accessible and understandable to, as well as usable by, everyone, to the greatest extent in the most independent and natural manner possible, preferably without the need for adaptation or specialised solutions.

> The aim of Universal Design is to make the built environment, communication, products and services accessible and usable to the greatest extent possible. It promotes a shift towards user-centred design by following a holistic approach and aiming to accommodate the needs of people with disabilities, regardless of any changes they might experience in the course of their lives.

> Consequently, Universal Design is a concept that extends beyond the issues of mere accessibility of buildings for people with disabilities and should become an integrated part of policies and planning in all aspects of society.

The political discourse has charged Universal Design with an institutional meaning and in the process reduced the scope of its application. This book aims at exploding that concept into an inclusive concept, one that brings in culture, research, and design into a single domain.

There are evident barriers in lack of training or low literacy levels that pull users away from the Internet, and these must be addressed in the appropriate context. What this book seeks to address is another aspect of the digital divide, that being the localization and globalization procedures of digital products.

Cultural and linguistic bias can place additional pressure on international Web users, making it harder to use and read information that can otherwise be assimilated easily by people in the same cultural context as the producer. Having software in the appropriate language, and understanding the habits of the users in the area, can play a decisive role in a product's success and overcome key usability issues like specific text input requirements via keyboard or touch layouts.

Design for actual needs is the solution that can answer challenges in the poorest and less well-educated regions of the globe, and it constitutes a boon to overcome the challenge of differing languages and expectations.

The goal of making pages as accessible as possible is not the end of the journey, for, as Tim-Berner Lee stated during the launch of the Web Accessibility Initiative in 1997:

> The power of the Web is in its universality. Access by everyone regardless of disability is an essential aspect.

The grand purpose for universal web design is to design in an inclusive manner, for all in society and, for international businesses, for *all societies*. There is a sea of good intentions, and many open questions about the implications. But as companies are becoming aware of the importance of design thinking, the need to understand the client across all business channels and international marketsgrows. This is allowing designers and researchers from California to Beijing to hone their expertise into a finely crafted symphony of experiences both micro and macro which resonate with the targeted users. Far from a pipe dream, inclusive design is a requirement in a world where all groups have a voice, and all voices demand to be heard.

1.2 REDEFINING LOCALIZATION

> Long human words (the longer the better) were easy, unmistakable, and rarely changed their meanings ... but short words were slippery, unpredictable, changing their meanings without any pattern.
> **Robert A. Heinlein, Stranger in a Strange Land**

As an essential component of human-centered design, UX is often defined as the set of emotional and evaluative perceptions and responses that a user goes through while interacting with a given user interface (UI).

User experience is at the forefront of the emotional link between a digital design and the way somebody interacts with it, with key components being the look and feel, the perceptions and feelings towards the design, and the practicality of achieving the intended goals.

The ISO 9241-210 norm defines UX as "a person's perceptions and responses that result from the use or anticipated use of a product, system or service." Broad in its target, the psychological implications of this definition are nevertheless clear: UX is less a well-defined discipline than the combined sum of the user's emotional response to a specific product. A typical user is not looking for the color scheme details of an app's interface or interested in the harmonious streamlining of the checkout feature in a website: only the full, integrated experience matters. And, for the user, the product is only as good as its experience.

With appropriate metrics and an integrated perspective on product development, UX can help to differentiate a brand and maintain its identity by promoting improved usability and a greater adequacy to the user's actual needs.

A design-oriented company stands a better chance of creating products that are not prone to feature-creep while remaining usable and attractive. As a result, support costs are reduced and customers are more satisfied. As an example, McAfee reported a 90% decrease of support calls after refactoring their UI. After consolidation and establishing proper searching tools geared toward better accessibility, IBM's complex internal information network acceptance improved exponentially.

A lot of Google's and Apple's success is owed to design. Interface minimalism and optimization with only what is required for the user's most common goals constituted the basis for sound success. These principles remained consistent between different locales, thereby maintaining the brand identity, regardless of the target language.

So the main question lies in asking whether localization is a part of the UX paradigm at all. This question actually incorporates two different aspects: Should internationalization be taken into account during the design stage and does localization impact the overall effect of a product's UX?

The answer is, obviously, yes. Text is an essential part of a complete multimedia system that includes image and text. Visually and linguistically, text plays a major role in the user's perception of a product.

The most refined and sophisticated UX can be wrecked by careless localization and haunted by issues and bugs. Fonts are lost, carefully complimentary labels suddenly appear juxtaposed, HTML is improperly adapted to target locales.

Therefore, internationalization is key to a consistent UX in a multilingual product. Internationalization defines the set of processes and techniques that are implicated in making a product capable of adaptation to different cultures. This is where UX implementation is at its trickiest.

No sound internationalization-friendly design can be adequately implemented without an accurate study of localization prioritization. Define which languages and cultures you want to localize into and include both immediate priorities and future plans. This will enable you to optimize layouts for culturally sensitive graphics and indications or—optimally—to change requirements in the light of new market strategies.

It is hard enough to achieve an optimal combination of consistent layout and sound text in any locale. Adapting a carefully laid out interface and its content to other target cultures requires thorough considerations with regards to branding and visual aspect.

A common misconception of localization associates it primarily with translation management of assets that are, to a very fixed degree, already established. However, incorporating localization already during the earliest design stages will lead to websites that are bound to offering a more direct UX.

If a company is not ready for a specific market, there is a number of things that it can do in order to work and establish that market:

- Develop a marketing strategy to appeal to people in the market
- Translate its websites and main services into the local language(s)
- Foster receptivity in the market by cultivating trust and understanding
- Increase appeal and relevance across the cultural boundaries
- Champion the cause by cultivating diversity evangelists in the company
- Unearth precedents in testimonials and case studies

1.3   UNIQUE AND UNIVERSAL

The key to good decision making is not knowledge. It is understanding.
We are swimming in the former. We are desperately lacking in the latter.
Malcolm Gladwell, Blink: The Power of Thinking Without Thinking

Indians are ambitious. Italians love their family. Chinese are great tea drinkers. Stereotypes are easy to fall into and even easier to creep into the assumptions of designers and researchers.

Cultural stereotyping comes in all shapes and forms, often relying on general conceptualizations of human behavior that are in no way exclusive to the group they are supposedly representative of. The word "stereotype" itself derives from the Greek term for "solid impression" and implies a "shared set of beliefs about traits that are characteristic of members of a social category" (Greenwald and Banaji, 1995, p. 14).

Stereotypes are inherently social, and they often refer to known social groups doused with some distinguishing feature: "technophiles," "trend-setters," "hipsters." This influences many of the assumptions interaction designers hold about their target users, and guides many a marketing campaign in the wrong direction. Examples abound, like introducing a Kitchen Entrees food line when you are the biggest toothpaste maker in the world (Colgate) or launching a caffeine-ridden fizzy soda aimed at breakfast lovers (Pepsi A.M) as a coffee replacement (Fig. 1.3.1).

It is essential for corporations to understand the variety of habits and preferences in users worldwide, especially their needs. This will help to avoid imposing their own values, corporate and ethnocentric, in what Theodore Levitt called a "marketing myopia." There is no room for stereotypes in a world where, Africa is the fastest growing market for mobile, 45% of all Facebook users are over the age of 35, and a quarter of all gamers are over 40 years old and 52% are women, according to a 2014 Internet Advertising Bureau UK report.

It is easy to fall into the fallacy of generalization of race, age, gender, and socioeconomic background. UX research plays a decisive role in understanding the specific needs of the users, enabling companies to undermine the possible negative impact of using stereotypes on designing a new product or service.

FIGURE 1.3.1
Gender stereotyping is sometimes used in segmenting users, but assumptions can easily be challenged. Knowing the audience you are catering for involves foregoing any previous restrictive models based on pop wisdom, and instead researching on their actual lives and how your proposition can complement them.

It is vital to aim at specificity and information coherence with valid sourcing and appropriate methodologies.

The success of Apple, Amazon, Google, and Facebook in the west, and Tencent, Alibaba, and Baidu in the east, have come to condition the expectations of billions of users all over the world, encouraging normalization, as the market becomes more streamlined and other companies seek to replicate the success and appeal of these worldwide brands. The design and proposition of these brands weigh on users and designers alike, especially as web templates become easier to use and more prescriptive. However, in order to allow the user experience fulfill its purpose of speaking to the user in an adaptive and appropriate manner, companies that do not rely on global domination must rely on a combination of approaches and methodologies aimed at understanding the local context of the user—and design specifically for that context. Design can be geared towards a normative ideal user, and the reliance on universal principles of accessibility and usability opens avenues of opportunity for equality and awareness, as well as designing for a world that is far more complex than streamlined approaches demand.

As an example, take a look at the nearest tabloid newspaper and leaf through the pages of sexy pop-quizes and scandal of the week reports, to find purchasing the horoscope section. With any luck, today will be a good day for your horoscope: "Expect great changes in your life. Money troubles will arise, but family will help you to gain control of your own destiny." Almost everyone can identify with this.

The general message is positive, but the specifics are nowhere to be seen. How can you prepare for these great changes? How to face this impending financial doom? Should you start looking into bonds, investments, pyramid schemes, or the ancient art(s) of busking?

This approach to generalization is known as the *Barnum effect*, where inclusive appreciations of specific groups are enunciated in generic descriptions that are actually describing the group in such broad swathes that it does characterize the group, but does not define it. In other words, horoscopes are correct by always being fuzzy enough not to be wrong.

These generalizations are easy to identify with, but seldom correspond to a particular time frame: who doesn't experience great changes in their life at one point or another? Who doesn't experience money trouble at one point or another in their life? Yet whenever these predictions fail to become true, we naturally disassociate the outcome from its source: coincidences are overvalued.

And the horoscope page lives to see another day, free of any correlating responsibility.

Similarly, a website design or an app may be designed *well enough* to be functional, but the added value that defines success comes with the *relevance* of the design, where consequence resides:

- Distinct and relevant branding identity imbued in the product,
- Usability accommodates the necessities of the general audience, with varying degrees of literacy and ability,
- Functionality and reliability (e.g., constant availability or "online" status);
- Content should be appealing and concise enough to create a lasting impression on the user.

Users are not given sufficient credit in many cases, especially in projects where usability tests are lacking or user research is deficient. Often they are pandered to with too much or repetitive information, even in the simplest of UIs, or too many features are made available at any one time. This is where the standard principles of user-centered design apply, as every activity and objective of a project aims at developing an appropriate and purposeful experience for the user.

According to the ISO 13407 standard (ISO, 2001), user-centered design includes four iterative design activities, all involving direct user participation:

- understand and specify the context of use, the nature of the users, their goals and tasks, and the environment in which the product will be used;

- specify the user and organizational requirements in terms of effectiveness, efficiency, and satisfaction; and the allocation of function between users and the system;
- produce designs and prototypes of plausible solutions; and
- carry out user-based assessment.

The key to designing for individuals lies, therefore, in accurate research of their abilities, preferences, and where they will use their mobile phones, smart wear, or any interactive device. Using a wealth of universal design techniques discussed later in this book, good design can be made self-explanatory by virtue of its own logic.

Furthermore, users are also quite savvy now that we live in a world where virtually every interaction with an electronic device is mediated through some sort of virtual interface. Smart homes, VR devices, and 3D printing are only some of the newest applications where facility of use is a key part of the generalized adoption.

This is the new democracy of a reality blanketed with a digital layer, brought about by the postindustrial world.

Welcome.

1.4   UNDERSTANDING CULTURE

You can't walk alone. Many have given the illusion but none have really walked alone. man is not made that way. Each man is bedded in his people, their history, their culture, and their values.

Peter Abrahams

Culture is a vague concept in and of itself, and its definition often dangles from the strands of contemporary history and society. As a consequence, there are literally hundreds of definitions of culture, each with its own merit. Already in 1952, Kroeber and Kluckhohn reviewed hundreds of definitions to find no conclusive answers, other than the "culture concept of the anthropologists and sociologists is coming to be regarded as the foundation stone of the social sciences" (p. 9). The emergence of culture thus coincides with the consolidation of anthropology, when the notion of "culture" suggested was heavily marked by then reigning slavery and the progressive stratification of the newly developed capitalist society.

It is hard to escape the dark undertones of the term at its inception. Throughout the 19th century, "culture" was, for a long time, an implicitly racist term associated with the contrast between the allegedly "advanced" nature of the cultivated Western civilization in comparison with the more "primitive" cultures of then newly discovered territories overseas. Even prominent intellectuals like Émile Durkheim (later appointed one of the forefathers of sociology) produced significant bodies of work in the early 20th century devoted to studying the "simple" religions (totemism) and communication of cultures deemed "primitive," like the Aboriginal and Sioux tribes. These societal groups were called "lower" as their values differed from those displayed by the imperialistic Western colonial perspective.

However, gradually, the term "culture" gathered a wider acceptance and came to be applied to all groups equally. Edward Tylor produced perhaps the most widely accepted assertion of culture in 1871: "Culture, or civilization, taken in its broad, ethnographic sense, is that complex whole which includes knowledge, belief, art, morals, law, custom, and any other capabilities and habits acquired by man as a member of society" (2010, p. 1).

The word itself derives from the Latin term *colere*, which can mean anything from cultivation to worship. Cicero had already introduced in common parlance the expression "cultura animi," literally meaning cultivation of the soul.

The word "culture" remained closely linked to education in the Classical sense, however. In 1869 Matthew Arnold published his extremely influential *Culture and Anarchy*, a veritable tome lauding erudition and "the study of perfection" as the ultimate goal of civilized "refinement."

Culture can be seen as a set of common values and goals distinguishing a community and its effect on the individual, but it remains hard to pinpoint and even harder to define in a self-contained manner.

Today, culture is used in various contexts: "corporate culture," "pop culture," "counterculture," "mass culture." The term has been misconstrued and applied; it is about the internal set of values and beliefs of a group, at others, the iconoclastic nature of the larger media ensemble blaring out the latest chart-topping hit (Fig. 1.4.1).

This book will handle culture as a single definition: in broad terms, the combined whole of the roles and beliefs the individual holds and in a larger group or context, and the constraints or influence that this context may have on the individual's beliefs and personal identity.

Most relevant to HCI, culture has been identified as a common system of communication that distinguishes us from other species:

> Culture is a technical term used by anthropologists to refer to a system for creating, sending, storing, and processing information developed by human beings, which differentiates them from other life forms.
>
> **Hall (1990, p. 193)**

The concept of culture is fluid, and it is impossible in modern society to expect a monolithic definition of "monoculture" to serve in an authoritative. More than ever, the world is divided into subtribes and subcultures. It is possible to be "African-Asian-American," or to have parents with Scandinavian roots while still being brought up in Brazil. People in these circumstances, like bilinguals, have a necessarily broader exposure to various different influences on their own tastes and aesthetics, as well as social interaction. Similarly,

FIGURE 1.4.1
The definition of culture is elusive and all-encompassing.

traditional cultures in emerging markets are being exposed to Western and Asian paradigms, particularly in technology acceptance. One example is the powerful role played by Chinese companies like Huawei and ZTE in over 30 African countries, where telecommunications equipment and infrastructures are largely owned and financed by the Chinese behemoths. These companies also lobby actively with local governments strapped for cash and have, as of 2015, established over six regional training centers in South Africa, Nigeria, Kenya, Egypt, Tunisia, and Angola. As a result, thousands of young African professionals trained by these Chinese companies have already entered the job market with an acutely different awareness of the world power balance and the international market as a whole.

The complexities of a wide world based on freedom of movement and trade cannot be ignored, and culture as a set of values is necessarily fluid and dynamic. Anyone who visits their local Chinatown can attest to that fact. Diasporas and ex-pat communities often keep their own habits and world-views, but it has been shown (Lee et al., 2007) that diasporas can be open to intergroup cooperation and thus the "us versus them" instinct that is sometimes quick to arise in more problematic sociopolitical contexts.

Like currents in the ocean, then, there is not only one culture or concept of culture, but many working together and influencing each other simultaneously. However, culture as a more straightforward geopolitical concept is still a useful marker, in particular for international marketing and research. By considering regional areas, and taking into account the local economy necessities, education, and overall technological index, it is possible to assess and identify preferences and biases in the overall processes of communication, representation, and interpretation of users.

We can therefore still assess differences between typically aesthetic choices such as color, pictures, and typesetting and identify larger tendencies informed by the cultural background of designers and the reception by intended audience.

In a broader sense, culture can be interpreted as what defines the "human" character of mankind, equating it with a learned method of processing reality, and relating between individuals.

Culture is the history of permanence, of what sticks between generations, of preservation, providing us a toolkit for our strategies of action (Swidler, 1986). In a world of consumerism run amok, that principle tends to be deemphasized. However, culture is more present than ever in the *vox populi*, in the political cleavages between nominal cardinal points: West, Middle-East, Far-East. In an increasingly divided world, technology and design are the common thread that unifies these poles of human endeavor. Designing appropriately for these hidden worlds is the next necessary step in the journey to overcome ethnocentrism. That is, the need to see beyond ourselves, our politics and values, and into the essence of design: solving problems and avoiding difficulties for fellow humans.

1.5   SPINDRIFTS AND UNDERTOWS

All the diversity, all the charm, and all the beauty of life are made up of light and shade.

Leo Tolstoy, Anna Karenina

Smog-covered skyscrapers peer ghostly in the morning light of Shanghai. The mega-metropolis rises early, and the sweaty masses find their way into cramped offices. UX is still an early practice, but China has shown its remarkable adaptability with the adoption of Western technology and methodology, combined with the power of a highly educated worker class. The gigantic economy manages to sustain its growth even when economies worldwide take a downturn (Fig. 1.5.1).

"It is still a bit like the Wild West," says Aurélien Rigart, as we chat over a sturdy French brandy. "Companies are quick to rise and equally quick to fall, but there is plenty of room for quality. Digital China is evolving at the speed of light, much more quickly than in the West."

FIGURE 1.5.1
China is at a technological and cultural crossroads as its tech power rises in the mobile and web markets.

China is often seen as an unstoppable world power on the rise, but its journey to a landmark economy only started relatively recently. In late 1978 economic reforms were introduced to reform its economy, steering it closer to a capitalistic model with the government loosening its restrictions. Since these reforms, the growth rate has reached a solid 10% since the 1980s, only recently slowing down. This led to a number of social changes, with the newly available disposable income allowing a new middle-class to rise, and pushed the traditional economy to a new height of production and consumerism.

The rise was meteoric. In 2015 it took the title of the biggest mobile economy on Earth, with over 1.28 billion users registered as of February 2016, according to a Statista report. However, China is still undergoing a major telecommunications improvement and its potential has not been exhausted yet. China's penetration rate in mobile and web technology exceeds that of the United States or Europe, sporting the most profitable e-commerce revenue in the world (over 580 billion dollars in 2015, almost 50% more than the United States in 2015) and a very young user base: 55% of its users are under the age of 29 years. "This is just the result of an exponential boom that has been taking place over the past couple of years," concludes Aurélien with a wave over the shimmering skyline.

Over the last century, China continuously walked the tightrope between its lengthy history and strong identity, and the technological influence of the West. Baidu is an example of this dynamic. Arguably the most popular search engine in China with almost 80% of the search market according to Expanded Ramblings, it was established in 2000 by Robin Li and Eric Xu, then recently returned to China after stints studying in the United States. Both men brought home the knowledge and know-how of website indexing and crawling, but their biggest prize was another: how to compete with Silicon Valley on its own terms. Bringingan extremely competitive approach to the corporate development *ethos*, and enjoying the benefits of a protectionist economy, Baidu went on to become the prime player in the market, while the behemoth Google met with increasingly frustrating resistance and political tension in its efforts to enter the Chinese market.

This is a sign of the balance between the world economies and the influence it holds over web design. Thanks to its particularly strong economy and inexorable rise to become a world super-power, China, like Japan and the USA, benefit from a privileged economic position that sees them sponsor a qualified web development and UX force directly aimed at a growing and substantial internal market.

In the global confluence, web design aimed at the same country in which it is produced has a privileged position in catering for a domestic audience, eager for new products, but with familiar preferences and tastes. UX and web design for internal consumption is very different from that produced for international audiences. Despite the constraints of web and device standards, domestic UX has a greater possibility of developing its own quirks and unique identity, like in the case of Japan.

Latin America is on the Rise as a Mobile Market

Smartphone users and penetration in Latin America, by country, 2014–19 (millions and % of mobile phone users)

	2014	2015	2016	2017	2018	2019
Smartphone users (millions)						
Brazil	39.7	49.1	57.8	65.8	72.5	77.6
Mexico	31.3	38.5	45.2	51.7	57.9	62.4
Colombia	14.4	16.7	19.0	20.9	22.6	24.3
Argentina	11.0	13.3	15.5	16.9	18.3	19.8
Chile	6.3	7.1	7.9	8.7	9.3	9.8
Peru	5.1	6.2	7.3	8.3	9.3	10.1
Other	19.8	25.0	29.7	34.0	38.1	41.5
Latin America	127.6	155.9	182.4	206.3	228.0	245.6
Smartphone user penetration (% of mobile phone users)						
Chile	49.7	55.5	60.9	65.7	69.7	72.8
Colombia	45.3	51.4	57.4	62.1	66.0	69.7
Mexico	40.1	47.4	54.1	60.4	66.2	70.0
Argentina	36.7	43.5	49.3	53.0	56.7	60.2
Brazil	31.3	37.6	43.3	48.2	52.0	54.8
Peru	28.7	33.5	38.2	42.5	46.5	49.7
Other	22.4	27.6	32.0	35.9	39.5	42.3
Latin America	33.1	39.3	44.9	49.7	53.9	57.0

Note: Individuals of any age who own at least one smartphone and use the smartphone(s) at least once per month.
Source: Used with permission from eMarketer.com

Portrayal of LatAm UX scene

There are other markets where web design is thriving, but for different reasons. Central and South America in particular have been experiencing a boom in the past decade. In a 2015 report, eMarketer predicted that over 245 million people in Latin America would own a smartphone by 2019, a significant increase from the estimated figure of 155 million in 2015. The biggest markets are arguably Argentina, Brazil, Chile, Colombia, Mexico and Peru—which hold over 84% of smartphone users in the region.

This yields the potential for a qualified young slew of web professionals local design companies are quick to snap up: "[Companies] are not competing for clients, they're competing for talent," stated Ricardo Arce, a local entrepreneur, in a presentation concerning the burgeoning web scene in Costa Rica (YouTube, 2011).

Much of the design work developed in the region is for US businesses "near-shoring" work to LatAm design companies. "Near-shoring" is the practice of offshoring to a nearby country or location, and it has become one of the big drivers of the Latin American tech scene. Central and South-American design teams are often tasked with developing the front- and back-ends of apps and websites to be marketed in the United States (Fig. 1.5.2).

However, the strategic bearings of UX design can sometimes be more difficult to implement. The distance between the company and the outsourced company often places user research and understanding at the managerial decision-making level and away from LatAm teams. Sergio Nouvel, partner of the UX and development studio Continuum, present in the US, Chile and Peru, has an insider's perspective:

> UX as a guided process which involves managing stakeholders and interviewing/testing users requires physical presence. In fact, many American clients off-shoring their design work to high-end LatAm companies require the team's willingness to travel to the US and a good level of English fluency. That is probably what end up driving off-shoring efforts to tasks that are easier to accomplish remotely, such as front-end, branding or visual design work. In that sense, LatAm offers no shortage of talent at competitive costs. On the other hand, there are many American clients that offshore their app or website design to LatAm in the hopes of saving some bucks. If that's the case, a client looking for savings in their UX work may indicate an immature or underfinanced project, or a lack of willingness to invest in a full-fledged UX consultancy.

However, while the technical work is often easy to handover due to its standardization, it is usually harder to ensure cultural consistency in design and marketing work without the proper cultural sensibility:

> The cultural gap that UX research firms sometimes fail to bridge may occur both ways. For instance, one of our top Peruvian clients worked

with IDEO before working with Continuum, and one of their main complaints was that, despite the high quality work, the American consultants were not able to capture the subtleties of Peruvian culture and decided to prioritize local consultants for future projects.

And conversely, some multinational US-based firms have recurred to us in the hopes to better meet the needs of their Latin American customers or help localize or tropicalize global solutions.

For mature multinational companies requiring a deep understanding of their client, local knowledge of their market is essential, and this often can only be provided by an assured team on the field that is sensitive to these issues. Doing otherwise risks compromising the entire brand relationship with the customer with an experience that can be offensive, innappropriate, aloof — or, at the very least, boring.

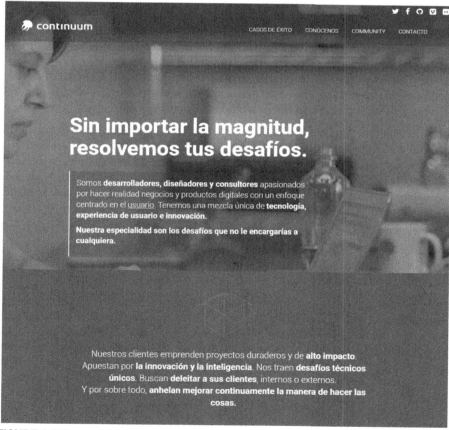

FIGURE 1.5.2

Continuum is one of the Latin American UX and development firms making inroads with the American market.

1.6   THE AUDIENCE IS NOT LISTENING

> It is a profoundly erroneous truism, repeated by all copy-books and by eminent people when they are making speeches, that we should cultivate the habit of thinking of what we are doing. The precise opposite is the case. Civilization advances by extending the number of important operations which we can perform without thinking about them.
>
> **Alfred North Whitehead**

Snap decisions are a primer of modern life. We swim in an ocean of consumerist possibilities, always reachable with minimal effort. Cheapest bar? Yelp it. New tablet? Amazon it. It's late and raining? Uber it.

These choices and the material abundance that comes with living in affluent societies is a direct consequence of the exponential diversification of production means that we as a civilization have attained.

The evolution of technological artifacts in civilization tended to be closely linked to our ability to manipulate and transform our environment. Information technology in particular has been associated with the evolution of applied technology. Since cave paintings and written signs on sand, information has been passed through the molding of materials combined with a symbolic language. Now, the passage of information through external materials relies on the reception as much as the production.

The variety of the choices available around us enables us to live in cultures of minimal effort and maximum reward. So it is little wonder that researchers have found our attention span shorter than the average goldfish. A Microsoft study held in 2015 surveyed over 2000 Canadian participants and analyzed 112 other participants with electroencephalograms, finding that the average attention span was 8 seconds. By comparison, the average attention span length in 2000 was over 12 seconds.

Anecdotal evidence seems to support this idea: authors like Nicholas Carr have argued that the cognitive load imposed by the abundance of stimuli in web design tends to slow down or even impair long-term memory.

Whatever the extent, it is clear that the performance expectation is changing drastically with every computer generation. In the 1980s it was common to take 5 minutes to read a tape onto a game or app that would take only 48 K in a Spectrum. In the 1990s, chaotic 56KB modem sounds served as the other half of the Gen X soundtrack (in addition to grunge), and website navigation was an adventure in and of itself. Only those with significant time and motivation would risk a file download.

The current situation is immensely different. A site's performance plays a huge role in user acceptance, and research shows that users have no patience: European and American users tend to abandon a video-streaming website after *2 seconds* if the video does not start in that period (Krishnan and Sitaraman, 2012).

Users tend to be particularly unforgiving in websites with more text, and evidence suggests that the perceived slowness of a website has a subconscious effect. Harry Shum from Microsoft suggested that a mere 250 milliseconds difference is enough to prompt a user to visit a competitor's webpage if the user is looking for specific concrete information.

Is there a difference in these expectations between different regions of the globe? Given the relative imbalance in terms of communication infrastructure, people tend to expect less responsiveness in countries with poorer infrastructures. The need to analyze the local conditions and adapt the web presence to these conditions is paramount in order to keep your users interested. The immediate reaction does differ between regions and devices.

This difference in infrastructure also highlights the different data necessities in a mobile-first world where connections are unreliable and inconstant (besides slow, depending on the user circumstances). As an example, the worldwide coverage of LTE (long-term evolution) networks is growing exponentially, and is present as of 2016 in most territories, but the domestic signal coverage still varies wildly, as you can attest when that last bar goes missing from your connection strength during a countryside trek. Culture-driven expectations also play a major role in user behavior.

For example, Impulsivity is not a quality that tends to be associated with Chinese culture. Professionally, the Chinese are famous for relying on a measured and somewhat bureaucratic decision-making process, with snap decisions seen as signs of a rash temperament rather than a display of competence. However, according to a China Internet Watch 2016 study, this is not a tendency shared by the Chinese people at large: over 30% of e-commerce users make an impulsive purchase (7 Habits of China Online Shoppers, 2016).

In other markets the dynamic is different and there is a distinct tendency for the social motivation to assume a particularly important role. Social media and word-of-mouth recommendations are key to a product's success in Asia, Africa, and South America. "When friends post something cool on their feed, it gives you a reason to check it out," stated a Bangkok user in a session for an international electronics company. "You always want to be on the cusp of what's new."

"What's new" plays a major role in decision-making. Companies should have a very active role in social media like WeChat if they are to thrive, as the communication playground is levelled and customers expect to interact with services in the same quick, off-the-cuff manner they might chat with their friends. Channels are funneled into the same medium, and user convenience stands only to gain.

1.7 ACCULTURATION AND GLOBALIZATION

As for me, I am tormented with an everlasting itch for things remote.
I love to sail forbidden seas, and land on barbarous coasts.

Herman Melville

America is a country aligned with the definition of "cool." Despite economic upheavals in 1949 and 2008 and its military and political influence in world events, the country has successfully marketed itself as the epitome of "coolness," a myth that Hollywood, music, and merchandising have helped to perpetrate throughout the second half of the 20th century. From denim-wearing gunslingers in the Wild West to the deep space exploration of NASA programs, America poses itself as a land of possibility and risk, where the potential of reward is worth any chance of a crashing failure.

This national character is indelibly related to the positioning of most of its companies, particularly in the digital arena.

The story behind giants like Apple and Microsoft is well documented, but similar garage-to-skyscraper stories apply to companies like Amazon and Salesforce. This sort of emboldening success story has placed the American digital economy firmly on top, with 7 of the 10 biggest IT companies in the world flying the star-spangled banner. However, for every success story, there are 10 failures that remain obscured by history. Despite the famous dictum that 8 in every 10 new businesses fail, according to a 2014 CB Insights report, companies typically die around 20 months after a final financing round, and after raising over $1 million in revenue. The competition for startup funding competition is difficult and the success rate of any new startup in the USA is about 50% in the first year. These numbers are consistent across other markets, although some countries protect new companies, attempting to grow the local economy and develop domestic value. Across Europe, startup hubs benefit from public support, particularly in Germany, Scandinavia, and the Benelux area.

However, outside of the IT industry, and particularly for smaller economies, stories are rougher. This is one of the reasons why many entrepreneurs prefer to franchise, or assume the guise of a branch of an international brand, for their new businesses.

It is a relatively low-risk way to get a small business up and running, and the use of internationally well-known brands acts as a honey-pot attraction for potential customers. It is therefore telling that, among the top 10 largest global franchises, seven are from the United States (7-Eleven, Subway and McDonald's as the top three), and only one is Asian (the Japanese Kumon, specialized in children's education).

Part of the reason for the success of American franchises is the perception of the products, and the powerful branding that companies like KFC and Hertz have come to master.

There is a definite correlation between the country of origin of a product and its perception. Successful prosperous countries enjoy a certain "halo effect" with emerging economies, with their products being branded, for the most part, more attractive than those of poorer countries. Attributes commonly associated with a country tend to be generally transposed to its products. From the German precision of engineering with Volkswagen "Das Auto" to the solidity of Japanese design, cultural expectations and generalization often dictate reception and, ultimately, success. However, what happens when a product is appropriated locally and becomes its own entity? What happens when users adopt foreign habits as if their own?

Part of the answer lies in the quick absorption of habits that a successful service brings to an existing need in a social group, or the role a new international service plays in a market it expands itself to. Social media is a perfect example of the double-edged impact of a digital presence in the local habits.

Research has consistently shown that ethnic social networking plays a positive role in the emotional stability and acculturative stress (the psychological impact of adapting to a new culture) of students and first-generation family members in foreign countries (Oh & Ogawa, 2014). The stress involved with the integration in a new national culture is mitigated by increasing contact with remote families, prompting an increase in video calls and messenger apps communication.

One of the reasons behind this positive effect is simple and universal: people like to use the Internet. Using data collected in the University of Michigan World Wide Survey, which was taken by 35,000 people between 2005 and 2007, Michael Willmott from the British Computer Society managed to successfully trace a correlation between the frequency and intensity of the time spent online, and general psychological indicators of happiness: well-being, awareness, and comfort. The study also found that this effect is especially significant for three groups:

- people with **lower education levels**,
- **women**,
- people in **developing countries**.

This is not a coincidence. Although there is a degree of entertainment to web and device usage that can play a role in these findings, the main thread that weaves these three groups together is altogether different.

Most of the activities that these users carry out online were of a social nature and impled communication with others. The ability to communicate easily with anyone, to have one's voice (figuratively and literally) heard, and the building of an online identity, are all factors of an assertive stance of self that helps to build and solidify a sense of autonomy and independence (Castells, 2007).

Using the Internet is psychologically associated with a sense of freedom, and seemingly constitutes a way to link one's self to the pulse of the world. Several studies have strongly suggested that the Internet reinforces sociability and the desire for communication (Castells, 2007; Rainie & Wellman, 2012), a conclusion that is also featured in the 2012 World Internet Survey.

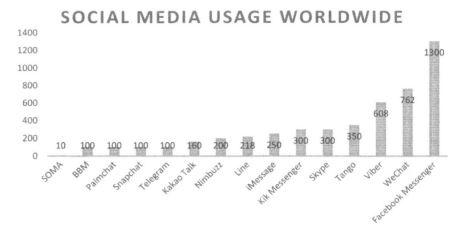

CHAPTER 2
The Universal Totem Pole

ABSTRACT

Technology optimization and miniaturization have successfully broken down most common frontiers to usage: literacy, accessibility, and applicability. The pervasiveness of modern technology has allowed emerging economies to get on the fast track of the latest technological innovations. Technology is the great equalizer and the driver of development. This is at the root of the explosion of mobile in developing nations. There is a changing logic of globalization relationships at work, and the triumph of design as the prime methodology to impart global thought on corporate action.

Keywords: Technology; user; diversification; brand localization; interface; marketing; culture

2.1   METABOLISM OF A DIGITAL PRODUCT

> One minute was enough, Tyler said, a person had to work hard for it, but a minute of perfection was worth the effort. A moment was the most you could ever expect from perfection.
>
> **Chuck Palahniuk, Fight Club**

According to the International Federation of the Phonographic Industry, there was an aggregate of US$6.7 billion in global digital revenue for the music market in 2015. That represents a growth of 10.2% over 2014, with streaming increasing over to represent over 19% of the global industry revenue. Music streaming has constituted a contentious market over the years, overcoming initial doubts and fears of the music companies to become a staple of modern user habits over the world. Spotify, Rdio, Google Play, and other similar services have become ubiquitous in the households of 68 million subscribers

Universal UX Design. DOI: http://dx.doi.org/10.1016/B978-0-12-802407-2.00002-2

that, according to the IFPI, use these services all over the world. Despite the increase in music streaming all over the world, sampling and remixing still constitute legal wildernesses subject to judicial entanglement. Artists from amateur to authoritative require access to common platforms of sharing, however, and licenses like Creative Commons allow creators to share music freely without risk of copyright infraction. Sites like Soundcloud and Freesound allow access to a world of music for open sharing and appropriation by other (re-)creators. And there are a lot of them: over 90% of all artists are undiscovered and unable to capture an audience. Only 0.2% of all artists can be considered "super-stars," according to a 2013 Next Big Sound report.

This is a reflection of how accessible and flexible sound technology has become. There were past premonitory predictions of this evolution, however. In 1624 Francis Bacon depicted the "sound-house" in The New Atlantis as specialized quarters where scientists would manipulate audio at will and "practice and demonstrate all sounds and their generation." In effect, Bacon was anticipating the modern electronic capabilities of the recording studio, where sound can be designed and repurposed at will. Digital audio manipulation is a ubiquitous presence in the modern world, its presence felt in every audio manifestation, from bombastic Hollywood blockbusters to the catchy jingle playing in the local radio station (Fig. 2.1.1).

Compare this level of customization and manipulation to what the average phone or laptop offers: we can generate soundboards from audio recordings, edit photos with Instagram and Snapchat facial recognition, and even enact your own digital paintings with specialized apps. The massive infrastructure

FIGURE 2.1.1
Francis Bacon's "New Atlantis" anticipated the modern university and the rise of the scientific method.

that was to become the "sound-house" now conveniently fits into one hand and is completely flexible to purpose.

Technology optimization and miniaturization have successfully broken down most common frontiers to usage: literacy, accessibility, and applicability. According to the 2014 OECD report on global well being since 1820, the world literacy levels have seen an exponential increase in the past few decades, from 42% in 1960 to 83% in 2010, and the pervasiveness of accessibility and usability has allowed emerging economies to get on the fast track of the latest technological innovations higher rate than the richest markets. This is one of the reasons behind the explosion of mobile as a premier device range in developing nations, and why Uruguay and Kazakhstan, among other smaller economies, were in the top 10 countries with best LTE coverage in 2015.

This is partly not only due to the changing logic of globalization relationships, with the expansion of worldwide commerce facilitating the exchange of goods and services, but also due to the triumph of design as the prime methodology behind innovation (Fig. 2.1.2). According to the World Intellectual Property Organization, the amount of industrial design applications worldwide amounted to over 1 million, with Asia (particularly China and South Korea) at the top of the list, with over 750 thousand design applications in 2013. However, the number of patents filed has dropped considerably since then, suggesting that the emphasis is not on innovative technologies, but rather

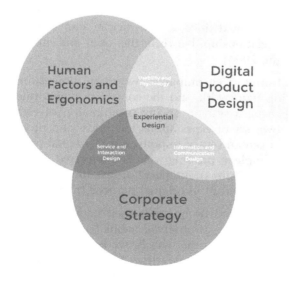

FIGURE 2.1.2

A wilderness of fields: UX design as a cross-section of HCI, service design, and strategy. *Source: From https://venngage.com/templates/. Used with permission from Vengage.*

improving and maintaining the existing ones. Research is expensive and prolonged, and the law of diminishing returns is met with a stabilizing market, which can account for some of this reduction. However, Africa and Latin America have surged in industrial design applications since the early 2000s with 22 thousand patent applications combined, and there is a combined investment effort in technology research, particularly in Brazil, Mexico, and Argentina.

In all of these scientific communities, human–computer interaction occupies a significant role, and the interactive aspect surpasses that of web and app development: industrial and large-scale systems are also implied. However, user experience (UX) crosses many of the key areas in industrial design with other, more specific applications. It is an all-encompassing set of methodologies that absorbs the entire spectrum of user interactions and contexts, including psychology and human factors. UX is largely the art of optimization and maximization, in an attempt to answer the needs and requirements of *how* to interact with technology. UX is largely about the hedonic dimensions in utilitarian use cases, and iterating on design and presentation to make interaction simpler, more gratifying, and focused. UX is seldom used in the context of videogames, and there is a simple reason for it: the term itself is embedded with the instrumentalism inherent to supporting external (or real-world) tasks. One does not "use" a game, so much as play it. Similarly, interfaces and services are not (usually) played, so much as "used".

The relationship between an interface front-end (or, all that is visible and on the surface) and the user is one of status and power. An "user" can be considered an actor, an agent who explores an utilitarian side of the technology. The user is not a creator or an inventor in any known or accepted convention of the term. The "user" is, as defined, a construct: it is an abstraction of an actor and a subjective relationship between the user and the product follows (McCarthy & Wright, 2004).

Usage of a digital product encompasses two main dimensions: the actor, the afforded interaction framework, and the context or ergonomics involved. The actor can be a person, a system, or any combination or escalation of both. They bring their own set of expectations, methods, and processing methods: their actions trigger certain sets of responses in the digital product itself. These actions may be as simple as pressing what is interpreted as a button (arguably the simplest of metaphors in an interface) or installing a new object that alters and expands the product from its original purpose (like updating an app).

These actions are influenced by not only their native intuitive cognitive processes but also the influence of observed habits (cultural influence) and internalized behavior patterns. In other words, we learn that a button is a button in a fairly universal way, as a simple trigger for a desired consequence, but the manifestation of the button is cognitively wider and not linked to our interpretation of it. For instance the user can interpret a button as a text link, a call to action, or even as a visual nuisance, given the ubiquitous nature of banners and other "dark" patterns in modern web design used in betting websites and other persuasive contexts. This contextual interpretation is driven by previous knowledge of what constitutes a button (a push or click-down event), how it can be represented (an actual button with color, shading, or a rectangle, or simply the text label), and its contextual raison d'être (the content, layout, and purpose of this page tell the user that a button should be present). And this alone allows for massive individual variation in the usage of a user interface. The metaphors and esthetic principles that allow us to identify a button as an action are built by context, education, recognition, and cognitive appropriation.

Until the early 2000s, the web was a vast mosaic of choice, which prompted users to visit several websites in order to get the information they needed or were accustomed to receiving. This has since been replaced by networks of content that are deeply linked regardless of the website they are on. Sites like Reddit, Facebook, etc. (a permanent fixture in the top 3 most used websites in nearly every country in the world) perform the indexing of this content, allowing the user to jump between assorted curated content at will on miscellaneous and often random posts. It is easy to spend hours navigating the static of these seemingly mindless posts, which has been interpreted by users by "entrancing".

On a wider scale, there is a "state of flux," carried through onto personable disembodiment, which occurs when a user engages with a user interface. It is the result of the conflict between the combination of an established mental model and set of expectations. When using a user interface, we are interpreting its internal logic, its affordances, and its visual disposition as a model that we need to interpret and our actions are subject to. Our center of decision submits to its model as the user bends to adapt to the kernel of this framework.

Culture bends these dispositions and the values assigned to the interpretation, so if the friction between the act of interpreting and the plan of design is the result of models imposed by the interface and those internalized by the user, as UX attempts to bridge cross the gap between what is expected, what is relevant, and what is efficient.

2.2 UNIVERSAL AND LOCAL DESIGN

I paint mostly from real life. It has to start with that. Real people, real street scenes, behind the curtain scenes, live models, paintings, photographs, staged setups, architecture, grids, graphic design. Whatever it takes to make it work.

Bob Dylan

IKEA is usually identified as a case study in proper acculturation and adaptation to local markets. This is primarily linked to a general quest for simplicity, where content is stripped down to its most basic features. The Swedish company's market strategy is based on broadening the appeal and understandability of its product range by stripping customizable content to its minimum. However, this does not avoid cases like in Thailand, where the product name Jättebra was changed in order to avoid associations with its vulgar counterpart in Thai. In Saudi Arabia this concern translated in radical decisions like removing all female presence in the photos of the local catalog.

The success of the IKEA ethos is also a consequence of changing housing conditions and demand. As many have come to rely on rented housing, the need to express oneself through decoration of a personal domestic space has taken a step back into oblivion. Apartments have become transient spaces, and young professionals (aged 25 to 35) renting furnished houses are restricted in making any changes for the sake of personal decoration. The concept of "home" has changed, along with its traditional association with past memories or nostalgic family gatherings. The urban lifestyle leaves little time or inclination to assert a space of our own.

This is one of the reasons why Ikea enjoys such global success: it represents a limited vocabulary from which to draw from, enabling its buyers to focus strictly on the application of the various furniture elements in their environments.

This is the case with most of the usage scenarios around the world. There is a limited device portfolio available across the world, and the popularity of mobile devices has brought with it a streamlining of available interaction options. Regardless of processing power and screen size, iOS and Android phones constitute most of the global market's choices and preferences with over 95% of installed mobile systems all over the world, according to a 2015 Gartner study. However, the software and webpages designed for international environments often fails to take into account the variety of hardware and specialized use case scenarios a good local version may require. And this is where designing for the world implies knowing the world's users as well.

The uniqueness of the Japanese market demands specifically designed products that take into account Japanese culture and society. Products that take a Western-centric point of view and impose it on Japanese consumers are doomed to failure.

Starbucks is an example of a brand that has successfully transcended its identity and reinvented itself as a temple to "high-end cool" in Japanese cities. With over a thousand stores in the country, SUTABA (a Japanese-friendly adaptation of the iconic brand name) is more expensive and decidedly more Western than other traditional tea houses, but the brand has successfully associated itself with a high-end social status. Its perception as a classy caffeine den for well-off individuals has been aided by the ubiquitous presence of glowing Apple logos at its tables. As in the West, the distinctiveness of a Starbucks store riddled with brand-new silver laptops has become an aspirational image in Japan, with the same bearings of a digital-based lifestyle in a comfy cocoon laced with the aroma of roasted coffee beans (Fig. 2.2.1).

FIGURE 2.2.1
Starbucks is ubiquitous all over the world, but the brand strategy is to customize the establishments to their local reality. A Starbucks store in Shanghai is not an alien body, but a taste of an exotic beverage for tea-loving locals and a welcome place of comfort for foreigners.

The emphasis that the brand places on space and context has cut through the very strategy of the company. Its elements are consistent across its stores and the basic components of the store experience are predictable: a comfortable place to sit, a nice cup of coffee, a welcoming environment. However, the brand has retained its leading position not by settling for the baseline of its business, but by reworking its product offer, with seasonal offerings and a wider variety of beans, thus retaining interest for casual and regular coffee drinkers all year long.

However, these are classic approaches that thousands of coffee haunts, big and small, adopt every day. As a standard suburban cafe or train station hot beverage stall, Starbucks stands for a standardized coffee experience. However, the brand has retained its market leadership not because of its spicy pumpkin latte concoctions, but by becoming the single biggest coffee store design firm in the world. No other detail of the Starbucks coffee experience has been more important in its enduring international success as it has carefully constructed store layout and decoration.

"The moment when you share a cup of coffee with someone is different in different parts of the world", stated Bill Sleeth, Starbucks' VP of Design for the Americas, at the 2014 Specialty Coffee Association of America Symposium. "Our goal was to create store designs with locally relevant design."

From Seattle's 15th Avenue to the Care Center in Beijing, Starbucks has endeavored to turn selected stores into unique design experiences. Daring oak patterns line the ceiling of a historic bank on Rembrandtplein Square in Amsterdam, in a nod to the meaning of the country's name, as the Germanic origin of "Holland" is holtland (wood land). The brand's image is translated into a contextual experience that pushes an eclectic design vocabulary which incorporates the local sensibility. This long-term strategy ultimately aims to personalize the design of every one of their 23,000 stores. Certain key elements of the store experience are to be kept intact (down to the pervasive burned bean smell so common to smaller shops), but Starbucks is developing a business strategy of differentiation by design. This is a threat to smaller and local coffee houses, but the growth of the Starbucks empire is directly related to a general trend: customers welcome the safe bets of familiarity and reliability, while being delighted by the design novelty of the environment. This mass personalization of Starbuck's physical stores is part of a larger trend that also rings true for the digital market. The most widely used websites are not awash with bombastic innovation, but rather subdue their design to content and experience: Facebook, Amazon, YouTube, Reddit. Designing for mass localization on a digital platform on a scale is a fruitless endeavor unless it is correlated with quantitative data: analytics and tracking can help designers and Information Architects in finding the best structure for a site map or flow for transactional websites and customize it to suit the user needs. Like a Starbucks coffee house, make available all that is expected, and have excess trigger surprise, not confusion.

2.3   ERGONOMICS AND STANDARDS

Know the rules well, so you can break them effectively.

Dalai Lama XIV

In the late 1970s, screens were called visual display terminals (or units). The then recent proliferation of screens generated a widespread concern over the effects of prolonged use in the eyesight of the users, particularly for screens with lower image quality. However, studies have reoccurringly shown that the main impact on eyesight comes from aging and working with screens merely makes the users aware of these problems sooner. Nevertheless, there are tangible (pun intended) issues with ergonomics, particularly in an age of touchscreens and gestural interfaces. Natural user interfaces are beginning to overtake the traditional paradigms of keyboard and mouse, and the old metaphors designed at the Xerox PARC research facility, that were later appropriated by Apple and Microsoft.

This has caused a number of standards to emerge, and despite being only partially successful in accommodating for the emerging needs of users, they remain in force:

ISO 9241-3:1992 Ergonomics requirements for work with VDTs: Display Requirements

This standard has been successful in setting a minimum standard for display screens on an industry-wide basis. It focuses on Cathode Ray Tube (CRT) display technology, which is arguably obsolete. Compliance based on a performance test (therefore making it technology-agnostic independent) was approved in the early 2000s. It has since been revised with standard ISO 9241-302:2008, on *Ergonomics of human–system interaction—Part 302: Terminology for electronic visual displays.*

ISO 9241-400:2007 Ergonomics of human–system interaction—Part 400: Principles and requirements for physical input devices.

This standard was slow in redaction, but remains valid as of 2015. It describes generic ergonomic principles and requirements for the design and use of input devices, such as keyboards, mice, and joysticks. It is aimed at exploring the terminology for other parts of the ISO 9241-9 standard and includes several touchscreen and hedonic technology definitions. However, a definitive standard for that technology is still more implicit than openly available.

Over the years, ISO has published a number of standards of interest to digital designers and architects:

Usability and usage: ISO/IEC 9126-1: Software engineering—Product quality—Part 1: Quality model
ISO 20282: Usability of everyday products
ISO/IEC TR 9126-4: Software engineering—Product quality—Part 4: Quality in use metrics
ISO 9241-11: Guidance on usability
ISO TR 18529: Ergonomics of human-system interaction—Human-centred lifecycle process descriptions
Interface and interaction: ISO/IEC TR 9126-2: Software engineering—Product quality—Part 2: External metrics
ISO/IEC TR 9126-3: Software engineering—Product quality—Part 3: Internal metrics
ISO 9241: Ergonomic requirements for office work with visual display terminals. Parts 10-17
ISO 13406: Ergonomic requirements for work with visual displays based on flat panels
ISO/IEC 14754: Pen-based interfaces—Common gestures for text editing with pen-based systems
IEC TR 61997: Guidelines for the user interfaces in multimedia equipment for general purpose use
ISO 11064: Ergonomic design of control centres
ISO 14915: Software ergonomics for multimedia user interfaces
ISO 9241: Ergonomic requirements for office work with visual display terminals. Parts 3–9
ISO/IEC 10741-1: Dialogue interaction— Cursor control for text editing
ISO/IEC 11581: Icon symbols and functions
ISO/IEC 18021: Information technology—User interface for mobile tools
ISO 18789: Ergonomic requirements and measurement techniques for electronic visual displays
Documentation:
ISO/IEC 18019: Guidelines for the design and preparation of software user documentation
ISO/IEC 15910: Software user documentation process
Development process:
ISO 13407: Human-centred design processes for interactive systems
ISO/IEC 14598: Information technology—Evaluation of software products
ISO TR 16982: Usability methods supporting human centred design

Other standards of interest:
ISO 9241-2: Part 2: Guidance on task requirements
ISO 10075-1: Ergonomic principles related to mental workload—General terms and definitions
ISO DTS 16071: Guidance on accessibility for human-computer interfaces

Other standard for touch screen technology have been created in the meantime, including the American National Standards Institute (ANSI) and Human Factors and Ergonomics Society (HFES) 100-2007 standard.

These standards all differ in recommendations. One of the key aspects is button size, which varies significantly between the different expert authorities. ANSI/HFES recommends a button size of at least 9.5 mm with a gap of 3.2 mm, and advises against using button sizes larger than 22 mm.

The ISO 9241-9, on the other hand, recommends a button size similar in size to the breadth of the distal finger joint of a 95th 87 percentile male (which consists of roughly 22−23 mm in diameter). The 1996 Monterey Technologies standard, on the other hand, recommends a button size of 19.05 mm with a 6 mm gap.

These differences in international standards reflect the changing user needs and the rapid pace of hardware change for end-users. Nowadays, people reach, hold, view, and extend their limbs and digits during an interaction, which may involve the full body. The fact that more children and elderly than ever are also using devices entails new concerns about posture and accessibility.

The issue with designing for difference, however, is how much of it there is about it. Human beings are naturally diverse in size, height, fingertip height, elbow measurements, and the natural preference that each individual prefers. An ATM screen to be available to different viewers on the street can be optimized for an adult's average height, but this hardly accommodates for vertically challenged people like dwarf populations and children. Eye height, like other factors in urban and industrial design, is usually designed for the mean, and not the exceptional audiences. This is also a sign of the designer bias, where the design tends to reflect and be adapted to the needs and preferences of the population creating the particular design. This is a fundamental issue of designs that ignore anthropometry (meaning, without specific knowledge of human body measurements) and consequently compromise the importance of the practicality inherent to a product for a universal audience.

According to Molenbroek (1994) and Dirken (1997−2004), this problem translates into eight design types:

1. **Design as Procrustus** The user adapts itself to the product, like the ancient Greek myth of yore about a rogue smith. The expression "Procrustean bed" itself refers to forced conformity with an arbitrary standard.
2. **Ego design** The designer fits his or her own designs to his own size and assumes they will be fine for everyone else.

3. **Design for the mean** Variations in size and height are overridden in favor of designing for the average and minimizing the extremes. Groups outside of the mean are excluded.
4. **Design for the small** The design is made with smaller or weaker populations in mind, but becomes ineffective with the mean user.
5. **Design for the tall** The designer assumes the user is tall and fits the design to that segment of that population.
6. **Design for more types** This is a targeted type of design, taking into account the anthropometrical aspects of a population, and fitting it for a reasonable range within the population (typically from 5% to 95%). This helps to exclude more extreme segments of the population, that would require significant design changes.
7. **Design for adjustability** The user should be able to adjust and adapt the equipment to their need. Although it is more difficult to know what the average limits are, this approach is more akin to the actual purpose of design, which is to enhance by adaptation and suit the users' needs.
8. **Design for All** This is not the same as universal design for everyone, but instead it is an attempt to make a design as inclusive as possible.

2.4 BRAND LOCALIZATION

"I am not an angel", I asserted; "and I will not be one till I die: I will be myself."

Charlotte Brontë (Jane Eyre)

Perrier water is one of the most popular fizzy waters in the world. From shrimp cocktails to creamy lasagne, it accompanied millions of overpriced and filling meals all over the world. Its image was one of class, elegance, and sophistication—much like its advertisement depicting a female hand caressing a growing bottle of Perrier until it exploded (an advertisement which was eventually banned from French TV), the brand aimed at having a glitzy, sexy image. This is why you would never expect it to taste like gasoline. However, in 1989, millions of unhappy fizzy water lovers found out that their meals were not in need of additional seasoning by way of refined petroleum. After a contamination spurt, the company was forced to withdraw billions of bottles from the shelves and face huge costs in compensation. This also sets the scene for an outstanding come back that allowed Perrier water to become one of the top fizzy water bottlers worldwide, with a renewed emphasis in mixology and targeting a younger demographic.

Happy consumers are trusting ones, and even when, like Perrier, a successful brand sees its image tarnished in the face of unexpected hardship, the "halo effect" is maintained. Companies that aim their marketing powers at a broad socio-demographic spectrum deal with perception tarnishing better than others, more niche ones. This is because a brand acts like an affordance, setting the expectations of the customer interaction. A positive character can be defined as the "intangible values created by a badge of reassurance" (Feldwick, 1996, p. 86).

A brand is stronger than nationality or culture. Most companies are multinational enterprises owned by consortiums which often are nationality-agnostic. Nationality is not as evident for the end-user as the perception of its origin and cultural setting. In other words a company is not necessarily European, Japanese, or American, but it can still sell its products as part of a distinctive cultural setting of origin. As an example, for several years, Sony, a Japanese multinational, has owned the movie rights to Spider-Man, an American superhero created by Stan Lee, founder of the all-american Marvel Entertainment media company. Heineken is often considered one of the top beer brands in America and a distinctively German beer, despite the fact the brand is actually Dutch.

With their complex production chain and international distribution systems, companies should be the first to acknowledge the importance of guarding brand perception against typical human bias, particularly when it comes to the sensitive nature of culture. Even when the origin of a brand is imminently local, however, indulging in cultural stereotypes for advertisement seldom works:

> The British bottler of Kirin, a Japanese beer, ran an advertisement of two geisha girls with a slurring samurai crooning this caption: "My karaoke singing used to sound rike fowsand howring banshee but now I sing rike spawo and hafe recod contract with Wonco [after drinking Kirin Beer]."

> We saw nothing offensive about the ad — we thought it was quite funny, actually," said Alasdair Fraser, who worked on the ad for Team Sacchi, a subsidiary of London-based ad giant Sacchi & Sacchi. The spots were pulled after they were criticized by Japanese newspapers, and Kirin executives in Tokyo became enraged. "We wanted to appeal to British lager drinkers," he said. "We thought a Japanese character who spoke the way a Japanese person might speak would be funny — certainly more interesting than putting a beer bottle in front of Mount Fuji.
>
> **(Kline, 2005, p. 158)**

Cultural sensitivity is one of the major factors for ethical advertising, but the real hallmark of a popular brand is its response to the real-world concerns and interests of the local users. This is nowhere more visible than with international markets, where copycatting and appropriation are sometimes commonplace. Brand squatting is a real issue in China, for instance, where Hermès was denied registration of its Chinese company name after a local company successfully managed to register the brand word in 1995. There is a complete segment of industry in Shenzhen devoted to absorbing the best ideas from Kickstarter and developing the products at an accelerated pace before the funding is even finished for the European and American entrepreneurs populating the platform.

In the postmodern globalized world, ownership is diffuse and hard to pin down, particularly in international settings where copyright might mean very little. A brand's ownership is always partly crowd-sourced, as the multitude of appropriations and subversions in advertising, art, and the media show. One

FIGURE 2.4.1

Rarely have bug sprays been celebrated with such musical gusto as "Super Timor." The ad was a phenomenon in Ivory Coast, and was later appropriated for memes in French social media. Like many other content, it had a new lease on life in the social web, where it was assigned new meaning and popularity. The "Super Timor" brand lives on.

example is the tongue-in-cheek advertising of products like Carl's Jr. Most American Thickburger commercials, a brand whose very name borders on self-parody, are designed directly to appeal to the millennial "meta" crowd, one that is aware of the ironies of advertising, yet recognizing the appeal of exaggeration as a distinguishing factor in the face of market saturation. The ads are heavy-handed and bordering on offensiveness, while still avoiding it by being self-aware. This is nothing new even for smaller and emerging markets, however, where a tongue-in-cheek tone is common and even mandatory to command attention. For instance, the 1986 "Super Timor" advert from Ivory Coast became internationally known for its rollicking play on African stereotypes and the trappings of television clichés. Similarly, the song "Gangnam Style" became infamous not only because of its catchy chorus, but also because of its parody of the pretentiousness associated with a neighborhood in South Korea. The local audience did not laugh at these portrayals as much as laughing with them, and their intended message was very different in foreign territories, that valued primarily their viral novelty (Fig. 2.4.1).

Perception changes with distance—physical and cultural. Similarly, brands are localizable and depend on a close relationship with their target markets for their success and intended message to thrive. As a representation of combined values and perceptions, brands depend on the consumers' beliefs to deploy an inherent trust that speaks to the intimate world of the individual. The "Share a Coke" campaign launched by Coca-Cola is a direct translation of this attempt to appeal to the individual by putting the most common names in markets around the world on the soda bottles. The campaign soon went viral (Fig. 2.4.2).

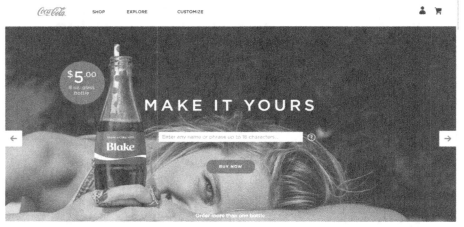

FIGURE 2.4.2

Coca-Cola tried different personalization campaigns over the years but struck gold with the 2011 "Share a Coke" campaign. The simple use of common names in the bottle revitalized the brand in a progressively shaky fizzy drink market. A new typeface called "You" (as in you, the customer) was created for the names, inspired by the Spencerian font of the logo.

What does a brand represent at its core? The term "brand" comes from the original practice of cattle branding, protecting the livestock as private possession against theft. Capitalism has prompted the term "brand" to evolve from this act of possession to a noun depicting identity, a symbol that lives within a cultural continuum and is appropriated by markets around the world. Peter Doyle has defined it as "a name, symbol, design or some combination" thereof, and this is a significant departure from the original implicit meaning of the term.

Consider how a brand may have a specific combination of factors that renders it absolutely unique: as the representation of a certain commercial segment, it has a voice of its own and a unique identity that resonates with the intended target.

Broadly, three frames of reference can be drawn:

- *Corporate positioning*: what is unique and distinct in the user's mind about the brand compared to its competitors;
- *The retailers*: often having as much or more visibility than the brand itself, the retailer partnership should be well considered and weighed, as well as the impact it carries on the consumer's mind;
- *The consumer's perception*: the sum of past experiences, accumulated knowledge from other sources, and the way the brand both presents and communicates itself.

There is one common principle to all of these three aspects. Thanks to the ubiquitous nature of contemporary information, a brand does not exist in a vacuum and is challenged every day by competitors and customers alike. A negative reaction on Twitter or Facebook can easily become a rallying cry for other unsatisfied users. Unresponsiveness tends to be almost as damaging as an uninterested or a cold response.

It is therefore essential to communicate on a small scale, keeping the tone personal yet not invasive. A personalized answer is guaranteed to generate a much more positive image of the brand in the consumer's mind than any form of automated customer support, like a cold "we are working on your problem" message would imply.

A 2011 study by the Umeå School of Business found that the three main dimensions of service quality are "responsiveness," "empathy," and "reliability."

Today's modern world is all about short attention spans and a quickening pace. It is important to be as concrete as possible regarding the wins and advantages of your particular product or service. In an expansive worldwide market, it is more important than ever that the individual feels connected to the general logic of a world that is huge, yet so close and accessible. The world is a village: try to talk to your users as you would to your favorite neighbor.

2.5 EXPECTATIONS AND LOYALTY

> I loved her against reason, against promise, against peace, against hope, against happiness, against all discouragement that could be.
>
> **Charles Dickens (Great Expectations)**

In an age where nearly every single marketing and psychological trick has been used, shock effect speaks louder. When the KFC Double Down was first launched in 2010, it seemed like a joke—and indeed the greasy creation was unveiled to the public as an April Fool's prank. However, the infamous fried chicken sandwich with two pieces of fried chicken serving as buns was an instant hit (Fig. 2.5.1). Other companies like Taco Bell and Jack in the Box followed suit with foods designed to shock and allure. The trend quickly

FIGURE 2.5.1

New Double Down Sandwich. *Source: Used with permission from KFC.*

expanded to other countries, including Japan, where the Kuro Burger, served on black buns tinted with squid ink, met with a rapturous reception.

All these companies were able to introduce new and highly successful product because of their established position in the market, and their deep knowledge of the local market. Kentucky Fried Chicken has been one of the most successfully established fast-food brands in the world and its expansion to other countries reflected its flexible approach to local markets. For example, in China, it has been one of the perennial stop-over joint for Chinese teenagers before an evening out. This comes on the hot steps of a campaign that explored Chinese cultural values and succeeded in growing the brand in the country from a tentative opening in Beijing in 1987 to opening its 1000th restaurant in 2004. Companies like KFC have succeeded in "clothing their brands in local costumes" (Belk, 2000) in order to fulfill a complete "localization of language, product attributes, advertising content, and even product meanings" (Zhou and Hui, 2003). KFC achieved its success not by the quality of the food, which was met with an initial lukewarm reaction, but rather through the entire experience surrounding it: a friendly and efficient staff met customers on clean, well-lit, and flawlessly air-conditioned spaces. Western food has gradually become more acceptable since the early 1990s, and KFC's use of poultry has been seen as more relevant to the Chinese cooking traditions than the heavy beef used in McDonalds. However, KFC's success was achieved by a savvy advertising that played to the different "China markets," which reflected the country's complex diversity of social groups, climate, religion, economic status, and language. Their advertising became more family-oriented, emphasizing social value for large groups (e.g. KFC bucket), as well as the importance of young boys in the family structure (a perspective that has since slowly changed). However, the real appeal of the brand was to design an offer that included locally-influenced dishes like Old Beijing Chicken Rol, as well as typical Chinese breakfast, alongside Western novelty foods like New Orleans Barbeque Wings and Mexican Chicken Warp. The success of a product is heavily influenced by the perception of its country of origin (Nagashima, 1977). Stereotypes play heavily into acceptance: a positive mental model can often determine whether or not a product is not only accepted, but its degree of success. Customers are more forgiving toward successful brands. Strong branding can overcome the individual negative feelings.

This may sound like a contradiction, but there is a specific reason behind how brands can consistently defy their customer's negative perceptions and remain in the game.

The fast food industry is one example of this type of behavior. Fast food has been indicted almost universally for its lack of healthy options, unethical behavior, and low wages toward its workers, and yet yearly results are through the roof.

Part of it is due to advertising which, to a large extent, expects a harmonization of the audience. Top brands spend millions every year to launch massive advertising campaigns that are recognizable from Magadan to Buenos Aires, expressing a unique set of values and beliefs about the brand that supersedes cultural or political borders. However, it is very recognizable in very different ways, with the same products generating different reactions in different contexts.

The end product is only part of the story, and our expectations are everything. These unweighted anticipated impressions are related to who we are and what our experiences were. They are preconscious and relate directly to values. We latch onto the familiar, and there are several values that are universally appealing: order, fraternity, respect, and awareness.

The most successful companies live by well-defined internal principles, but these can sometimes be mysterious even to the most business-savvy executive. Consumers do not seek to align themselves with values that could be excluded from their lives.

This applies to how we see brands as well. A brand is not only a symbol or a representation of values: in its best assertion, it acts as a rallying agent. It is an indirect recruiting platform. Its brick-and-mortar stores are temples. Its logo is an adored icon. Its personality is complex and layered, and it can be anthropomorphized in our thought.

2.6   ASPIRATIONS AND BRAND IDENTITY

Loneliness is the human condition. Cultivate it. The way it tunnels into you allows your soul room to grow. Never expect to outgrow loneliness.

Janet Fitch

One of the reasons for the success of Apple products, though, is their inherently universal appeal. Apple barely changes its product portfolio in different territories, because its overarching principles are simplicity and minimalism: universal qualities that are easily identifiable and marketable. When assuming the reins of a waning Apple in 1997, Steve Jobs excised most of the previous product line to focus only on a few select products, stating that Apple needed to get back to basics: "great products, great marketing, great distribution." Marketing became a core aspect of the company, and with it a new campaign emerged: Think Different, a watershed moment that associated the Apple brand with some of the important and representative thinkers and artists of the past century. This became a hallmark of the company, who successfully leveraged this early success to pave the way for the more daring and innovative products that would follow in the forthcoming years: the iPhone and the iPod, which were a smashing success worldwide.

The Apple iPhone 5C campaign in 2013 recognized the potential of the product in foreign markets and was a clear indicator of the brand's international strategy. The main TV advert displayed a succession of iPhone users engaged in a call, each emitting a greeting or an expression of surprise in various languages. Each caller was of a different age, gender, and race, located in a different part of the world, and in different situations (sailing, waiting on the taxi, in the middle of a yoga class) while making the call. After a canopy of idioms, the ad concludes with the caption "For the Colorful" before introducing the iPhone 5C model, which went on to sell over 35 million units all over the world. Its unique selling point was the light customization allowed with the steel frame–reinforced case color.

Apple's strategy never focused on customization or personalization, but rather aimed at pushing audiences the world over into assigning a different personal meaning to a fully standardized and instantly recognizable range of products. The fact that Apple's prices are uniformly high in every market and its unwillingness to cede control on their devices speak of monopoly but are actually one of the many strategic decisions that allowed them to reach their domineering role in the market.

The company also knows when to assume a more passive role and cede control. In 2015, Apple managed to achieve a total of $59 billion in revenue for China alone not only because of the attractiveness of big sellers iPhone 6S and 6S Plus, but also because of accommodating political requirements, like censorship of the News and Maps apps and using China Telecom servers owned by the state. However, the company also worked hard to establish itself, by signing with the biggest telecommunication provider in the country, China Mobile, and directly tapping into a market of 760 million subscribers. The company also pushed their then biggest phone, the iPhone 6 Plus, for millions who had no television at home and used their phone as a streaming device, a game console, and communication center.

Reliability and flexibility are more important than snazzy design. Companies often run into the mistake of increasing familiarity in their content tone to appear more familiar. But there is more about being more accessible and friendlier to users than to increase the number of exclamation marks in a copy.

Familiar tropes and buddy expressions should be avoided if they are not in line with the audience's expectation. If the customer segmentation shows that there is a significant 40–50 age group accessing the website, would familiarity work better than reassurance?

For some brands, however, the question is not even about content subtleties. Sometimes the user expectations subvert the interpretation of content. Some brands are more "forgivable" than others. Why does this halo effect help to distinguish between a "cool" brand and one that is not?

On his book *Brand Is a Four Letter Word*, Austin McGhie lays out a perception of brand as a combination of positioning and eccentricity, and a construction that requires both work within the company and raising the expectations of the unsuspecting audience. He also reminds companies that a youthful, multisided appeal is not only not always possible, but not even recommended in some cases:

> Cool is ... not an inherently desirable characteristic. Remember that so-called cool brands, while fun to talk and write about, tend to be on the smaller end of the business scale. It's tough to be big and stay cool. There are exceptions, of course. Apple and Nike have certainly managed it, Starbucks still does pretty well for such a well-distributed

brand, and Twitter and Google are still going strong. But no one ever mentions MySpace these days, and Facebook, while still increasing its audience, is losing its edge. At the end of the day, big does not coexist comfortably with cool, so the list really isn't that long. Cool ubiquitous brands are rare. (p. 244)

Larger corporations have a more complex ecosystem and as departments grow and hierarchies become more layered, it is more difficult to remain focused on a single business vision and still appeal to the target audiences with a personalized flair. Apple, Starbucks, and Nike managed to keep their image fresh not by adopting high-street popularity fads as their own, or a portrayal of desperate unconformity. These brands have one thing in common, and that is their insinuation of aspirational appeal, and their aura of social exclusivity.

Few products carry more of a social meaning (or stigma, to some) than an Apple product. It is a representation of status, and it embodies a sense of belonging that is often fiercely defensive. For proof, look no further than an argument between Windows and Mac users, a division that was partially promoted by the company itself with the Get a Mac campaign, which had a string of adverts depicting a PC character as a stuffy bookish-looking nerd awkwardly confronting or attempting to deceive a smart-casual laid-back Mac. The campaign consistently depicted the PC as a system for work and "boring presentations," whereas the Mac was meant to be used for fun, easy communication, and entertainment. These characters were also played by different actors and with different emphasis depending on the country they were played, with John Hodgman as PC and Justin Long as Mac in the US and Robert Webb and David Mitchell in the UK (Fig. 2.6.1).

FIGURE 2.6.1
Windows and Mac side by side, as seen by Apple.

The perception of the product relationship and the community building and positive reinforcement aspects. Richardson (2013) labels community-driven innovation and product support as elements of the tribal following that Apple has successfully rallied around its products: "less [of a] computer, more a statement of creativity, style, and difference from the grey and uninspiring world of the PC" (p. 7). The Apple consumer tribe that populates the trendiest Starbucks coffee houses is a truly global one: a collusion of high-tech style drenched in fair trade beans sourced from South America or Southeast Asia. It is a tribe that feeds off the brand's reputation and nurtures it.

Aspirational brands fit with the millennial crowd. A 2016 study undertaken by GlobeScan found that aspirational consumers make up 40% of potential shoppers. Aspirational are primarily empowered by the search for style and status, rather than focusing on price-quality efficiency or loyalty to a single brand. On the other hand, generational perspectives are easily put into conflict. A 2014 US phone poll revealed that over 60% of Americans considered millennials, aged 18–29, were "entitled" and "selfish" (http://reason.com/poll/2014/08/19/65-of-americans-say-millennials-are-enti). Rather than GenX's navel-gazing, hipster GenerationMe is staring at their digital pin board and endorsing the value of social media communication and the positive effect of supporting movements and companies that improve the state of society, like anti-pesticide petitions and alternative fuel policies—with the power and conviction of an easy, single click, or tap.

However, this European and American reality also finds its way into the wider reality of a worldwide economy. GlobeScan's research also found that aspirational consumers are more prevalent in developing economies: Nigeria (58%), India (53%), China, South Africa (52%), Indonesia (51%), Ghana (49%), Peru (49%), Kenya (44%), and Brazil (42%). The richer economies with the largest groups of aspirational consumers found were: Canada (42%), the United Kingdom, Russia (41%), Greece (40%), Spain (37%), and the United States (36%). The aspirational element of international consumerism serves as a mediation layer between the local reality and a global repertoire of hedonistic images as influenced by Hollywood, advertising, and the full brunt of capitalist institutions, enabling "progress through pleasure" (Mazzarella, 2003, p. 101). This is exemplified by the popularity upswing of fashion and jewelry brands in Southeast Asia and India, resisting economic slumps and consumer fatigue elsewhere in the world.

2.7   DIVERSIFICATION AND COMMUNITIES

Strength lies in differences, not in similarities.

Stephen R. Covey

The impact of brand on multicultural environments is becoming more important and recognized as an independent field of marketer work, but keep in mind that multicultural audiences are not necessarily international. An institution recognition factor can be the result of its importance and recognition within the mainstream. One example of this is the US Marine Corps, which launched in 2013 a campaign with the title *A Warrior's Education* aimed squarely at the Asian communities in the United States. This was part of a wider diversification effort within the army, and it pitched a human angle, showing the testimony of Asian-Americans soldiers in active duty as a way to increase relatability for audiences.

Weaving a story for the audience with identifiable faces is essential to achieving personal identification. Brands often hold more enclosed meanings than they seem. Look closely at the current FedEx logo and you will notice a small arrow in the midst of the simple design, deceptively pointing toward the accuracy and precision of the service.

The increasing complexity of demographics is prompting more specific targeting of ethnic demographics, as the social landscape becomes more fluid. "Understanding the nuances of multicultural markets, yet maintaining inclusive brand message is essential for brands to thrive in our increasingly multi-ethnic economy," explains Andrea Van Dam, CEO of Women's Marketing. American marketing agencies have increasingly specialized in a number of markets, targeting minorities, genders, and age ranges as the demographics become more complex.

One of the immediate consequences of this diversification is the use of social media in grassroot organizations and activism. Movements like Africans in the Diaspora promote social change in African countries by reaching out to Africans all over the world to reinvest in local projects. Other projects, like Invisible Children, aim at upholding human rights and freedom for youngsters caught in conflict situations.

The impact of acculturation is not limited to those who strive to maintain a landline to their background: it also happens with those who are integrated in larger cultural streams and affect their context with new habits and routines. *Attitudes* and *behaviors* are the two main components that determine the level of acculturation (Berry, 2005): the first one must stimulate the second one in order to be affected positively.

Communication is always two-sided and bilateral, even when dropping a 140 character message onto an unsuspecting legion of followers. Twitter conditions the nature of messages by way of the very medium, with the character limit and hashtags. A feedback loop is inevitable with comments and retweets, as that is the basis of the entire value proposition. This is one of the reasons why social media has taken a heavy role in the realization of international communication. Facebook is a perfect example of a dominating internationalization strategy that relies on excellent internationalization tools and sound modular architecture. Server-wise, the isolated components of the web front-end are layered in an independent manner and distributed across different machines in order to alleviate processing and data access. The site also has a mobile-only version with a dedicated URL at m.facebook.com instead of relying on a responsive version, which allows greater control over the layout and features made available to mobile users. It is impossible to overestimate the impact of Facebook on lives across the globe. Even in China, where the service is blocked by the local government, there are almost 2 million users who are able to access the latest news on their friend's activities and outings. Facebook is consistently the most widely used website on the planet, with more than 1.3 billion users, and acts as a central platform for social communication and economic activity. However, the variety of social media available is correlated to geographical preference as well. While Facebook is relatively omnipresent in every country except China and Japan, WeChat is the Chinese equivalent that has seemingly taken over mobile communication, the main driver of traffic in the country. Chinese immigrants living in the West have the app installed on their phones in order to easily communicate with friends and family back home. Mobile preferences are another factor of distinction of diasporic communities in foreign countries and contribute even more to a kaleidoscopic variety of communication patterns.

CHAPTER 3
Across the Dashboard

ABSTRACT

Global companies can easily fall prey to diffuse goals or corporate politics when it comes to their globalization practices. Everybody wants to sell a relevant product to their target markets, but often there are geopolitical and culture-related issues to think about. Should a product be sold in both Hebrew and Arabic? Should a map note Taiwan as part of the Chinese territorial expanse? And how to execute the necessary research to avoid a commercial failure and public opinion backlash when insensitive decisions are made? A concerted and thought-out strategy is necessary in order to place the proper strategic emphasis on the globalization and international awareness of a project or product line.

Keywords: Globalization; markets; product; corporate; software development; culture; research

3.1 ESTABLISHING A GLOBAL PRODUCT VISION

No matter where I go in the world, although I can't speak any foreign language, I don't feel out of place. I think of the earth as my home.

Akira Kurosawa

It is essential to ensure that content released within your products is always consistently "locally appropriate, and globally relevant." The right move is to anticipate reception and not to defraud expectation. There is a tendency for ethnocentrism in software design that can easily overshadow the entire development and release cycle. There are markets, however, that are outside of the proverbial box. Clients do expect the right language and experience for their local needs, and it is necessary to harvest these from the actual users.

A software development or service design cycle is an organic process, and the right pieces must fall into place. The same goes for the flexibility and openness to communication that such a department must hold even in the strictest strategic sense.

Pursuing a fully global product vision combines not just the commercial objectives, but also to understand what the reality of people using the product is. This involves user research, globalization processes, and an international strategy. These play a key role in corporate strategy and project planning for what are usually relatively small teams. The vertical or "meta" teams proactively endeavor to enforce cultural awareness across all areas of the company, which in complex multinational decentralized structures, can be a daunting effort.

A process shift such as this requires distributed ownership and corporate responsibility. It is not possible for any one isolated team to review effectively the work put into a product by the entire corporation, regardless of its size, without risking three factors (Fig. 3.1.1):

The principal step toward a healthy outward-looking attitude toward international customer bases is to train people to spot issues as soon as possible. In this sense, by the very nature of user experience (UX) work, this type of work encourages a cross-pollination of multidisciplinary skills, often calling teams into a collaboration model.

The communication facilitated by multifunctional people in the organization is a key to the "natural liaison" concept introduced by Adam Polansky. Individuals sustain and represent functional areas that are overlaid and complement each other, and fulfill a vital role in clustering disparate departments and key points of product development consistently. Paul Sherman (2011) suggests that these individuals carry the weight of initiative and evangelization in the corporation, and certainly UX, a field where multifunctionality and the ability to have expertise from various sources converge, lends itself to this active role within the corporate structure. UX incorporates ethnography, design, research, psychology, and human factors: it has become the proverbial kitchen sink for product development and corporate alignment, and the natural response to a primarily consumer-driven culture. However, teams often struggle with the inability to promote UX in the corporation beyond the scope of usability or even esthetics (Fig. 3.1.2).

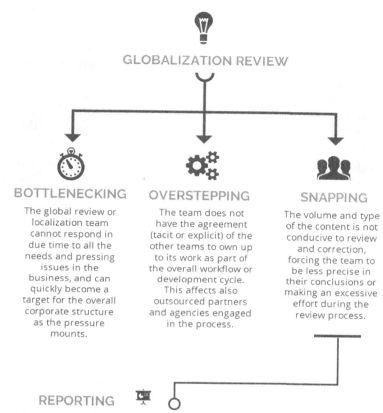

GLOBALIZATION REVIEW

BOTTLENECKING
The global review or localization team cannot respond in due time to all the needs and pressing issues in the business, and can quickly become a target for the overall corporate structure as the pressure mounts.

OVERSTEPPING
The team does not have the agreement (tacit or explicit) of the other teams to own up to its work as part of the overall workflow or development cycle. This affects also outsourced partners and agencies engaged in the process.

SNAPPING
The volume and type of the content is not conducive to review and correction, forcing the team to be less precise in their conclusions or making an excessive effort during the review process.

REPORTING
Depending on the corporate hierarchy and structure, as well as the number of resources in the team, results may be rapidly and lightly reported on, which involves developing very good communication with all stakeholders, or heavy on formal reporting, which can theoretically cover all the bases, but delays the implementation of actionable insights.

FIGURE 3.1.1
A review of the pain points attached to the typical globalization review process.

FIGURE 3.1.2
Research sits at the table with the other functional units and should be an integral part of every business decision.

The misunderstanding over the role of UX derives largely from the inability of companies to understand its customers, a field that UX should be accountable for. Trust is not a one-way street, nor is it a self-sustaining organism that can be left to its own devices after initial implementation. Trust is about making the pieces fit, and, like a jigsaw puzzle, finding out the side where the ridges are slotting in more easily. This process always starts with making the fundamental question: how can a business know its customer base reliably and develop a continuous and consistent perspective of the evolving customer needs?

Research is the obvious answer, both quantitative and qualitative. Interviews and surveys are the most often used methods of understanding users, but they paint a limited picture due to lack of context and practice. Any method relying on people describing what they think or do is limited to a fault, as both can easily contradict each other. People often do things out of habit and might have a limited perception of what motivates their behavior.

The best way to overcome these hurdles is to understand that the road to experience is paved with different pictures and stories and rely on observational information coupled with actual quantitative information. By gaining an insight into the user behavior on your website, the actual streams and the channels that play into your user's habits, you will find the basis for a sound international strategy.

3.2 KICKSTARTING CORPORATE CHANGE

Every man takes the limits of his own field of vision for the limits of the world.

Arthur Schopenhauer

Since the mid-2000s, UX has quickly risen to become a defining field in user-centered design and research. However, its prominence is indebted to the popularity of computers starting in the 1990s. The emphasis on usability as a differentiation factor was directly related to the success of early versions of PC and Mac in the 1990s, allowing for companies to be perceived as different not only by core product proposition and price but also by a renewed emphasis on customer satisfaction and ease of use. This allowed behemoths like Amazon and Apple to become market leaders.

However, many companies are still caught in self-centered paradigms that do nothing to reduce lack of efficiency during development and design. Research has proved systematically (Jones and Sasser, 1995, Prokesch, 1995) that sales increase proportionally to the investment in usability and design research. Investing just 10% of a project's budget in usability can yield up to 100% on sales and conversion rates (Nielsen, 2003).

The value of user-centered methods in improving the quality of computer systems is paramount to all stages of project development (Fig. 3.2.1):

The general issues faced by a user-centered project are only compounded when combined with the need to develop for international markets. The

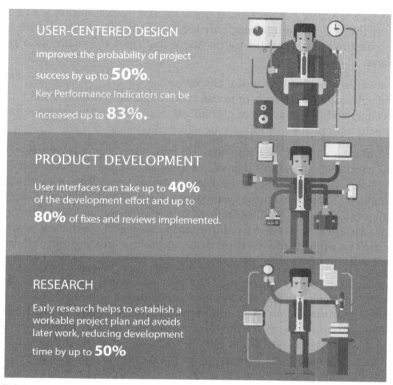

FIGURE 3.2.1

Different aspects of a project interacting: research, user-centered design, and product development are all simultaneously vertical and cross-functional in digital projects intended for end-users. *Keil and Carmel (1995); Bossert (1990).*

development of a global vision for a corporate strategy is a perilous zone of discussion that deals with several concurrent aspects. Lots of companies have good solid ideas about products that can appeal to international markets but lack the experience or the adaptability to make a specific product work in markets beyond their normal breadth of experience. This is where the involvement of all the stakeholders is crucial to face the challenges of becoming user-focused, especially on an international level.

Business structures and workflows should support the overall objectives of developing actual products for real people in the real world. When companies have to coordinate globalization projects over different regions, and multiple offices, there are inevitably differences in operation methodology and vision. No company is "born global," regardless of how acceptable and popular their products may appear to be. The need to have a sustainable globalization operation program is a key component of the wider company strategy. As IBM stated in a 1999 report on "Cost Justifying Ease of Use": "It makes business effective. It makes business efficient. It makes business sense."

Regardless of whether the globalization team has responsibilities and stakeholders in the UX, content strategy, or localization sides of the business, the core globalization team should follow these few steps to ensure their role in the process:

- be well-connected within the enterprise,
- actively collaborate with in-house copywriters and transcreators,
- evangelize for awareness of globalization strategy within the company,
- pursue independent audits on design and content.

It is important to realize the role that UX plays in corporate strategy. Many high-end executives make the mistake of considering UX as "whatever makes the site pretty" or a magical step into user's minds regardless of methodology and execution. These perceptions can only be countered with consistent and persistent evangelization and education. It is a constant source of frustration for many designers to have to educate an occasionally immature workflow, but it is also an opportunity to apply your empathic skills to improve an organization from the inside.

Companies have a nasty habit of looking sideways rather than ahead. Competitive analysis is often used to generate feature requirements and investment in the roadmap often tags along with other companies in the same segment. This is due to one of the core problems in the market: *reactivity*. Reactivity is essential to stay afloat in very competitive markets, but it can also stifle internal innovation as original ideas get squashed in favor of following in already trodden paths.

In this context, UX is often framed as a way to optimize conversion and retention. The best way to justify investment in the area and to build a strong business case is to directly correlate it to growth.

3.2.1 Lessons from the Field: Globalization According to Sony

As a company, Sony has forged a long and influential path. Its distinctive minimalist industrial design was an anomaly in the marketplace for decades, but the company used its design philosophy to promote a unique image of high-end simplicity. This proved to have a significant impact on entrepreneurs like Steve Jobs, who studied Sony's marketing materials attentively when Apple shared its first official headquarters with one of Sony's US sales offices in the early 1980s.

Times have changed, but Sony's strategy has remained relatively consistent. Sony's offices are now distributed worldwide, from Tokyo (also the headquarters of the company) to San Francisco (where most of the company's UX is designed). With the need to decentralize resources, the company faces a challenge that other major players are also subjected to: the processes and methods for ongoing projects and programs worldwide are not developed in tandem.

In terms of content, for legacy reasons, products are actually developed with 2 source languages for a total of 33 target languages. The company operates in over 70 countries, which implies a massive logistical effort, which is the culmination of a transnational strategy that took over 20 years to implement. In the 1980s, Japan was the first country to successfully open production facilities in the United States and was rewarded with a massive success based on the customer perception of its products as distinctive high-end designer items.

This success was largely due to the time that Sony spent studying markets before setting up operations there. It learned the local reality before investing more heavily in the market, and this research helped it to become one of the most pervasive brands on the planet.

Like most companies, Sony operates by setting up sales operations on a new territory first and only later implementing local operations, which may include development and design teams. This helps to distinguish approaches for the European, Latin American, Asia-Pacific, and Asia markets. Apart from the different market adjustments, products line are introduced or maintained depending on their market performance and their relevance to local audiences. This mandates a careful design strategy, which caters to local requirements yet still preserves the company's distinctive minimalist style. For instance, the earliest presence of Sony in Germany was focused on establishing a perception of quality, and with this objective, the company focused on understanding the market before setting off on any commercial concerns.

Sony also coordinates global launches across different territories over a period of up to 24 months (longer in some cases) that extends through the following phases for content-sensitive projects (Fig. 3.2.2):

These projects are released in waves, with each wave focused on a different region. Content localization relies on an internal translation system, which is closely integrated with internal CMS and translation partners. Content operations are performed in bulk, and the translation system includes basic automatic QA processing on character length, terminology inconsistencies, fragmented sentences, and automated capitalization issue. This integration allowed Sony to reduce their work volume by up to 50%.

3.3 AGILE GLOBALIZATION

> Grand principles that generate no action are mere vapour. Conversely, specific practices in the absence of guiding principles are often inappropriately used.
>
> **Jim Highsmith**

Agile has quickly become one of the main project methodologies in the software industry, taking both companies and agencies by storm.

Agile is a design and development process framework of a "lean" nature. It is often associated with a certain philosophy underlying a set of guidelines

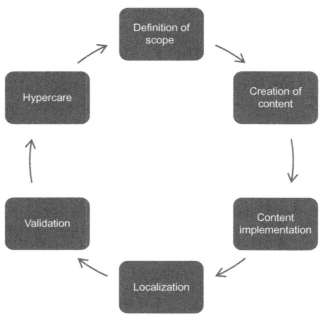

FIGURE 3.2.2
The content workflow at Sony.

which emphasize close integration and communication, as well as a goal-oriented collaboration among corporate, design, and engineering teams. Agile focuses on goals and actual value, rather than processes, and is inherently a responsive methodology. The document that started it all, the Agile Manifesto, was signed at the Snowbird ski resort in Utah in February 2001 by a group of disgruntled developers and engineers, disappointed with the lack of focus of lightweight methodologies. It is still used as a watershed reference across the industry, unchanged for over 15 years (available at agilemanifesto.org): individuals and interactions over processes and tools; working software over comprehensive documentation; customer collaboration over contract negotiation; responding to change over following a plan. This is also a methodology that is inherently reactive and devoted to rapid development. By reducing the load associated with long requirements documentation typical of Waterfall systems, it is possible to achieve quick and tangible results. This suits UX developments, as work activities can be parallel rather than serial, but the quick and flexible approach can also support quick development and reaction to changing priorities or the logic of the market. Another aspect of Agile that favors UX research and design is its iterative nature. By focusing on the true customer value, rather than internal processes, Agile UX allows for a quick approach to research. This includes the ability to run qualitative studies, like user interviews and testing, or quantitative, like surveys, heuristic analysis, and competitive analysis, in order to make quick decisions on feature prioritization and development focus, and get fast feedback on implementations over the results of the earlier iterations.

Localization is frequently linked to the end-of-chain stage, interspersing time constraints with role diffuseness, leading to severe quality compromises in most cases. However, localization is an essential step in designing and planning for a consistent UX in international markets.

In this context, internationalization and localization becomes an essential component of the overall globalization process. Corporate-wide linguistic strategy is a must in this case and localization departments can work in tandem with the UX teams to help drive this effort by supplying much-needed geopolitical assessments and assessing the effort behind localizing a given product in a given language (Fig. 3.3.1).

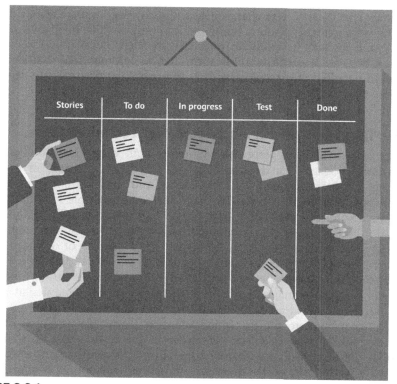

FIGURE 3.3.1

It may be hard for globalization to carve its own corner in Agile planning. The trick is in integration and communication. Regardless of the revenue generated by international markets, the end result will always depend on internal lobbying, and perception of value.

This counters the frequent perception of localization as a more or less sophisticated translation management process applied to software development. Not only is this untrue, it is dangerous in Agile environments. In an Agile environment demanding constant responsiveness, responsiveness, and the ability to adapt to changing requirements in a constantly shifting context, the project development process is never really over.

This implies the necessity to change requirements at late stages, which can represent a major hurdle for teams. However, if research and design work together in knowing the market and the user requirements, a key cog of a chain that relies on communication and stable interchange of information is then set into motion. While monolithic development and requirement lack of specificity often compromise results in traditional development structures, Agile's focus on productivity and decomposable work items enables a richer and more quality-oriented development process.

From a design point of view, localization (or, in cases where both are owned by the same team, globalization) must be one of the stakeholders in the User Story if it is determined that it affects any kind of text resources in the application, either directly (i.e., text changes) or indirectly (i.e., impact on UI design or graphic arrangement). From a maintenance point of view, this relies on pre-planning and resource assignment from an early stage. Localization is the primary link between a software application and its international marketability and should be taken into account as early as possible in the software development process.

3.3.1 Team Dynamics: Rockstars and Technical Gaps

However, unlike the view perpetrated by many Agile evangelists and coaches, Agile is not a godsend for development and UX. It is the source of many a frustrating and tense moment in some teams, and depends not the internal corporate structure: the quick pace is often deemed unsuitable for finding the best creative solutions. Although Agile games and methods are used, there is no actual mindset in the team, prompted by distrust and resistance to change; there is a general sense that Agile implementation consists of a "cargo cult" where the benefits will come eventually with sufficient ritual devotion; a typical criticism is that Agile is better suited to smaller teams where the dynamic is higher and easier to manage than with larger corporations. Agile design is not easy to track and even harder to account for in a standardized manner. Agile does not accommodate for the individual and many Lean experts actively advocate against having "rockstar" elements in the team. Agile resistance is also about the barriers that workflow adaptation and management migration must face. On this last point, there are numerous tensions to having cross-functional teams, especially when human nature determines that the individual reward (either material or in recognition) is at the base of most of our behaviors. A team is a psychological mix of combined influences and behaviors, and maintaining a dynamic balance is a hard task for any team leader or manager. Developers provide Luiz Fernando Capretz, in a 2003 study, argued that the most common personality type amongst developers was the so-called ISTJ (introverted, sensing, thinking, judgment), while other studies found that there are correlations between product quality and the dominant personality of team members, with extroversion having a positive effect (Acuña, Gómez, & Juristo, 2009). Designers and developers often have a contentious relationships, as they can sit in different countries, and only really communicate systematically through ceremonies like the daily stand-up. This results in a difficulty of ownership and accountability, as the conflict between both sets may contribute to slow down progress and reduce the odds for productive conversation in the midst of the team. Designers (particularly of a visual nature) may not feel empowered by the development workflow, and if there is a systematic approach to having their tickets or tasks deprioritized by developers so technical or back-end issues are addressed, there may be a growing feeling amongst designers that there is a technical "gap," whilst developers may well feel that designers throw wireframes "over the wall" to them with little motivation to back it up. In these circumstances, there is no replacement for personal presence and face-to-face communication, particularly when discussing the technical intricacies of a specific design. Having even one full-stack member in the design team will fuel productivity and awareness, serving as an anchor to edge the team closer to understanding the demands of the design and communicating with developers in a more productive manner. Sponsoring co-location (even if temporarily) and visits among the teams can definitely improve the prevalent relationships. Having lean analytics to track implementation success, as well as a shared pattern library and style guide for all project members can also help.

3.3.2 Agile Roles

Actors and stakeholders in an Agile project come together in a unique way that is a departure from traditional workflows. For companies in transition from waterfall to Agile, User Stories can follow an acceptance criteria and function like small, manageable requirements. Any User Story implemented in a product has several components that demand different expertise from a multi-specialized team, which can be either contained in different departments or, optimally, working exclusively together on given parts of the product. In this setting, global strategy is a concern from the get-go thanks to constant involvement with the core design and development teams, as well as the product stakeholders. Project management duties are distributed and the Product Owner's vision is instrumental in the whole process.

The naming of roles often varies between different Agile methodologies, but some commonalities can be identified.

Customer
It can be a combination of the Product Owner and the end-customer. They specify the product requirements, regardless of the actual final plan.

Product Owner

Fulfills a similar role to the classical perception of the Product Manager in waterfall methodologies:

- creating and collecting the general requirements of the project,
- establishing clear objectives for ROI,
- releasing schedule,
- having responsibility over the Product Backlog prioritization and management.

Scrum Master

The role drives and supports the work developed by the team, helping the team to overcome potential obstacles to completing the project stages. The role is of the main facilitator and implementing the process for the whole team.

An iteration typically lasts 1−4 weeks and has four distinct phases:

Planning

The preparation of the project involves prioritizing and handling items in the Product Backlog that will be implemented during the iteration, in case one is used. For noniterative approaches like Kanban, the team gets together regularly to review and plan the next batch of items to be implemented. Normally, if the iterative model is used, it should have a clear theme or goal.

This is where the UX teams can be most influential. Insights from research and preparation for both visual and experience design set the stage for development for implementation. This is also where user testing can be most useful, working on hypothesis and implementation ideas before.

Development

During the Development phase, there is also a daily status meeting known as the daily stand-up. In this meeting, each team member states what they did the previous day, what they are going to do today, and identifies any existing or foreseeable roadblocks.

Review

When the iteration nears completion, a review meeting is held with all stakeholders to demonstrate the new software and receive feedback on it and the functionality that has been developed.

Retrospective

The last phase, or Retrospective, is a postmortem for the team to discuss how the process could be improved.

Localization and design are not separate worlds. Text is an essential part of a complete multimedia system that includes image and text. Visually and linguistically, text plays a major role in the user's perception of a product. The most refined and sophisticated UX can be wrecked by careless localization and haunted by issues and bugs. Fonts are lost, carefully complimentary labels suddenly appear juxtaposed, HTML is improperly adapted to target locales: all are little product nightmares that can only be countered by a combined approach that makes UX and localization part of the same combination.

Therefore, internationalization is key to a consistent UX in a multilingual product. Internationalization defines the set of processes and techniques that are implicated in making a product capable of adaptation to different cultures. This is where UX implementation is at its trickiest. No sound internationalization-friendly design can be adequately implemented without an accurate study of localization prioritization. You must define which languages and cultures you want to localize into and include both immediate priorities and future plans. This will enable you to optimize layouts for culturally sensitive graphics and indications or—optimally—to change requirements in the light of new market strategies.

3.4 THE ROLE OF GLOBAL AWARENESS

The Chinese use two brush strokes to write the word 'crisis.' One brush stroke stands for danger; the other for opportunity. In a crisis, be aware of the danger—but recognize the opportunity.

John F. Kennedy

Global companies can easily fall prey to diffuse goals or corporate politics when it comes to their globalization practices. Everybody wants to sell a relevant product to their target markets, but often there are geopolitical and culture-related issues to think about.

Should there be language parity within a region? How do maps account for geographic territorial disputes? And how to execute the necessary research to avoid a commercial failure and public opinion backlash when insensitive decisions are made?

Global awareness is related to the whole enterprise and affects every single process in display. With that in mind, Paige Williams, Director of Global Readiness at Microsoft, classifies the work of her team as helping to ensure that content is "locally appropriate, while globally relevant." According to her, the right move is to anticipate reception and to be considerate of user expectation. "Understanding cultural and language needs is complex when you consider that people using technology are mobile, bringing their culture and language, or languages, with them wherever they go; be it to the office, in the home, or as they travel to various destinations."

A software development or service design cycle is an organic process, and the right pieces must fall into place. The same goes for the reliability that such a department must hold even in the strictest strategic sense.

We spend time researching and remaining current on geo, cultural and language topics, to assess not only the correctness of various scenarios, but also to understand where there are complexities or sensitivities to factor in. When things are "right" with a content experience, it's seamless for users. If things are not quite right, or in fact would be considered "wrong", it's more likely to face risk in the marketplace. We would rather vet these scenarios as a part of our overall process of quality, rather than learn about a concern too late in the cycle.

The concept of Global Readiness as a combination of sociopolitical research, internationalization QA, and cultural markers review ensures a key role in corporate strategy and project planning for a relatively small team. The vertical department proactively endeavors to enforce cultural awareness across all areas of the company, which in a complex environment offered by a multinational giant, can be a daunting effort (Fig. 3.4.1).

FIGURE 3.4.1
The Microsoft Language Portal has been active since 2009 and is one of the reference tools openly made available by the company. *Screen shot(s) reprinted by permission from Microsoft Corporation.*

However, according to Williams, "we cannot possibly cover the entire company from one team; instead, we train people to spot issues as soon as possible and from where they sit in the organization." In this sense, by the very nature of UX work, this type of work encourages a cross-pollination of multidisciplinary skills, often bringing teams together under the initiative of a corporate strategy toward global readiness.

According to Paige Williams, imagery analysis is also a source of global inspection. The origins of the Global Readiness team began with analyzing the assets shipped with each product, in the beginning starting with products like Encarta, where geoculturally sensitive materials were a likely source of market risk in certain territories. Digital or analog, an encyclopedia always has aspirations of universality, and the correctness of the content is essential to its success.

Cartography was also an important geopolitical concern, where maps often had to accurately portray the contemporary status of international politics in a nonconflictive way. An international company cannot afford to alienate major players, both political and economical, in the international market.

A team involved in cultural assessment has by principle to be multidisciplinary, and to be aware of the actual expectations of the target markets. They have to know what is "locally appropriate, and globally relevant," and the weight of this process in corporate strategy and project planning is second to none.

The origin of the Microsoft Global Readiness team lies on imagery review with the early product Encarta software, a popular staple of desktop OEM systems in the 1990s. The software was originally provided in CD-ROM and, as a read-only media, it did not benefit from hot fixes and live content updates as most web products do today. The shipped product was expected to last at least 9 months on the shelves, depending on reception and audience demand, and getting the content right before the release was essential to its perceived quality. The maps, borders, names of cities, and other geopolitical markers were a critical aspect of quality assurance in packaged software.

Now, given the dynamism of global politics, local expectations are as critical as ever, especially with the migration to a primarily online experience. This has implications on the release process, particularly with a rigorous compliance process.

It is impossible to avoid issues with released software unless an actual corporate policy is in place that allows cultural review to assume a primary role in the product's development and final acceptance. Releases are never validated unless checked and approved by content reviewers. According to Williams, the product as a whole has to reflect "what it means to be outside of a (packaged) box, especially when customers do expect the right regardless of where they are originally from, where they are living now, and which language, or languages, they may speak."

3.5 ITERATIVE REFINING

I wanted a perfect ending. Now I've learned, the hard way, that some poems don't rhyme, and some stories don't have a clear beginning, middle, and end.

Gilda Radner

Local websites of global consumer brands often use a global template that is specialized locally. This allows the brands to keep the layout and navigation consistent by usually relying on the same template. This consistency comes at the cost of specialization, but can be cost-effective if the market is still developing or if your website is not the main channel to enter the company's value proposition. This is the case with the Opel website, which uses a standardized layout for nearly every market, except the ones it goes by a different naming, like Vauxhall in the United Kingdom and Buick in the United States. Like other car brands, the website can be low-context, focusing on technical data exposition and providing an authoritative reference that relies little on the previous knowledge of the product (Fig. 3.5.1A–C).

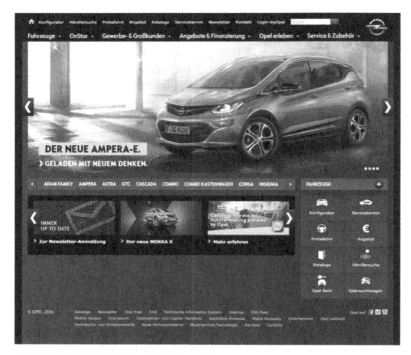

FIGURE 3.5.1

Opel is one of the top European brands, and as part of the General Motors group, it is sold under a number of guises around the world, including the Buick brand in the United States. The official website uses a global template that is then adapted in multiple territories, depending on campaigns and the models that best appeal to local markets. The more expensive models are appropriate for more individualistic cultures where cars are seen as status symbols. The three websites shown here are the local versions from, in order, Germany, United Arab Emirates, and South Africa.

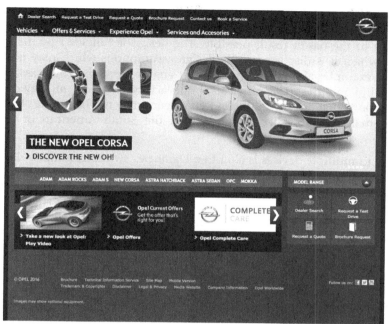

FIGURE 3.5.1
Continued

These brands exemplify that the best approach is often to have a modular approach to both widgets and CSS elements, with front-end and back-end modules available for multiple configuration for different markets.

For corporate webpages, even with transactional areas, this type of globalization process usually relies on a "master design" with a "post-release" international adaptation, and can be treated as a separate project for each territory. However, working on a "simship" (simultaneous shipment) basis for apps and software products requires an altogether more sophisticated integration between teams.

This implies the need to break with the traditional model of a waterfall-based model where UX teams hand over designs to developers for implementation with minimal communication after that hand-off. This leads to a separation of duties that is not beneficial for the workflow as a whole. Designers and managers can easily lose perspective by being unaware of the necessary adjustments and adaptations that their designs may require in development. The problem is compounded in responsive design projects, especially those who span a multitude of platforms. The possibilities that a single design may suit dozens of browsers and mobile combinations, as well as a variety of use cases, are minimal.

The technical drawbacks and necessary depth of testing involved in catering for all these disparate markets implies that the end result will be leveled according to the basest result possible. The design is hindered by the conditions in which it is displayed or by design assumptions which may not hold true. For example, although a metasearch engine developer may assume its top-usability intuitive page runs at a satisfactory speed in all devices, the search options that are key to the user experience may not be visible above the fold in smaller devices like those used in the South American or African markets.

Adapting to multiple devices is akin to a Damocles sword, constantly dangling over a layout and threatening to completely disrupt the experience. Modern UX design focuses largely on a two-dimensional approach to design, similar to a typographical workflow, where sizes and layouts are adjusted continuously, but in this case, instead of a single page size, these designs will hang precariously on thousands of prescriptive and highly variable canvases.

Similarly, features do not come out of a development sprint deliciously garnished and ready to consume, especially in the earlier stages of the development. In fact, often the result is downright disgusting: half-baked and barely functional lumps of code are thrust into testing, but the scope remains the same and the expectations do not change. Add to that the pressure of time in tightly wound environments and the whole thing threatens to unravel.

Too many teams adopt a "stand-by and pray" attitude, where the final release in the cycle is the first user release. However, in order to face the situation constructively, the best approach is to decompose the testing in parts and focus on the parts of the flow of the user journey and to test only the changes made by development.

Traditional *rapid prototyping* can assist in developing a quick iteration of the project, but it will eventually pigeonhole the process, as it focuses on optimizing a design, rather than uncovering fundamental issues with the product or questioning the validity of the feature designed. A good example is app security and password logic, which have grown into one of the more complex full-stack conundrums. Front-end logic limits password rules, whereas the encryption system takes care of the storage and protection of the passcodes. Many form designs have convoluted rules for password checking, yet these seldom amount to an actual increase in app security. According to a 2015 TeleSign report, 73% of online accounts share duplicated passwords, and 54% of people will use less than 5 passwords throughout their entire digital life. The beauty of the design (regardless of how many rules are used to validate passwords) is hindered by the user habits, reducing the value of the effort put into security.

Analyze what effectively works in the context of your team. Frontloading design and prototyping work may be seen as ineffective, and a hybrid approach may benefit the team's relationship with development and managers. Design can be iterated initially, or validate concepts continuously as the project progresses. The end goal should always to validate the best possible UX, rather than to increase efficiency at the expense of usability or optimize small parts as opposed to developing sustainable scalable workflows.

Rapid prototyping can also benefit from a decentralized corporate structure, where facilities working with an interval of several hours can work on the same front-end design or module on the same time frame. In ideal cases, this can lead to a round-the-clock 24-hour cycle arrangement that can benefit the project as a whole. There is also the risk, however, of misunderstandings and delays due to poor coordination or misunderstandings over knowledge and content ownership.

When possible, use low-fidelity wireframes and do not invest time in high-fi mockups until the needs of both core and secondary audiences are defined and agreed by all the stakeholders' requirements (Fig. 3.5.2).

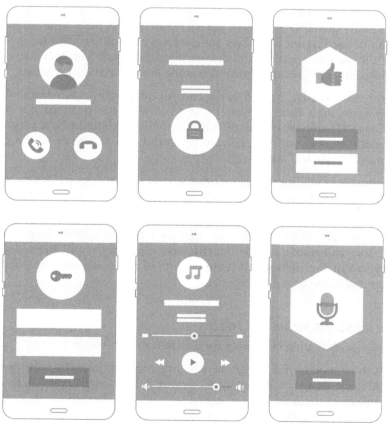

FIGURE 3.5.2
Wireframes and mockups vary in size and fidelity but provide vital project and testing support to iterate ideation and validate concepts.

3.5.1   Wireframes

Wireframes consist of simplified representation of designs, which can be made into prototypes. These prototypes can be either analog or digital, either for demonstrational or interactive purposes.

Often times, wireframes are represented with lines and text, on paper (hand drawn) or electronic. They should already highlight content and structural elements that are represented with lines and text, as well as a hierarchy and priority of elements.

They are not focused on visual design, and in case visual choices are already making their way into the wireframes, this can sometimes work against acceptance. It depends on the team and stakeholder culture. While early wireframes can set up wrong expectations, it is sometimes useful to illustrate your design solutions with some spit and shine in order to translate a specific product vision properly to the unsuspecting teams. Just be careful on how this may condition very early decisions.

Wireframes are generally devoid of color and styles and serve as a "stick draft" which can be used to test with users and perform heuristic evaluations, as well as to allow the team to visualize and discuss interaction strategies. It is a schematic and a blueprint, and essentially meant to guide feasibility and early testing.

The fidelity may change, as well as the content quality, but a wireframe should translate more than that: it must be in sync with the goals of the project and audience. Therefore, questioning any early details should be a progressive and mindful process, with the priority being the true adherence of the design to the project goals and audience.

Many alternatives will inevitably be produced in the process, so it is important to stay focused on the right issues and try design alternatives.

Any user-centered workflow design will rely on the feedback and analysis of the customers and target users, with this data informing the design process directly. This will maximize the benefits and the adequacy of the redesigned platform to suit the wishes and requirements of the customer, allowing for a smoother and more engaging experience.

3.5.1.1   *LESSONS FROM THE FIELD*

A few ways of designing effectively for different devices are as follows:

- *Focus on product*: for designers, it is important to keep in mind that the intent of design is primarily to deliver a **core user experience**, which consists of the base level group of features that the product is supposed to deliver. Do not worry about redundant or secondary features, and prioritize those that are at the center of the product.
- *Divide devices by groups*: analyze the markets where the product will be sold and develop a shortlist of the most popular phones for each

territory you will target with your designs. More information on how to accomplish this strategy is available elsewhere on this book.

- *Be input-agnostic*: privilege a "fat finger" approach when designing. Think of the least practical and optimal pathways through a design, and optimize from those. Users will break things, and every flaw can be maximized.

3.6 INTERNATIONAL RESEARCH

We have met the enemy and he is us.

Walt Kelly, *Pogo* cartoon strip

User research is a relatively recent discipline of study and analysis. It is the combined product of techniques used in anthropology, ethnographic studies, market research, and industrial engineering. It is partially the result of a long-standing trend to approximate actual usage observation with intended design, and has been heralded as the best way to get in touch with the audience using an objective methodology and a consistent framework. In most of its assertions, it involves collecting information directly from the users (Lafrenière, 2008) rather than insulating product development from its audience or lacing user feedback with procedural red tape and biased observations.

The field involves a continuous appreciation of the evolution of both usage and technology. User habits change quickly in a day when the average urban dweller has an average of 3.64 devices (GlobalWebIndex, 2016) and not all adopt new products or technologies at the same rate. People differ in social standing, economic power, preferences, emotional responses, and a multitude of other factors that can be attributed to both social and psychological causes.

Rather than to accommodate for individual variation, user research is primarily centered around tendencies and bias in group results. One interview is not enough to make a defensible report, and a sizable and representative sample is needed in order to produce any kind of meaningful results. Sometimes, researchers adopt an holistic approach, "eyeballing" a result or seemingly steering a study toward a certain hypothesis that appears obvious or a common tendency based on past projects. This is a common problem of reliability and validity in ethnographic research (LeCompte & Goetz, 1982), but it can be minimized by taking special care with all stages of the research process:

- study design,
- data collection,
- data analysis,
- findings presentation.

For example, aspects like the researcher's gender and social status can play a decisive role in the data collection stage. Depending on the dominant culture and surrounding environment, a female study participant may provide inaccurate or merely different feedback to a male moderator during a test session. A young student might feel constrained by a significantly older interviewer, or too comfortable and seeking social approval with an interviewer who is too young.

Rule of thumb: For any study, it is strongly recommended to have more than one researcher. The average study should involve at least two researchers, if possible of different backgrounds. All the researchers should be exposed to a varied subset of the tested audience (e.g., hold interviews with the same number of men and women and with varied backgrounds) as that will guarantee a better analysis of the multivariate research. Mix and match the entire study as much as possible, rather than assigning "specialized" parts of the study to the same researchers.

To get more meaningful information from participants, the study should have a facilitator who is very familiar with the demographic and background of the participants.

The use of an interpreter during the testing can assure the end-client of the quality of the interview and provide the "gist" of the testing as it occurs. This is particularly relevant during sessions broadcasted directly to stakeholders, as it allows them to take their own notes, discuss observations, and start posting observations on the wall. However, it also has three main disadvantages:

1) It takes more time in the interview session which could otherwise be used for the actual testing.
2) It slows down the responsiveness rate when users take different paths during testing, and may compromise observations.
3) It may create a more difficult atmosphere for the user to communicate openly and for the tester to create a climate of empathy with the user.

The facilitator should, whenever possible, speak the language of the user being tested. It is important to be aware that even when the testing session is perfectly conducted in the original language. It might be challenging to find the right skills in a closed market with limited UX training, such as countries where the practice of UX is still maturing.

3.6.1   Lessons from the Field: International Phones Corp.

An international communications company started a study to understand the users' perception of its own pages versus the competitor pages, and common retailer websites visited in five different countries: Germany, Spain, Netherlands, United Kingdom, and South Africa.

The study goals involved website benchmarking and usability testing for each country with up to nine websites:

- the communications company,
- 4 most successful competitors,
- 4 retailers.

The methodology was centered around an unmoderated online usability study using participants who were otherwise unfamiliar with the proposition or brand.

Each user performed up to six tasks for each website, based around:

- shopping for a device,
- comparing similar devices across competing websites,
- analyzing quality of service,
- consulting a help article on device support.

The user feedback was overwhelmingly negative for the company's website as well as the competitors for nearly all countries. The users tended to prefer the retailers' websites, which had a smoother user journey and ironed out many of the usability flaws that the company's own website displayed.

Users also had a negative reaction toward the inconsistent experience offered by the localized website, particularly in terms of performance and differing layouts and templates.

PART II
Magnum Impulse

CHAPTER 4
Worlds Within Worlds

ABSTRACT

The Internet has become accessible to over 3 billion people worldwide. It has become an aphorism to say that the world is a connected village. However, even in a small group, there is significant variation within a roomful of people, let alone billions spread over the globe with different habits, connection speeds, social networks, and necessities. Designing for these markets holds many different challenges and demands a deep knowledge of the constraints at hand as well as their habits, demographics, and local context.

Keywords: World; credit card; China; digital portrait; social media; demographics; connectiveness

4.1 A GLOBAL USER JOURNEY

> You can't walk alone. Many have given the illusion but none have really walked alone. Man is not made that way. Each man is bedded in his people, their history, their culture, and their values.
>
> **William Shakespeare**

In 2015, the Internet has become accessible to over 3 billion people worldwide. There are over one billion websites registered worldwide (with 75%

Universal UX Design. DOI: http://dx.doi.org/10.1016/B978-0-12-802407-2.00004-6

of them parked domains), and over 90 trillion e-mails have been sent since the dawn of the digital age. All of this is the result of human activity and connection. It has become an aphorism to say that the world is a connected village. The implication is that physical distance is transcended by way of our digital connection, and that we are closer than ever before. However, there is enough variation within a roomful of people, let alone billions spread over the globe with different habits, connection speeds, social networks, and necessities. Designing for these markets involves many different challenges and demands a deep knowledge of the constraints at hand.

Not all countries use technology in quite the same way. Cultural specification underlines many of the prevalent behaviors and habits, especially when it comes to how people use and share their devices. Knowing the audience that one designs for is paramount to designing effectively, like an old adage from ancient scripts: know your users and the rest will follow.

4.2 DIGITAL PORTRAIT: EUROPE

As a territory, Europe is vast, extending from Lisbon to Moscow, but it is actually the second smallest continent, with barely over 10 million square kilometers and a population of around 740 million, according to a 2012 UN report. Information and communication technologies have become an integral part of everyday life in the continent, from e-commerce to education. This has generated ongoing conversations and legislative initiatives concerning privacy protection and antimonopoly laws.

According to a 2014 Eurostat report, over 81% of all households have access to Internet, marking an upward trend that has followed on from previous years. Luxembourg and the Netherlands recorded the highest rate of households with Internet access, at 96%, followed closely by Denmark, Finland, Sweden, and the United Kingdom, where approximately 90% of households have Internet access and individuals make an average of 50 online purchases each year (Fig. 4.2.1).

In Spain and Portugal, like in other Latin countries, messaging and communication apps are commonly used among friends and family. Whatsapp is one of the most popular services in these countries, due to the fact that local phone companies usually do not provide unlimited calls and charge for SMS. The picture is slowly changing, but it is still cheaper and more accessible to use a VOIP or chat-based app like Whatsapp. This has led many companies to adopt the app for customer contact and support, and many businesses, large and small, actively

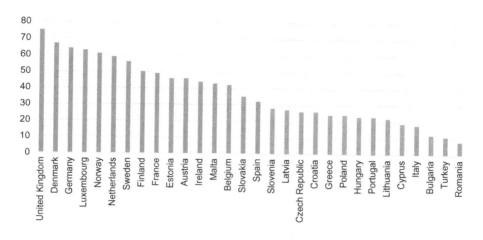

FIGURE 4.2.1

An average amount of purchases made by individuals in all European countries in the third quarter of 2016. *Source: Eurostat, September 2016 © European Union, 1995–2016*

promote their services on Whatsapp as a customer support tool. Several support desk tools integrate with the app in order to provide a "switchboard" to track individual customer cases.

There is a relatively low concern in these countries with the impact of media and technology on children and learning, unlike France, for example, where public discussions over children's technological overexposure are relatively common.

In the United Kingdom and France, devices tend to be shared among the family, but accounts and credentials remain relatively individual and private, whereas in Latin countries, access accounts are often shared by the whole family. France has a more diverse approach to technology, with some families relying on very high-tech solutions for their everyday life while others rely on traditional means like analogue note-taking when talking on the phone. However, parents also tend to moderate their children's usage of mobile devices, especially before the age of 16 years, due to concerns with health.

4.2.1 Housing

As several countries in Europe rely on a renter's market, housing is often seen as an impermanent space and there is a trend toward minimalism and pre-made decoration. Given the economic and political tensions in countries like France and the United Kingdom, there is a high prize on mobility and portability.

4.2.2 Family

The concept of family is not the same even in a relatively homogeneous continent like Europe. While Western Europe tends to equate the nuclear family a fairly traditional definition, the model of the average family is quite different in Eastern and Southern Europe.

In countries like Poland, the concept of family tends to be larger and to include not only immediate extended family like grandparents, uncles, aunts, and cousins but also ancestors. There is a continuity to the individual that extends into the past and contextualizes the present.

Families are also more communicative and interactive, and this infers a very specialized use of technology. Multimodal interaction is not as common in countries with a weaker economy (Ghosh & Joshi, 2013). Most European countries tend to multitask while using mobile devices at home. Although "mobile-first" is a much repeated mantra since it was introduced by Eric Schmidt, then Chairman of Google, users are far more likely to use a range of devices for different tasks and choice of content. According to a 2015 comScore study in the US, 77% of users aged 18−34 used a combination of mobile and desktop, with only 3% stating that they only used desktop platforms. This number increased systematically for older audiences aged 55+, where nearly 26% stated that they depended on their desktop machine only for Internet access. The 2016 comScore MMX Multi-Platform study also found that users differentiate per content and scenario: weather was far more likely to be checked on the mobile phone, whereas newspapers could be checked on both desktop and mobile. On the other hand, banking and retail were predominantly done on desktop machines, a trend, however, that is changing in favor of the mobile phones every year.

Throughout Europe, the importance of quality of life and family is relatively high, with children's school vacations often arranged in order to coincide with holidays.

Poorer economies also tend to rely on "hand-me-down" devices for relatives, particularly youngsters or senior citizens. Depending on the family preference, mobile phones can be passed over between members—e.g., the teenager gives his or her iPhone to the grandmother once the phone is replaced. The turnover rate for devices is much lower and devices on average take longer to replace. Due to this emphasis on cost, refurbished phones are very common and free services like Whatsapp or Google Hangouts are popular. Skype and other similar VOIP platforms are also extremely popular, particularly for long distance or overseas calls, whether personal or business. However, the inconvenience of setting up a video call and the need to stay in-camera and in a stable position is a factor that can reduce the frequency of the calls. Using tablets for videocalls is a common way to overcome this situation.

There is also a marked difference in the communication between partners and former family members. Communication with ex-partners is relatively rare in most societies, except when children are involved. The communication patterns tend to be more frequent and reliable with couples and children than with more distanced family members.

Extended families in Poland also sometimes do the shopping for their older relatives and are very influenced by personal recommendations.

Landline calls are most often used with older members of the family, as most older households have landlines. Although the panorama is slowly changing, elders for the most part do not yet communicate by text or message with their children or grandchildren. Telecommunication providers differ in tariffs and contract value between countries, and apps like Whatsapp have become more popular as a result, as they sidestep the potential cost of SMS and other phone costs pushed by the network.

The variety of devices and apps used imply that the initiator of the contact has to know what device the receiver has (Android or iPhone) and what the conditions of the receiver are. For instance, a daughter may have pictures of her holiday to show their grandmother but, knowing she is not on Whatsapp, opts to send them to the aunt who lives with her granny instead.

Videocalls are particularly important for communication between the younger and the older generations of a family, in order to determine how "healthy" or "safe" their relatives are, particularly when traveling or away.

Family relationships are sometimes strained by professional obligations, as there is no overwhelming feeling of responsibility or economic obligation that prompts families to live together with the elder members in the same household. Consequently, there is sometimes a perceived emotion of guilt associated with not being able to obtain more feedback on well-being or physical status of elder family members on the ensuing communication.

Sharing accounts in digital services like Amazon, eBay, or Spotify is also common between couples and families sharing the same household.

Russia has fairly dissimilar habits concerning messaging from the rest of Europe, as the most popular app for the category is Viber, initially launched as a direct competitor for Skype.

4.2.3   Social Media

The use of Facebook is heavily dependent on demographics as well. In France, families tend to use features like groups and events in a much more inclusive manner, whereas in other countries, communication over Facebook tends to be more direct.

4.2.4   Most Often Used Communication Channels

SMS (France, Eastern Europe, Germany); Whatsapp (Portugal, Spain, Italy); E-mail and Skype (for long-distance communication with absent and younger family members).

Reliance on voice commands and speech recognition is moderate and on the rise, but self-awareness inhibits many speakers from using it in public. It is very useful in the household, especially for family members engaged in other tasks.

4.3   DIGITAL PORTRAIT: NORTH AMERICA

Recently, a friend of mine was stuck in Atlanta on a 3-hour layover. His flight was delayed, and aching to check his work e-mail, he was desperate for a quick shot of Wi-Fi. He decided to ask for assistance. "That cafe has it," waved a bored security guard dismissively. Disheveled and unkempt, he was chasing that fabled two-bar signal that can take one from incommunicado to engaged. He waved his weathered Macbook in the air as if awaiting a transmission from the heavens: alas, the electronic deity informed him that a monthly subscription was due if ever he was to see his inbox refreshed again.

However, Canada and the United States are two of the best connected countries in the world, ranking consistently in the Top 10 of every Digital Access Index and Internet statistic. Silicon Valley has consistently set many of the digital trends that have taken other markets by storm, from Apple and Nvidia to Facebook and Netflix. The individuality and self-reliance that are an inherent part of the national character have helped the entrepreneurship spirit to grow beyond its borders, allowing the American presence to grow the world over.

User habits in North America tend to be wildly variable, as they can differ substantially between large areas such as New York and San Francisco, to more remote locations in the Midwest and even northern Alaska. Although connectivity is very good throughout the country, there is a clear difference in the usage of standard services like social media. According to a Statista report, North America is the global region with the highest penetration of social media at 59%. Facebook dominates the proceedings, as 44% of all social media access is stamped on the company's servers. As of 2016, it is estimated that 185 million people use social media. Suburban areas and high-income users (over 75,000 dollars per year) lead the overall access statistics, with almost 30% of inhabitants accessing their accounts several times per day.

Although traditionally, SMS was cheap and accessible across operators, this communication channel has since been replaced with iMessage and Facebook Messenger. iMessage has latched onto the success of the iPhone and allowed users to use instant messaging between Apple devices without using the carriers network. Facebook Messenger has grown over the past few years and is set to continue domination on the Android market as well (Fig. 4.3.1).

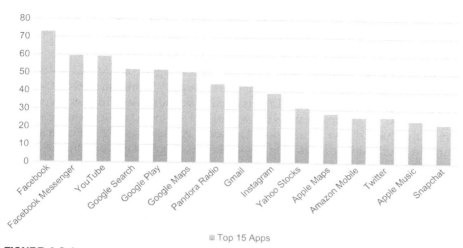

FIGURE 4.3.1
2015 top apps in both iOS and Android platforms. *Source: comScore ranking in the United States, July 2015.*

4.4 DIGITAL PORTRAIT: SOUTH AMERICA

Internet access in South America is unbalanced, reflecting the sometimes extreme contrasts that afflict developing markets. Its biggest economies are Argentina, Chile, and Brazil. Of the three, Brazil has the largest Internet penetration and digital access index. More than a combination of overblown costumed celebrations and an amalgamation of football excellence, Brazil has grown to be one of the promising new world powers in terms of prime materials and social mass. Its investments on carbon emissions control and environmental sustainability policies have attracted attention all over the world. Historically, the country has been plagued with mediatic corruption scandals, entrenched criminal activity, and internal recessions. Yet, according to the IMF, it is also the eighth largest world economy and holds the high mark in South America for new technology adoption. The country has successfully transitioned into state-of-the-art telecommunication networks and continues to improve its infrastructures on a yearly basis.

And most of it is used by the poorest segments of the population in the country. The lower classes have the upper hand in their access and usage of computers, and poorer people use communication technology more extensively: phones, laptops. A 2010 report by the Datapopular Institute reported that 87% of people with a monthly income under $2040 BRL (approximately $580 USD) had a computer at home, with a total of 28 million Brazilian families having access to at least one such device in the household. Nine out of 10 favela dwellers owned at least one mobile phone by 2013, and the Internet penetration on the country was 64% by 2015, totaling over 130 million Internet users in a population of roughly 200 million.

The average low salary and inflation prompted Brazil to have a uniquely shifting social landscape, where 65% of slum inhabitants were already considered to be a part of the new middle class. Over the years, socioeconomic indexes have also demonstrated that rather than move away from the slum areas, more families are becoming comfortable with the low rent and the closeness of the neighborhood of the "favela."

The same can be said of Mexico, where, according to a AMIPCI (Mexican Internet Association) 2015 study, there are over 53.9 million Internet users, with a 51% penetration in inhabitants aged 6 or older. Also in Mexico, social groups of a C or D classification (lower middle or low class) constitute up to 77% of the Internet user community. The social gap between the different social groups in South America is closing in—and technology is largely to blame.

Digital experience in Brazil, like elsewhere in South America, is heavily social—and predominantly young. In Mexico, at least a quarter of all Internet users are teenagers between 13 and 18 years old, with 75% of all Internet usage coming from millennials aged 6 to 34 years. This implies that younger segments of the population are the main targets of actual web design, mainly in a home setting.

According to the same AMIPCI report, most of the Internet usage is social in nature: over 83% of users in Mexico use it for social networking of some sort. The most popular social media websites in Brazil and Mexico are Facebook, followed by Twitter and Whatsapp.

Facebook Users and Penetration in Latin America, by Country, 2014–19						
Facebook user (millions)	**2014**	**2015**	**2016**	**2017**	**2018**	**2019**
Brazil	72	79	87	92.5	94.8	97
Mexico	40	45	52	57	61	65
Argentina	18	20	21	21.7	22.4	23
Other	63.9	73.2	81.5	87.5	92.9	97.4
Facebook user penetration (% of social network users)						
Argentina	94.8	94.8	96.3	96.3	96.4	96.5
Mexico	94.1	94.5	94.7	94.8	94.9	95
Brazil	92.2	91.4	93.3	94.5	94.2	94.1
Other	89.6	88.4	90.9	91.1	91.2	91.1
Facebook user penetration (% of Internet users)						
Mexico	67.3	70	73.3	75.3	75.8	76.2
Brazil	66.9	69.5	72.6	75	75.3	75.5
Argentina	67	68	70	71	72	72.6
Other	57.6	61	64.3	66	67.5	68.6
Facebook user penetration (% of population)						
Argentina	42.2	45.4	47.6	49	50.3	51.2
Brazil	35.5	38.7	42.2	44.6	45.4	46.1
Mexico	33.4	37.6	42.4	46.1	48.9	51.4
Other	26.5	30	33	35.1	36.8	38.2

Source: eMarketer, July 2015. Used with permission from eMarketer.com.

4.5 DIGITAL PORTRAIT: ASIA

The Chinese are among the most avid travelers in the world. You will be hard-pressed to find an attractive destination anywhere that is not regularly visited by Chinese families, aiming to record the whole experience for posterity (and online outlets) with thousands of hazy Polaroid-emulating shots.

Given the emphasis on a hard-working ethic, Chinese consumers tend to take precious little time away from work and often holidays go incomplete when employees return to work earlier to demonstrate their commitment to the company.

For these reasons, choices in traveling and products are very well thought-out, with an in-depth premeditation. When booking hotels and holidays, Chinese people tend to carefully research international hotels, and consult both search engines as well as travel guide sites. Some of the most popular choices include CTRIP, Booking.com, and Baidu searches. These searches are often conducted on social media and forums as well: word-of-mouth and personal recommendation play a major role in making a purchase choice.

India has developed its own smartphone infrastructure dramatically in the past 10 years, and the most popular messaging app in the country is Nimbuzz with 150 million users in the country. The app features various chat rooms and Nimbuckz, a specialized currency used to buy gifts and others.

Online audiences are getting older, with over 40% of Internet users aged 25 years or older as of 2013. Also, there is a trend to increase the number of female users online, which will have an impact on the economy, as women are incharge of over 44% of budget choices at home in India.

Social units in India tend to be small, and the population density in the country implies the need for smaller homes. Living rooms tend to be small, but are usually equipped with television and DVD or Bluray players.

Families tend to share devices, and it is very usual that younger members of the family are given hand-me-down smartphones and tablets. The content in Indian websites also tended to use the English language, as the Internet in India largely started in the urban areas, typically accessed by a more affluent segment of the population. A 2016 study by W3Techs on usage of content languages for websites clearly puts English atop the Web pyramid, populating over 52% of all websites. Hindi has less than 1% of the total worldwide

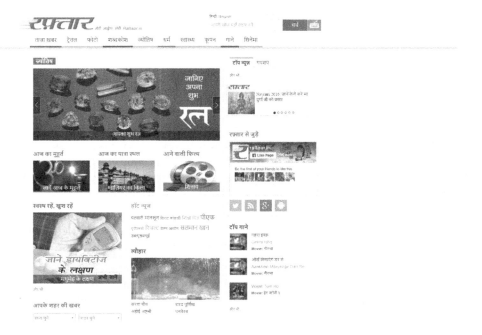

FIGURE 4.5.1

Raftaar is one of the oldest websites in native Hindi, having pioneered the complex script of the language for search engines at a time when there was little standardization on the subject.

web content, Now that mobile phones and accessible technology are more popular, however, social diversification can lead to a growth of Hindi and Tamil on online content and the proliferation of sites like Raftaar.in (Fig. 4.5.1).

Most of the popular equipment in the country tends to be low-end or with limited Internet functionality. Internet cafés were traditionally the center of the online activity in less urban areas, and are still very popular. Given the reasonably low speed of communication, the use of pen drives is also a popular resource within small groups of users. Electricity plugs might also be a concern.

Depending on the social makeup of the group, it is possible that any research in Asian markets involves a cross-channel approach, involving both desktop, tablets, and mobile phones. Desktop is no longer a dominant approach in the continent, in light of the growth of mobile in Asia. However, connection issues and data bandwidth (along with pricey data packages) sometimes prompt users to spend longer on their devices at home. This, coupled with occasional difficulties in accessing international websites due to national firewall restrictions, can render the experience frustrating at points.

The reliance on personal validation also implies that larger purchases, like a holiday, may be subjected to the opinions of others. This is also a social constraint on many other Asian countries, where the emphasis lies on social acceptance and agreement.

Credit cards are not universally used throughout the world as a preferred means of payment, and the Asia-Pacific has in the past shown a slow rate of adoption for credit cards and other credit solutions. However, one notable distinction is China, which according to a 2015 McKinsey report on Asia-Pacific payments, has seen their credit card revenue (27%) surpass the transaction fee revenue in absolute numbers (21%).

Credit card usage is increasing in China, where traditionally prepaid cards enjoyed great success. This is partly due to an increase in B2C sales, but also the development of certain payment alternatives, including Alipay.

Alipay has risen on the back of the Alibaba Group, which has become over the past 15 years one of China's most striking success stories. It has since been made in an independent enterprise which is involved in over half of all the online transactions in China. This is especially relevant as the e-commerce market in China has quickly doubled from 10 to 20 trillion yuan since 2013, and much of it is paid with Alipay methods.

Due to the novelty of the method, Chinese users tend to use their credit card as banks offer various loyalty rewards and benefits based on their expenditure, especially for larger sums. Given that holidays and travels might incur large sums, credit cards offer a flexible and reliable means of payment that absorb the financial shock for the payment of a large amount of money. WeChat and Union Pay are also popular means of payment.

4.5.1 Lessons From the Field

A record-holding company with the largest IPO in history, Alibaba is at the center of an ecosystem that incorporates financing and marketing affiliates:

- social media: Weibo
- location browser: AutoNavi
- entertainment: Youku
- logistics: Cainiao

The Chinese market is a two-way door, with traffic flowing in both directions. Just as Western companies attempt to find a foothold onto the Chinese market, so are Chinese companies seeking out their markets in the West in order to expand their market. Over 40% of Alibaba's customer base is split between North America and Europe versus 30% in Asia.

4.6   DIGITAL PORTRAIT: AUSTRALIA

The tech scene has been developing in the Australian and New Zealand ecosystems for quite some time, and has matured rapidly. Despite the remote geography of the continent, Sydney and Melbourne have developed buzzing development hubs as the society at large caught up rapidly with the latest innovations pushed by international big players.

Most of the tech work developed in the country is directed at international clients, and the location can be beneficial in that regard. Sydney and Melbourne partially overlap with the US West Coast and most Asian capital cities time zones. The prevalent multicultural workforce in the country and its buzzing business atmosphere make it an exciting destination for tech companies. However, the cost of living and housing is still unfathomably high, even by comparison with expensive cities like New York and London.

Australia and New Zealand are typically closer to the American reality than the Asian technological figures. Whereas South Korea and Japan boast average connections of over 15 Mbps, the average in Australia is around 8 Mbps.

Still, in terms of connectivity, the country has one of the best rates in developed nations, and it shows in the digital habits in the country. Television still plays a major role in the country's entertainment options, but Australian consumers are savvy and prefer streamed options over bloated subscriptions and packages. Netflix and YouTube are two of the most popular options in the country.

According to the 2015 Deloitte Media Consumer Survey, reading and watching television are still leading activities in the lives of an educated population with a high standard of living. Nevertheless, 55% of the population uses accesses the Internet over 5 times a day, and 87% of Australians access it on a daily basis. Social media has developed a strong presence in the country, with Facebook clearly emerging as the winner with 95% of all social media accesses. Instagram follows at 31% and LinkedIn at 24%.

Australia also has a particularly restrictive policy on censorship and privacy. This can make videoing interactions in commercial areas a dicey affair.

Like elsewhere in Western Europe, phone users tend to buy a plan or contract for mobile phones rather than buy the device in full. It is possible to break the contract with a penalty fee, but this is highly variable between providers.

4.7   DIGITAL PORTRAIT: AFRICA

Africa is the most ethnically diverse continent in the world, and its multitude of languages, customs, and habits pose a challenge to designers. The difference in digital literacy and experience in ICT is changing in several places in the continent, which as a whole continues to move further and further away from the grim imagery of famine and war that plagued its perception in the West for decades.

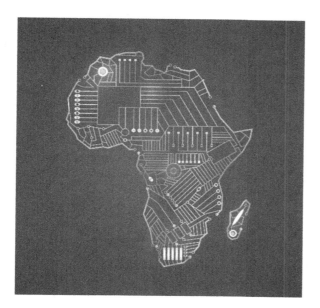

Nigeria in particular has experienced a dramatic growth in connectiveness since the early 1990s. According to the DHL Global Connectedness Index 2014 report, it is actually one of the 50 best connected countries in the world at number 38. (As a comparison, the United States are ranked 23rd.) This is partially due to the important role played by the Nigerian economy in international trade with other partners worldwide, particularly in terms of oil derivatives. Even though it has done little to bridge the economic disparity of the local population, the country continues to thrive.

4.7.1   Infrastructure

The mobile communication network is generally improving, with fixed lines still lagging behind in rural areas. Urban centers are predictably much better connected. South Africa is one of the exceptions, with the fixed-line and mobile phone networks being of general good quality throughout the country. Mobile phone subscription is on the rise, and competition is fierce in various countries.

4.7.2   Communication Style

In Nigeria, the high-context communication style often leads to a reliance on verbal cues and implicit messages. The conversation tends to be more direct when dealing with individuals perceived as social lower status.

4.7.3   Family

Most African cultures tend to be group-oriented. Multigenerational family households are common, and the emotional support provided by grandparents and cousins is crucial to everyday living. The importance of personal relationships cannot be overstated, since a lot of businesses rely on stable and reliable partnerships that often extend beyond the professional sphere. On the other hand, hierarchies are still respected and upheld in most European-style businesses, and short-term goals are often the priority in light of political and military tensions.

Privacy is less of a concern than in more individualistic societies, but countries like Kenya tend to prefer to work individually. Tensions between different ethnic groups are still rampant, due to the struggle for access to limited resources. Social media is blooming across the continent.

4.8   INFRASTRUCTURE AND TRUST

Here in your mind you have complete privacy. Here there's no difference between what is and what could be.

Chuck Palahniuk

Hardware cost is a problem in emerging markets. Often, it is more cost effective to use older systems and smart phones. Some projects aimed at introducing affordable smartphones in these economies have relied on outdated technology or refurbished devices. One of these projects was the Freedom 251 phone, claiming to be the world's cheapest smartphone with a retail price of about $4, although the production cost exceeded $40. In 2014 Google also entered the Indian market with its own low-cost "Android One" project, retailing at 6399 Indian Rupees.

How sustainable is this business model? Companies defend smart phones by targeting burgeoning growth markets, particularly the poorer social segments which cannot afford a glitzy (even if outdated) iPhone. This represents a significant opportunity to build a presence and even a controlling monopoly with markets that are just starting to awaken to the possibilities of the digital lifestyle.

It also helps that these markets are *huge*. According to a 2015 GfK forecast, the largest growing tech markets are also significantly populated (in USD $billion):

1. India: 34.8
2. China: 200.8

3. Nigeria: 5.7
4. Pakistan: 4.8
5. Vietnam: 6.1
6. Bangladesh: 3.8
7. Brazil: 39.3
8. Egypt: 5.0
9. Indonesia: 12.7
10. Philippines: 4.1

Over the years, major communication companies made several attempts at breaking the bonds of poor infrastructure in African countries. Vodafone was one of the first companies to do so, by introducing the WebBox in 2011: a keyboard that included a GSM/EDGE receiver and could be connected up directly to a television. The company attempted to pitch the WebBox at developing countries, starting with selected countries in Africa, including Kenya and South Africa, as well as India and Turkey. The expansion of the mobile infrastructure slowly overtook the investment in the area, but the WebBox, like other products in its range, led to a slew of products aimed at the poorly connected areas of the globe with a focus on robustness and low building cost.

The communication breakdown concerns about security and privacy are rampant, with the media and public opinion both, but what does this mean? Is there a general discomfort toward monopoly? Data collection? Is it a matter of trust toward corporations like Google or Facebook? Or is it something deeper and more malleable?

This is one of the reasons why monopolies can actually assist the user journey, and China leads the way in this seamless experience: from the incipience of wanting to the target of satisfaction. The integration between purchasing and payment is one of the reasons behind the success of Amazon, and the major Chinese services are following a similar recipe.

Western users are accustomed to a mosaic of services which bounce them from the midst of a purchase to the payment website, e.g., between eBay and PayPal. Monopolies are growing in the East, and consumer demand is actively growing with them.

4.9 CUSTOMER SUPPORT AND SERVICE

Here beyond men's judgments all covenants were brittle.

Cormac McCarthy

In some quadrants of the industry, marketing is seen as a world apart from user experience. Consider, however, that marketing plays a key role in establishing leads, reaching out to prospective customers, and setting up their expectations and idea of the brand. These are essential components of the prejudgments that the potential customer will bring when purchasing a product or using a service. Retaining and satisfying the customer is then a prime component of user or customer experience.

Expectations play a major role in the customer reactions to the support services in an international setting. For example, an English customer calls a brand's customer support contact number. The ensuing conversation with an Indian contact does not go well: the call quality is poor, the customer has difficulty understanding the support contact's accent, and the support service cannot reliably understand the nature of the problem. The experience is unsatisfactory for all involved, and as a result, negative feelings toward the brand are inevitable (Fig. 4.9.1).

This is in line with our own psychology as a social species. The sum of our experience and background constitutes its *subjective knowledge*, and this plays a major role in our assumptions. We tend to see things from one specific point of view, but this perspective has been influenced and affected by the country we were raised in, the companies we work in, and the expectations we have toward other services. Anecdotally, British and American tourists frequently vent their frustrations about local customer service when

FIGURE 4.9.1
Responsiveness and efficiency in handling a customer query should be optimized on a cross-channel basis.

going abroad in areas like Southern Europe or Northern Africa. The interaction is fairly similar to what they would experience back home: buying a meal or a souvenir, or going out on the town. However, the expectation toward a certain type of interaction and body language on the staff's part has been greatly set up by their own experiences in their original environment.

The Smiling Report, an international customer service quality assessment report specialized in shopping services, consistently places Asia at the bottom of their listings for smiling, greeting, and add-on sales. These are relatively universal indicators of good customer service in the West, and a common expectation for most indecisive customers sitting at the table of a modest restaurant or an upscale coffeehouse. However, in Asian countries, these interactions were for the most part curt and courteous at best. The 2015 report has placed territories like Hong Kong and Japan at the bottom of an international satisfaction survey with customer experience, while countries like the UK, Ireland, and Greece literally greet their visitors with a broad grin.

The difference between these countries is deeper than just cultural. Customer service in Asia was traditionally regarded as the modern equivalent of visiting a begrudging grandmother who has no qualms with identifying perceived flaws with your weight, clothes, and questionable life choices. This is not the universal reality, however, with the 2015 Avaya Asia-Pacific Customer Experience Survey highlighting that Thailand, Indonesia, and the Philippines praise their customer service, while Singapore are repeatedly disillusioned with the quality of their services. Sixty-five percent of them, in fact, rated contact with a customer service center as "always problematic." The trend toward higher expectations and customer-centric services is growing yearly in Asia. It signals a shift in the economy of Asian countries, which are increasing their service industry with tourism at the forefront, and product support as a firm reminder of the importance of reliable customer services.

The change in expectations also results directly of social upheaval in countries like China and Vietnam. The rise of a middle class with an increasingly solid amount of disposable income and the success of luxury brands and international retailers in these territories show the lingering social appeal that "lifestyle" products have, particularly in burgeoning societies where status and external signs of wealth are correlated.

Apart from the internal social and economic changes in these Asian countries, the rise of the service industry, with tourism at the forefront, as well as the implementation of some of the best airports in the world in Japan, Korea, Hong Kong, and China, brought about an increasing number of visiting Westerners, which also played a role in the growth of service quality expectations and demands.

4.10 CASE STUDY: WHAT'S IN A NAME?

Agency: IT Consultis

Client: Best English Name

When: 2014–2015

Methods: Behavioral, Attitudinal, Quantitative Qualitative, Exploratory, Generative, Evaluative

Type: New website

Imagine the typical mid-morning atmosphere of an office in Beijing. Twenty-two stories down, the traffic buzzes and whizzes by with chaotic mechanistic precision. In the office, a cacophony of its own can be heard. Angel, the receptionist, calls Ruby, a designer, to inform her that the legal consultant, Magnum Yuen, has arrived and is waiting for their 11 o'clock meeting. Gandalf and Eleven (first name Seven) are also invited to the meeting.

Although not commonly appropriate by Western standards, English names are often appropriated in Asian territories, particularly those with a colonialist past. They usually have an association with a concept or character that is deemed important or bringing great fortune, like "Pussy," "Cesar," or "Hitler." Celebrities are also extremely popular, but the correct spelling of their names is sometimes faltering.

This results from an altogether different naming strategy that takes place in the young and concerned parents' minds. Chinese names are decomposable and subjective in Mandarin, with the different characters enclosing hidden aspirational meanings of good luck and fortune. The novelty effect of appellations is also quite appealing, as proven by the existence of colorful names such as Devil Law, Moniac, Kinetic, and Lazy.

The practice is partly influenced by the British colonial past in the area, as the adoption of English names is also associated with social mobility and prestige in an area where international trade is ubiquitous and English is spoken on a daily basis. The difficulty in building familiarity posed by the Chinese language also helps to explain the reason behind English names and their popularity (Fig. 4.10.1).

Lindsay Jernigan came up with the idea for Best English Name after experiencing the bewildering variety and widespread popularity of English-sounding names in China. Until 2005, there were no Chinese sites made by English speakers, and upper middle-class young parents in the 20-to-25-year-old range looking to start or extend their young family were left without solid references regarding how to name their children with appropriate foreign-sounding names.

FIGURE 4.10.1

Best English Name provides a consulting service for Chinese parents looking to name their newborns with English and Western names. *Source: Used with permission from bestenglishname.com*

In seeing this, Lindsay devised a service meant to advise and help young parents seeking an appropriate name for their children. Being an ex-pat from the age of 12−19 in the United Kingdom, she returned to Shanghai to find an open environment. The presence of foreigners in China is now seen as normal, but was less commonly accepted in the past.

The resulting website was the product of a 1 year collaboration with IT Consultis. Although only 15% of the customer base used an initial iteration of the website to name newborns, later iterations started becoming broader in both appeal and usage.

"The website had to be colorful and interesting to appeal to a native Chinese audience," states Lindsay. "Our intention was still to keep a Western element to it, in order to reinforce our focus." Winks and ads are everywhere in normal Chinese websites. Although the website was directed at women initially, men have started to use it more often, namely because of the highly aspirational element of naming a child with a resonating English name that can beckon good luck and an auspicious future, according to Chinese lore.

The characters were designed purposefully with hybrid feature in order to depict them less as caricatures and more as international representations. That suits the international pitch of the site, which focuses on different countries.

CHAPTER 5
Mental Manifests

ABSTRACT

Aesthetics are governed by the influence of cultural imperatives. Humans think about shapes and colors differently, influenced by different perspectives of time and perception. These differences are motivated by the institutions and behavior patterns that we observe in those around us, and that we are exposed to since birth, but to what extent do they affect the way we think about inter-action, others, and ourselves? What role do we play in the stories we spin about others like us — and the rules that divide us? And how to leverage these differences in the realm of user experience?

Keywords: Mental manifests; cultural model; attitude; social value; storytelling; metaphors; culture; narrative

5.1 AESTHETICS AND CULTURAL IMPERATIVES

"I have known everything," said Lord Henry, with a sad look in his eyes, "but I am always ready for a new emotion."

Oscar Wilde, The Picture of Dorian Grey

Universal UX Design. DOI: http://dx.doi.org/10.1016/B978-0-12-802407-2.00005-8

One look at a Buddhist temple and one can see the materialization of Japanese aesthetics and its particular qualities of musicality and rhythm. However, this underlying principle reveals itself even in the way cinema is made in the region and, in particular, in the movie editing of one of their media exports: Japanese anime. Anime animation is usually characterized by an abundance of characters with exaggeratedly slim limbs, outlandish and emotional stories, and cartoonish facial expressions of surprise. However, some of the most successful animes are deservedly in the canon of best animated features ever (e.g., *Akira*, *Howl's Moving Castle*, *Spirited Away*, among others).

The way that these types of movies treat key scenes is worthy of attention. Each moment is carefully preceded of a single beat that allows the viewer to anticipate the reaction of the character, particularly in an emotional scene. Dramatic pauses are used sparingly in order to allow the audience to engage emotively with the situation, and to allow the scene to unravel before continuing the story.

Part of the reason behind the prevalent use of dramatic pauses in Japanese animation is the need for economy given the limited technical and budget conditions of earlier Anime, but their use also provides a berth to shore the audience's attention unto. Movie editors use a similar technique to give a scene emotional gravitas by changing its tempo and emotional punctuation. Timing is everything when you want to make an impact on the audience gracefully and in a lasting manner, and this is an essential principle of web design as well.

Regularity, even in the simplest of templates, allows the designer to maximize communication on a medium that demands balance and conciseness. This close relationship between rhythm and linearity plays an essential role in the different design strategies that a Japanese designer may adopt as opposed to its Western counterpart, and the way their minds may process information and formulate new ideas.

This difference in cognitive styles is a complex and contentious subject area with many conflicting theories and very many instruments to determine the different perspectives of cognitive style and in addition, the cultural background of an individual may affect the outcome of any cognitive test. However, there is a body of research (Markus & Kitayama, 1991; Witkin & Berry, 1975) that correlates cultural characteristics and the thinking or cognitive style of certain populations.

The relationship between culture and cognition has been considered in wildly different ways according to the dominant strands of social psychology. The concept that culture could influence basic mechanisms of thought was generally avoided by the prevailing psychological models and has only recently started to receive attention. To understand how culture can shape cognition, a little thought experiment applies: imagine in your head a door handle. Did you picture a door lever or a knob? Both are ergonomically different and prevalent in different areas of the globe. Door knobs tend to be more popular in the United States, whereas levers are most often used in Europe. This difference is even clear in our symbolic associations. Whereas the dove is the bird representing peace in the West, the white crane is the most popular symbol in Asia. This is but one of many differences that have loaded terms like "Westerners" and "Easterners," which are apparently differentiating and homogeneous, but carry their own share of stereotyping. Richard Nisbett, in his work *The geography of thought*, suggests that the cognitive style or intellectual approach have been influenced by centuries of separate sets of beliefs and aesthetic sensibilities:

> Like ancient Greek philosophers, modern Westerners see a world of objects—discrete and unconnected things. Like ancient Chinese philosophers, modern Asians are inclined to see a world of substances—continuous masses of matter. The Westerner sees an abstract statue where the Asian sees a piece of marble; the Westerner sees a wall where the Asian sees concrete. There is much other evidence—of a historical, anecdotal, and systematic scientific nature—indicating that Westerners have an analytic view focusing on salient objects and their attributes, whereas Easterners have a holistic view focusing on continuities in substances and relationships in the environment.
>
> **Nisbett (2003, p. 82)**

According to Nisbett, this distinction between holistic and analytic reasoning marks a difference in cultural identity between these two different cognitive styles. Nisbett distinguishes *holistic reasoning* as "an orientation to the context or field as a whole, including attention to relationships between a focal object and the field, and a preference for explaining and predicting events on the basis of such relationships" (Nisbett, Peng, Choi & Norenzayan, 2001, p. 293).

On the other hand, *analytic thought* "involves a detachment of the object from its context, a tendency to focus on attributes of the object to assign it to categories, and a preference for using rules about the categories to explain and predict the objects behavior" (Nisbett et al., 2001, p. 293).

These notions build on Witkin's definition of subjects as "field dependent" or "field independent" (1967), who pioneered the theory of cognitive styles. Later studies (Hayes & Allinson 1988; Nisbett & Norenzayan 2002) have shown the impact of cultural background on the way information is learned and processed, particularly in light of the holistic and analytical dimensions.

Both styles of thinking are deeply connected with their civilizational roots. The Greek favored a scientific method of decomposing Nature's elements into causality, consequence, and actors. Their epistemology was centered around analysis and the early scientific principle and Chinese rational appeals to a rounder perspective of data as nondiscrete elements.

This is directly reflected in the user attitude in China. Chinese culture is inherently polychronic (a definition first introduced by Edward T. Hall in 1977), where multitasking is common and tasks can be performed simultaneously. Polychronic cultures tend to rely on nurturing and constant attention to ongoing tasks, like scheduling meetings, as opposed to monochronic cultures, which focus on sequential or linear chains of events.

This is directly reflected in the attitude towards web design in China. There is a traditional perception of Chinese websites as hard to navigate with dense, cluttered pieces of content. The reliance on Flash technology, the tendency to have every link open a new tab, and an abundance of links seems to indicate an antiquated attitude towards web design in comparison with the tidy minimalistic designs inspired by Google.

In reality, most contemporary Chinese web design is adopting similar trends to Western design, with bold white space and a minimalism of same-page tasks (Fig. 5.1.1). The fact that the trends in China are more oriented towards sharing with their own social networks and are strictly mobile-based, with desktop sites becoming optional to most companies which instead choose WeChat as a suitable advertising platform.

Another reason for the difference in Chinese web design is the alphabet and its implications for information processing. Cantonese characters are graphically composed by a combination of strokes, and any given character can range from 1 to 60 strokes. The absence of capitalization and Latin indentation and paragraphs contributes to the perception of its "busy look."

The abundance of links still stumps the average web designer. One of the suggested reasons is that typing in the Chinese alphabet is a difficult task, and the links are supposed to encourage clicking. Chui Chui Tan, editor at Smashing

FIGURE 5.1.1
Didi Chuxing, the most successful ride sharing service in China, managed to upstage Uber at its own game and become the dominant player in the market. Part of the success is the alignment of the brand with a simple message: ride cheaper and more effectively. The company uses big data and complex machine learning algorithms to predict taxi demand and program routes more effectively, handling an average of 20 million rides a day. *Source: Used with permission from Didi Chuxing.*

Magazine, has a different opinion: "Chinese use the same keyboards as the West. They use 'Pinyin' to input Chinese characters using these alphabet-based keyboards. There are shortcuts. It is fast and easy. It could be slower for Chinese to type in English than in Chinese. Chinese also complain about not being able to find what they are after on a page due to the overwhelming content and links. Instead, they choose to use the search box and skip the homepage."

Links are often loaded on new tabs because of the traditionally slow connections. The pages continue to load while the users can still continue to read their current page. Flash is used because of its traditional ease to create colorful click-bait that generates ad revenue, but the situation is rapidly changing.

The use of Chinese fonts is also hard to judge at first, as there are still not too many choices on the market and emphasizing Chinese fonts is necessarily difficult because of the alphabet structure. Font sizes also make a difference, because of readability issues, given the complexity of each glyph.

The tendency for complexity is no longer a mainstay of Chinese design. Baidu's uncanny similarity to Google's cool minimalism is an example of success with an apparently unappealing Western design.

5.2 PERSONAL ATTITUDES AND SOCIAL VALUES

So, here you are

too foreign for home

too foreign for here.

never enough for both.

Ijeoma Umebinyuo, diaspora blues

Cultures are conventionally divided into traditional and nontraditional. An empirically-based scientific culture is often identified as nontraditional, whereas mythical belief-centered cultures are defined as traditional.

When thinking about modern beliefs and the role of science in our everyday interaction with world, it is difficult to uphold this distinction. The doctor is our shaman. Technology is our God. (And yet fundamentalism is rising and one of the main political issues of our time.) There is only one step of separation between this social arrangement and similar roles played by other actors in nonindustrialized societies, which present a variety of beliefs and the integration of age-old values and principles. It further blurs the line between what was conventionalized as "primitive cultures" and the "new" manifestations the same roles have come to absorb.

One important distinction between traditional culture and nontraditional culture is that the first one tends to be geographically restricted, whereas the latter has spread like wildfire throughout the world. Traditional cultures represent a fixed set of social roles, routines, and ideas about reality and the world.

Nontraditional cultures are, for the most part, fluid, interactive, and privilege individual social mobility, along with a strong prevalence of modern technology.

As an example, the Japanese perspective on entrepreneurship was traditionally quite negative. The *keiretsu* structure in Japanese society, which links different companies as a type of business meta-group, is still very prevalent in the economy, and the safety net for new entrepreneurs is extremely limited. However, the rise of young businessmen such as Hiroshi Mikitani, founder of the "Japanese Amazon" and local e-commerce giant Rakuten, served as the beginning of a mass interest in startup companies. Although working in a small company traditionally signaled either limited prospects or a family business, the rise of entrepreneurship allowed smaller and more agile companies to thrive in an otherwise very monopolistic market (Fig. 5.2.1).

Social psychologist Shalom Schwartz argued that "the prevailing value emphases in a society may be the most central feature of culture," stating that a singular value represents the "shared conceptions of what is good and desirable in the culture, the cultural ideals" (Schwartz, 2006, pp. 138–139).

FIGURE 5.2.1

Jumia, based in Nigeria, is one of the budding gems of the African e-commerce scene. Its homepage is easy to navigate and the IA categories are clearly separated. Unlike its American and European counterparts, the brand logos on offer occupy a prominent placing in the homepage. *Source: Used with permission from Juma.*

Schwartz has since developed a model of 10 fundamental values that determine the motivation and reception of interactive factors. These values are important to understand the role of these values in decision-making processes when the user is faced with a product value proposition. Schwartz defends that users make choices based on a set of wishes and goals, which can be traced to an hierarchy of perceptions of the actual product which, after interaction, correlate with a value. For instance, a user can perceive a website as having a sturdy encryption procedure during payment, which triggers a set of consequences, namely the confident use of a credit card, and correlates to the final or instrumental value, which is the general need to feel secure.

Schwartz suggested a value inventory that would be closer to grouping different values under one sole category:

- Power: Fundamentally correlated with social status and one's reputation, as well as the control over others. Public image and social recognition are key to the cultures associated with this.
- Achievement: The values from the achievement of goals and personal fulfilment. Associated with ambition and a sense of individual success.
- Hedonism: Solitary or egoistic gratification through self-indulgence.
- Stimulation: Thrills and the excitement of something new and difference drives individuals who are particularly creative or bent on artistry.
- Self-direction: Closely linked to more individual perspectives on social roles, this value category is related to the independence of thought and actions displayed by people.
- Universalism: Related to tolerance and mutual appreciation, as well the promotion of peace and equality. Socially tolerant societies are the most universalist.
- Benevolence: It is closely related to the preservation and protection of others and immediate connections (friends and emotional relationships especially).
- Tradition: Respect for what has come before, and keeping in with the previous customs in place. Normally associated with a more conservative mindset and averse to change.
- Conformity: Restraint and obedience to hierarchies and norms. Control is normally equated with self-discipline and obedience.
- Security: Associated with harmony and stability to a higher degree than normal. Health awareness and cleanliness of habits and personal stance are seen as primary concerns.

Understanding the values that matter to your users is paramount in order to adapt copy and content suitably. For instance, Spain consistently ranks highly on hedonism while the United Kingdom ranks highly in the achievement value set. This sense of achievement may be well perceived in Anglo-American culture, but the perception of an individual who displayed this type of behavior would be very negative in China and similar countries where these dimensions are not as pronounced (Fig. 5.2.2).

FIGURE 5.2.2

Statistical analysis of the structure of values proposed by Schwartz collated after a study with 68 countries and over 64,000 participants. *Source: http://valuesandframes.org/handbook/2-how-values-work/. Used with permission from Shalom Schwartz. Schwartz, S.H. (2006). Basic human values: Theory, measurement, and applications. Revue française de sociologie, 47 (4), 249–288.*

5.3   PERSUASION AND REASON

Character may almost be called the most effective means of persuasion.

Aristotle

Everything is a dialogue, either with others or the environment. The apps we use speak to us, either directly through the content displayed on-screen or with whispers in the background of our push notification list. We tend to engage with software as if they are a teammate or a person, and this can easily assume the role of communication accompanied with collaboration.

Similarly, as in conversations everyday, the systems we interact with everyday are trying their best to persuade us. We can be swayed by influence into buying something or accepting something. Our interactions are directly affected by the way we see reality, and reality is the compound of our expectations plus our influences, social, and otherwise.

As an example, take Steve Jobs. Hailed in many quarters as one of the greatest marketing minds of the 20th century, his path was obstinate and of single purpose. During his addresses for new product releases, he became known for creating what was called a "distorted reality field," where he was able to convince his audience that, among other unbelievable ideas, the iPad was a good product name.

Steve Jobs conveyed this feeling through rhetorical ability and technical acuity, but most importantly, he did it out with *conviction*. Jobs successfully persuaded audiences and markets the world over to change their attitude towards smartphones, touchscreens, and digitally-compressed music.

Like other aspects of interaction, persuasion is meant to convince the user to adopt a specific attitude or behavior and, like any method to convince someone, it can also be abused. An interface can convince the unaware user to click on an advertising banner, or to avoid reading terms and conditions that may spare months in a court procedure.

However, the basic focus of persuasive patterns is to address and influence *behavioral triggers* in users, priming their psychological biases to stimulate specific actions, which are positive either to the system or to the user itself. Applying a trigger in a micro-interaction or conveying the right tone is key to persuade the user to a single click that could mean conversion, and success in the ultimate goal of the buy-sell dynamic.

Theorists like Bob Cialdini argue that there are six basic methods of influencing others. These basic principles have been adapted into multiple interaction patterns, developing a unique set of attributes for each.

- *Authority*: Assume the role of an expert and a trustworthy authority on a subject or domain. More individualistic societies like Sweden and Denmark, where there is a low power distance between the members of the group, would tend to challenge authority more readily, an authoritative voice in the person of an expert would not necessarily resonate as clearly and quickly as a clear-cut minimal-fuss solution offered through experience. Scandinavia has a culture of consensus is in place and hierarchies are embedded in the group's relationships (Fig. 5.3.1).

On the other hand, high-context cultures like those prevalent in the Middle East, where families are extended and hierarchies are fairly rigid, have a greater bias towards the influence of those in their immediate network.

- *Commitment and consistency*: By allowing somebody to spend time or invest effort on an activity, it is easier to request a favor in return. For example, to request the full investment in a yearly subscription after offering 2 months for free. Past experiments in conformity studies have shown that there is a difference in commitment and conformity between different cultures. There is a strong relation between the

FIGURE 5.3.1
IKEA knows how to speak to its audience. Whereas the Spanish website features prominently an inviting portrait of blissful domestic life, appealing to families, the Swedish site features prominently a minimalistic collection set focused on design. Gone are the children's smiling faces: practicality and conciseness rules the day. *Source: Used with permission from IKEA.*

conformity in group consensus and collectivistic societies (Bond & Smith, 1996). The willingness to comply is also stronger in more collectivistic societies like those in Asian countries (Cialdini et al., 1999).

- *Liking bias*: We are swayed by personal preference into choice. We tend to pardon those we like faster than those we do not like. Brands operate

FIGURE 5.3.1
Continued.

across similar lines. The qualities perceived in the way a company communicates set the stage for the client's perceptions. This is one of the reasons why a familiar and friendly tone is used on apps and web services, building in colloquialism and humor in the communication between user and brand. There is a clear link between the perceived communication tone of a company's content, and being receptive towards the products or services it offers.

- *Reciprocity*: The principle of doing something in exchange for a favor or to repay an action. For example, we are more likely to retweet users who have retweeted us. Another example is the way that an interaction contrasts reward versus reciprocity. There is evidence that users tend to engage more in a situation of reciprocity rather than reward. For example, users tend to respond better when a registration form is presented *after* a complementary article, and the conversion rate is significantly higher than if the content is locked behind a register-first gate (Gamberini et al., 2007). Reciprocity tends to work better than reward in the case of free content, something that Radiohead and Pretty Lights can attest to with their pay-what-you-will experiments for otherwise free albums.
- *Scarcity*: Everything seems more appealing when it is presented as being in short availability. This principle can be coupled with *loss aversion*, which reflects our unwillingness to part with something that we already have over the possibility of winning something potentially much better. People feel a loss much more vividly than a win.
- *Social proof*: Reviews and validation by other trusted people play a major role in our decision-making. Social proof happens in particular when we are looking for validation of our own decisions with other people.

This is one of the reasons why we look at third-party sites and look at popularity indicators to feel confident about our own choices. In general, we feel more confident about comparing our opinions with those of others and these are instrumental in gauging our own perception. There is a clear difference in how this is manifested across the manifold of multiculturalism. Advertisements in Korea tended to focus on the advantages of buying a product due to the example of others rather than the inherent advantages of the product (Han & Shavitt, 1994), promoting group benefits rather than the benefits of the product itself. The tendency is countered by most Western advertisements, particularly in the United States (Fig. 5.3.2).

5.3.1   Researching

Qualitative research is key to understand the form and applicability that these triggers can have in the context of a user journey. Competitive benchmarking provides a good insight into the stimuli already in place in the marketplace, but in order to start with the source and not the consequence, a combination of methods (e.g., interviews and/or workshops) can provide a solid foundation on what the general biases and expectations of users are in terms of their behavior on the webpage.

By asking questions like "what are your greatest fears when it comes to booking a trip?" or "can you rate how important it is to you to have a recommendation on an hotel or a flight?", it is possible to group this input under actual persuasive themes that can be mapped to persuasive patterns. These themes can be groups: Cognition, Perception and Memory, Gamification, and Social.

You can approach each one of those persuasive patterns as "themes" and produce a set of recommendations on the general users' biases. This then can be used by the content and design teams in order to guide decisions on the actual placement, timing, and tone of the messages.

Designing for persuasion is essentially designing an interactive experience that influences and impacts behavior on a preconscious level. An influence analysis allows you to generate ideas on what the actual desired attitude and behavior changes are. By making these explicit, you can then manipulate and change these behaviors much more effectively.

5.3.2   Interview With Masaaki Kurosu

Dr. Masaaki Kurosu is one of the foremost thinkers in contemporary HCI research and author of "Theory of User Engineering" (2016). His works on the relationship between cultural usability and UI design have pioneered a new perception of User Experience and ushered in a new research approach more focused on triggering affective interactions, based on the Artifact Evolution Theory, which connects human factors specific to local populations with the progressive enhancement of technology objects (Table 5.3.1).

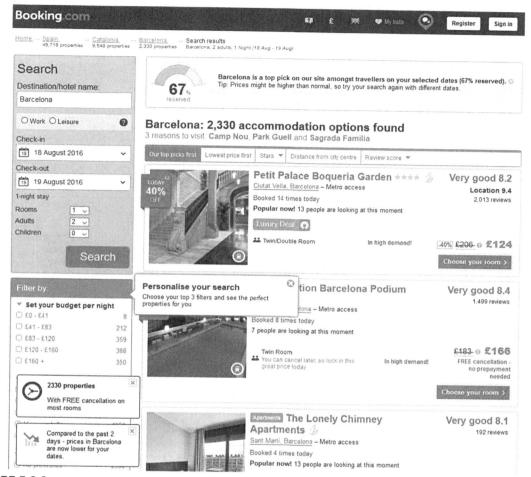

FIGURE 5.3.2

Travel sites are particularly deft at adopting persuasive design principles in order to promote user conversion and to push customers into the booking funnel. Booking.com uses similar persuasive patterns across their localized websites. In this case, the United Kingdom and the Chinese localized sites promote (1) the use of alternative dates in order to search for better prices, (2) the use of popular preset filters in the Chinese variant to play to the most popular requirements displayed by customers, (3) the promotion of filters in order to view preferred results as practically as possible, (4) an anchoring technique, showing the "full" price first and then a cut down "promotion." "Sold-out" results are also interspersed in the Chinese list, in order to promote urgency and impulse buying. *Source: Used with permission from Booking.com.*

Your recent research has focused on the importance of experience design. What is the importance of emotion engineering in comparison to cultural factors in user engineering?

> *In this figure, I classified quality characteristics into "objective and subjective" vs "artifact quality and quality in use." The quality in use is related to the UX and the artifact quality including usability is just clarifying the ability or the*

FIGURE 5.3.2
Continued.

potential of artifacts. The emotion engineering that is called as Kansei engineering in Japan is related to the subjective quality characteristics both in artifact quality and quality in use. As Hassenzhal pointed out, practical attributes (objective quality characteristics in my figure) and hedonic attributes (subjective quality characteristics in my figure and is related to Kansei engineering) are both important. Culture, in this context, is more related to the subjective quality characteristics.

What is your opinion on the emphasis in recent years on diversity- and usability-oriented design?

Diversity is a fundamental dimension that we'll have to focus on when designing artifacts.

Table 5.3.1	Qualities of Diversity Among Users According to the Artifact Evolution Theory (Kurosu, 2014)
Trait	Age
	Sex
	Disability
	Physical traits
	Race and ethnic group
	Personality
	Knowledge and skill
Tendency	Taste
	Attitude
	Emotion
	Arousal level
	Temporary condition
Context	Religion
	Culture
	Tradition
	Language
Environment	Physical
	Geographical

Government regulation on digital accessibility is not yet a universal trend. Do you think this will change in the future?

> *Yes, government regulations should back up the universal design. Just summarizing a guideline is just a one step toward the regulations and is not enough. The legal force is quite important.*

Seeing that culture can be interpreted as the common set of values and learned responses that affect the way we interact with objects and the world around us (it is known that culture can impact visual recognition and body language), can culture impact usability design in a meaningful objective way?

> *First of all, from the viewpoint of AET (Artifact Evolution Theory) that I'm establishing, there are various artifacts from culture to culture for achieving the same goal. For example, eating tools include, "knife, fork and spoon" in Western countries, "chopsticks" in East Asia, "spoon and knife" in South Eastern Asia and "hand" in various places in the world. Each tool has its own usability in relation to shape, size, weight, stickiness, etc. of the foods. Example is the chopsticks in Japan where the steak is sometimes cut as a piece of dice before serving it to the table and people don't need to use the knife and use just the chopsticks. Similar examples can be found so many including the artifact for toilet behavior, washing clothes, cleaning houses, etc. etc. They depend so much on the circumstances and serve to the improvement of usability.*

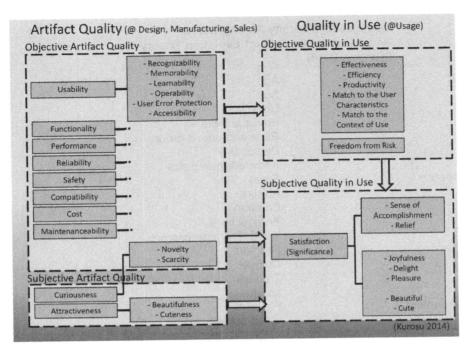

FIGURE 5.3.3

The Emotional Experience framework developed by Prof. Masaaki Kurosu is focused on the objective and subjective qualities of artefacts. The relation between the Objective Artifact Quality and Quality in Use relates the characteristics of the artifact, digital or not, with distinct emotional patterns in the user. Culture can influence the perception of the artifact, namely in its aesthetic, which could be deemed attractive and pleasurable or not depending on the cultural background of the user.

Concerning the diversities you listed, do you think that context can affect tendencies and vice-versa?

> *Tendencies are frequently characteristic to the person and generally are not much related to the context. But the exception is the case where a person with certain tendency selects the context from many alternatives. A good example is the case of selecting coffee shops - traditional café, Starbucks, etc.*

5.4   CULTURAL MODELS

The best teachers impart knowledge through sleight of hand, like a magician.

Kate Betts

Ma is one of the most prevalent concepts in Japanese tradition. *Ma* describes an interval between two or more spatial or temporal things and events. It is an ancient Japanese religio-aesthetic paradigm that brings about a collapse of distinctive (objective) worlds, and even of time and space itself. Richard Pilgrim states that "Ma takes us to a boundary situation at the edge of thinking and the edge of all processes of locating things." The acknowledgment of these "pregnant nothings" reinforces the importance of the mind-state of mushin (no-mind), and such "empty nothings" are absolutely central to Buddhist, Taoist, and Shintoist thought.

Emotions are universal, whereas facial expressions are relatively universal. A study by psychologist Paul Ekman where photographs of faces were shown to people in over 20 Western countries and 11 preliterate communities in Africa has shown a significantly high percentage of correct interpretations: over 90% of respondents in all the cultures successfully identified smiling faces.

But the question remains on whether these expressions are learned or innate. If we look at a baby on a crib, and put up a drop of vinegar on their lips, the reaction is quite universal: disgust. Neonates in general are able to smile and frown seemingly from birth, suggesting that facial expressions are an inherent component of being human.

However, interpreting facial expressions is a different matter. Several people claim to have difficulty recognizing members of another race, especially in a crowd, but culture influences this power of recognition to a deep degree. Research has shown that Chinese-Americans, e.g., can recognize the facial expressions of Americans more promptly than those displayed by other Chinese people living in China. The same findings have been observed in African-Americans. Respondents identified more quickly and more promptly the expressions on the faces of those they contacted with on a daily basis than those in other cultures.

The way we process information is largely related to culture, and the cleavage between the Western analytic and the Eastern holistic thought splits into different components. Nisbett proposed that the two intellectual approaches differ significantly:

> Analytic thinkers tend to see things as discrete individual entities, paying closer attention to the objects themselves rather than anything else surrounding them, and assigning things to categories more promptly. Formal models and rules tend to govern their thinking.
> Holistic thinkers focus on continuity and the relationships between things, as one thing in isolation is not necessarily the most important element when thinking about a concrete situation.

Both styles of thinking are deeply connected with their civilizational roots. The Greek favored a scientific method of decomposing Nature's elements into causality, consequence, and actors. Their epistemology was centered around analysis, whereas the Chinese rationale is holistic, worried about the context and the wider integration of elements.

This influences the way people of either cultural background may think about a problem, a piece of information, and themselves. Quantification is, however, an issue since there is a degree of fuzziness in the approaches. Cultural models were created as an answer to the unsurmountable problem of quantifying human thought in terms of their values and social contexts.

These models are primarily monocultural and thus necessarily incomplete, but they are useful to ascertain the role that certain values play in thought. The models proposed by Hall are possibly the most famous, as he has proposed a variable and quantitative definition of culture as a model composed of different dimensions. Each of these dimensions consist of a character or trait that all cultures possess to a greater or lesser extent, like their perspective of time:

- Low-context: Conversations should have all the information required for a successful interaction, with communication styles being more explicit.
- High-context: Not everything has to be explicit in the interaction. Roles and information are often subdued elements in the conversation, with an indirect communication style (formal/informal, written/symbolic).

Hofstede's model is based on five cultural dimensions, based on his work with 80 countries:

- Hierarchy
- Group orientation (Individualism and Collectivism)
- Gender roles (Masculinity versus Femininity)
- Trust
- Risk-taking (Uncertainty Avoidance)

The premise is that cultures with a high level of individualism have a low-context communication style, preferring a more explicit and formal communication style. Examples of this type of communication include the Swiss, Germans, Scandinavians, Anglo-Americans, English.

On the other hand, collectivism is correlated with high-context communication, where interactions are seen as more implicit and symbolic. Pictorial and visual communication is preferred by peoples like Japanese, Arabs, Latin American, Italian-Spanish, and French.

On this level, high-context cultures tend to be prefer indirect and transformational advertising messages creating emotions through pictures and entertainment (France, Japan). Low-context cultures privilege direct and rational advertising messages providing product information (Germany, United States).

Transposing these assumptions unto a layout and visual design, written text tends to be more informational and rational in nature in low-context communication contexts. High-context communication contexts tend to privilege layouts with visuals pitched with a more entertainment or emotional slant.

These models largely aim at providing a predictive framework for generalized patterns of behavior and their usage has been questioned in many academic quarters. The level of unpredictability and the complex nature of multivariate cultures even within a dominating discourse has given rise to a set of theories around effective brand communication across cultures.

For example, Cateora et al. (2012) has suggested an international marketing model split into two basic sets of factors:

- "Uncontrollables," which consist of everything that a corporation cannot affect or change, like laws, economic situation, geopolitics, standards;
- "Controllables," the actual marketing strategies and approaches that a company can manipulate.

There is arguably a correlation between content appeal and brand perception, and not only on a local basis. Local websites of global consumer brands are sometimes standardized on a worldwide basis. This allows the brands to keep the layout and navigation consistent by usually relying on the same template. This consistency comes at the cost of specialization, but it is cost-effective for certain markets. French food brands are sometimes compliant with a high-context style, whereas German car brands (Mercedes-Benz in Italy, Lancia in Germany) can be low-context regardless of the market. Websites of global companies tend to be strongly standardized and dominated by very linear value propositions.

Users seldom visit technology brand websites, unless they are looking for specific information on products, particularly of a technical nature, like specifications. For larger companies, the sheer website volume and deeply structured content can work in the favor of giving a good support resource for the end-client.

With the necessities of keeping a brand presence consistent on a worldwide basis, the "country-of-origin" effect can be difficult to achieve, unless the product depictions are already viewed in a positive light in the target countries. Ensuring a balance in the advertising and social media channels is key to ensure that local users across different markets capture the spirit of the brand. The brand can speak with many voices, but the message should be the same.

Some researchers have tried to correlate the relationship between access and receptivity to the Internet with cultural dimensions like uncertainty avoidance, arguing that individualistic risk-taking societies showed a quicker dissemination of their online presence (Capurro, 2006), especially with the quick rise of mobile in Asia and Africa.

5.4.1 Lessons from the Field:

Netflix is one of the leading VOD producers, streaming movies and series to over 190 countries. Its original productions, like House of Cards have earned multiple awards, and it is by far the biggest provider of high-budget content streaming outside of YouTube, with 34 million subscribers outside of the

United States. It has successfully introduced terms like "binge-watching" to audiences raised on television and video games across the world, and its aggressive international strategy has taken it to a new level.

Its design is also a master case study in iterative testing. Over the years, the interface has been subjected to a number of A/B testing iterations, with click rate and conversions analytics acting as significant factors of decision in the best approach to take (Fig. 5.4.1).

One of the most ubiquitous factors in the Netflix interface is the absence of a standard list of additions or the full contents of the collection. This allows the service to adapt and render recommendations based on previously seen content and the potential interests of the viewer. In a word, Netflix can push premium content and highlighted material on the viewer by encouraging conversions through convenient access.

Although there are a number of third-party websites and blogs that claim to provide the full list of the Netflix catalog, the service has yet to implement any similar features on its own website. Search engine indexing is also blocked to protect the opacity of its offerings with a paywall.

Netflix is arguably the biggest contender in the West for video-streaming services, but the variety of services worldwide is expanding constantly. These other VOD services are smaller, but have a strong focus on local content that acts as unique selling point when compared to Netflix. By comparison, in South Africa, ShowMax and OnTapTV are two of the biggest services in the continent. The former is backed by media giants Naspers, the largest company in Africa and one of the biggest digital companies in the world.

5.5   APPROPRIATION AND APPROPRIATENESS

The anonymity of typification is inversely proportional to fullness of content.

In the days preceding the fall of the Iron Curtain, technology was a limited good and new computer models were hard to find. The implementation of the CoCom embargo made the import of computer systems into the old URSS nearly impossible and, as a result, the new mass-produced personal computer models that flooded American and European stores in the late 1970s and 1980s were inaccessible to the Russian public.

However, that did not stop Russian engineers from finding their own solution to this particular problem. A few systems were smuggled into the URSS through Poland and Czechoslovakia, and found their way to university cities like Leningrad and Lvov, where engineers started taking them apart and figuring out how these particular computers ticked. Until then, Russian computers had been massive mainframe systems occupying that required both costly maintenance and a team of specialists. Now, small compact systems imported from the West allowed a glimpse of what mass computing could look like.

One of the smuggled systems was the ZX Spectrum, a small 48 KB unit running on a BASIC operating system (Fig. 5.5.1). This system was a worldwide

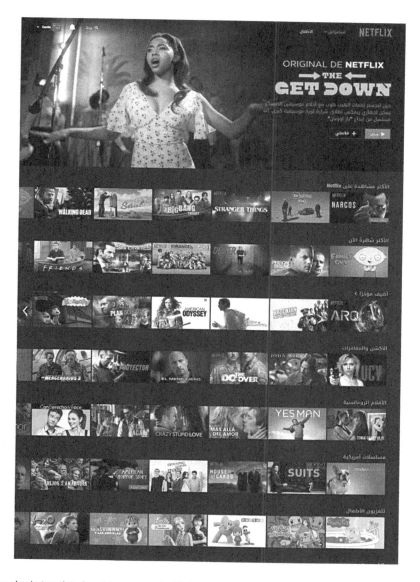

FIGURE 5.4.1

Netflix uses the same basic template for all languages. Arabic has a mirrored interface for the right-to-left script, but the basic composition is similar for all versions of the website. *Source: Used with permission from Netflix.*

success in 1982, leading to a knighthood for its inventor, but like many other appliances of its kind, failed to penetrate the folds of the Iron Curtain. However, in the early 1980s, homespun blueprints and schematics of the system soon started circulating and in the following years, Russian engineers in various points of the country started a myriad variations and clones of the system sprouted in the Eastern Bloc countries. Excluded from regular trade routes and capitalist imports, the local versions of these systems were adapted in order to work with easily obtainable Russian parts. Even the technological limitations of these homemade computers did not deter the budding home engineer. These devices had only a black-and-white display, broke down often, and were relatively expensive to build if you could not source the right parts. But they proved a success in a country where technology was constrained by ideological as much as economic reasons.

Russia exemplified one of the great equalizers of our time: technology. By appropriating the technology produced in another country and making it accessible, it created an internal domestic need for technology consumption. As a result, a specialized black market developed and became an essential resource for the budding home electrical engineer.

What Didaktik M and others like it exemplify is that demand will always circumvent limits in the offer if it is strong enough—especially with a bit of resourcefulness. The need for innovation comes as a response to the local needs rather than a drive unto itself, and that is the motivation behind, among others, many African design projects. In terms of usage, mobile money and small business lending were at their largest with the user bases in Kenya, Nigeria, and Uganda, particularly with the M-Pepea project, which focused on providing emergency credit to those without credit cards or bank loans on a purely mobile platform. Design can be calculated to fulfill social and financial needs, but it can also operate on a personal level, in our homes. According to Eurostat, rented housing has increased in the European market to 20% in 2014, and the need to express oneself through decoration of a personal domestic space has taken a step back into oblivion. Apartments have become transient spaces, and young professionals (aged 25−35 years) renting furnished houses seldom make any changes for the sake of personal decoration. The concept of "home" has changed and is usually associated with past memories or nostalgic associations for those who have lived in family homes. With little time or inclination to develop and endeavor on a new space of their own, their "language" of internal decoration is instead "borrowed" from an existing vernacular. This is one of the reasons for Ikea's success, according to Alison J. Clarke, Professor of design history at Vienna: "Ikea [is] the exact opposite of self-expression. It is self-expression within a limited repertoire" (in "Reflections: The real reason you still shop at Ikea," A Travel Blog About Home, July 28, 2016). In a world where the need for self-expression is becoming a global tendency, Ikea provides a good insight into the importance of an intimate canvas that can be assigned an emotional value. The Ikea furniture, as far as physical artifacts go, provides a minimalistic framework for emotional

FIGURE 5.5.1
Kellogg's presence in India was not an overnight success, as the brand's products had to adjust to a market with its own requirements.

and cultural expression. Values relevant to the buyers have been applied to the diffuse form of Swedish design that has crossed over the world in the past 20 years and appropriated cultural values implicit in the local maelstrom.

5.6 STEREOTYPES AND GENERALIZATIONS

Once you label me you negate me.

Søren Kierkegaard

A distinct British butler waddles tentatively around an empty dinner table with clearly too many neatly set plates in place. The dining room is swanky, and 19th-century crockery provides a neglected backdrop of high-class abandonment. The butler rings a dusty bell by the corner. An old woman in an elegant black lacy dress enter tentatively at the top of the staircase and is led by the hand to the head of the empty dinner table. What ensues is a 15-minute sketch with the ancient aristocrat hosting a dinner party for nobody at all, with the butler assuming the role of each guest in turn for both drinks and food, following the "same procedure as every year".

The 1963 comedy sketch is entitled *Dinner for One,* and despite the fact that both actors in it and the setting are distinctly British, it has been a staple of every single New Year's Eve schedule in German television and has gone on to become the most repeated program ever. This quirky piece of pantomime has since gone to gain similar staple holiday programming status in other countries like Sweden, Finland, and Australia. Yet, the sketch remains largely unknown in the United Kingdom and the United States, and it never actually aired in either country.

The popularity of the sketch has befuddled many English speakers. It was not conceived to appeal to an international audience like *Mr. Bean.* It indulges in a light parody of dementia, features acrimonious amounts of booze (which led to its banning in Switzerland for several years), and features the beguiled suggestion of senior citizen sex. However, yelling out "Same procedure as last year?" will likely get you a free round in a Bavarian *klappe*.

This example of distinctly European cultural contamination shows the illusion of single group identities. Our mind is biased towards difference. We perceive the world not by what is similar, but following the differences between the various elements. As a rule, our cognition is steered towards limits by contrast of colors, shapes, and identities. The hard sharp outlines of things allow us to interpret them and interact with the world more comfortably. We rely on contrast to know when a room gets cold and unpleasant, or when an especially spicy chili creeps into our food. As a race bent on survival, we do not like surprises (for the most part). Homogeneity and assuredness of expectations are not only widespread, but a condition of our reptilian brain.

In order to minimize the probability of jumping off a cliff, we also tell ourselves that we are special and often lie to ourselves about the actual worth of our achievements, looks, and actions. This plays a complex role in our social relations as well. This mental process is called *positive distinctiveness*, and it is particularly important in giving us our group identity. We perceive those closer to us and more similar to us as part of our group, and more relevant than other groups, and this encompasses different levels of separation between the designer and the actual audience.

5.6.1 Case Study: Curries, Cereal, and Masturbation

Corn Flakes is one of the most popular breakfast cereals in the world. It was originally created in 1894 by the ultra-religious Dr. John Harvey Kellogg as a breakfast food for the patients staying at his popular sanitarium and health spa. (Incredibly, it was part of a regimen of bland nutritious food meant to purify the body of the "solitary vice" of masturbation.) Over the years, it developed into one of the staples of American and European breakfasts and the best-selling brand of cereal in these continents. The brand experienced a tremendous growth during the 1980s, when it captured nearly half the United States market for breakfast cereals, generating an annual revenue exceeding 6 billion USD. However, in the early 1990s, Kellogg's found its U.S. market share eroded by its closest competitor, General Mills, and the company's growth began drooping (Fig. 5.6.1).

It made sense then that Kellogg's tried to expand to emerging markets, taking the success of its cereal branding to then-untapped economies—starting with India. According to Homi Bhabha, however, the brand did not research into local habits deeply enough: "Kellogg's set up a branch in India and started producing corn flakes...What they did not realize was that Indians, rather like

FIGURE 5.6.1

Kellogg's presence in India was not an overnight success, as the brand's products had to adjust to a market with its own requirements. *Source: Used with permission from Kelloggs.*

the Chinese, think that to start the day with something cold—like cold milk on your cereal—is a shock to the system. And if you pour warm milk on Kellogg's Corn Flakes, they instantly turn into wet paper" (Homi Bhabha in "A Humanist Who Knows Corn Flakes", 2005: 64–65).

Indian breakfasts usually involve hearty and spicy meals that include Puris, Dosas, and several types of curries.

The local habits initially did not support the appropriation of what had been a breakfast staple elsewhere in the world, and there were different reasons behind the low acceptance engendered in the market.

An exclusively sweet and cold breakfast was not common to the Indian diet, and Kellogg's initially positioned Corn Flakes as a replacement for the entire meal, rather than a complement.

The advertising focused on the its implication that traditional Indian breakfasts were not healthy was also not well received by a culture that attributed a deep familiar and communitarian meaning to the most important meal of the day.

In subsequent campaigns, Kellogg's backtracked and employed a combination of popular celebrities, cartoon mascots, and promotional events to grow the brand. Although it managed a sustainable, but slow, growth, the initial bad reaction still haunts the company's strategy.

5.7 CONCEPTS AND METAPHORS

The brain appears to possess a special area which we might call poetic memory and which records everything that charms or touches us, that makes our lives beautiful...

Milan Kundera

In 1996, Alvin Yeo suggested a way to categorize the different culturally-related components of interfaces into overt and covert factors. All of these factors would be relevant during the localization process. The overt factors are tangible, straightforward, and observable elements, whereas covert factors would be intangible and depend on culture or "special knowledge" (1996).

One of these "intangible elements" is the use of metaphors in user interfaces. From buttons to icons, an user interface is necessarily inferred from common knowledge, which makes them inevitably prone to being biased due to cultural assumptions. For instance, the image of a page turning in the Kindle is driven by a Western metaphor, as the spine is located on the left, with the pages turning right to left. The direction is necessarily inverted in the Arabic world, where books are read the opposite direction.

The appropriate reading direction makes a difference in information perception and processing. In a successful metaphor, imagery should evade instructional text and all information critical to the user should be clear in the context of the image. The affordances must be self-explanatory. On the other hand, in web design, placing a text frame on an image should also be done in a position relative to the image borders, in which case autosizing the text font to fit to the width is usually the safest choice. Communicating something to the user is the result of many factors, but metaphors can condense a huge number of semantic associations and spare the user of lengthy interpretations.

Metaphors are highly contextual, and function within two different modes: analogy and difference. Difference represents a mode of association: two elements which are unrelated or otherwise share any embedded property are equated as either the same or in the same semantic field. Since a metaphor is not a statement of fact, or otherwise truthful, there should also be a common understanding on the semantic field between the metaphor user and the audience. In other words, it means that something "is like" something else, and the interpreter needs to acknowledge the association by knowing both objects. Analogy, on the other hand, involves a comparison or the transfer of shared properties between both objects. Thinking of both objects in the equation becomes interchangeable, and the association becomes a part of the identity of both.

Despite being highly culturally-dependent, metaphors represent the bulk of user interface graphical output. Icons, logos, and headers rely heavily on symbolism and a complex network of semantic associations to provide users with guidance and visual cues as to how elements are used. This is represented by association with familiar aspects of the workplace and everyday

FIGURE 5.7.1
The American mailbox remains a popular metaphor for the mail inbox, even though it does not translate well visually to other countries.

life: the "desktop" or the "trashcan" are representations with an entirely different function in the user interface than in our analog everyday life, but the representation is similar and these semiotic traces are understood by the user as basic functionality due to the concrete and familiar concepts represented (Fig. 5.7.1).

Think about the last time when you saw a traffic sign that you could not recognize. For those who have driven in a country other than the one where they first wrecked their parents' car, the road has seemingly no secrets. We can cross the entire European Union by car and listen to over 35 languages in a single road trip.

Icons are not universal symbols. As metaphors, they are immediately recognizable in some contexts, but their inability to adhere to a unique international standard is clear in the use of different commands and cues. Sometimes, metaphors also transcend the use that initially brought them to life, like the use of a diskette as a symbol for saving data, whereas diskettes are hardly used in popular media since the mid-1990s. Other technologies have similarly influenced the choice of metaphors in UI design. The player metaphor is still used in web graphics, a reminder of times long past when the VCR ruled the world as the central point of contention for families fighting over the remote. This was, of course, before widely accessible digital streaming took over.

American traffic signs are heavily textual and reliant on contextual cues: the difference between signs like "Walk" and "Don't Walk" is primarily in the eyes of the beholder. The paradigm of mailboxes, as much a cultural artifact as traditional musical instruments, was a major source of adaptation back in the 1990s, when the Inbox icon came to be associated with U.S. mailboxes.

FIGURE 5.7.2
The crossing sign visual indication depicting a person was not an international standard until the ISO harmonized it.

Of course, the experience of British, Japanese, and French users was inherently different, as their mailboxes were not shaped like a tall oven. On the other hand, Japanese mailboxes were shaped as garbage bins for the most part. Telephone booths are another example of these transnational differences (Fig. 5.7.2).

Most metaphors used in UI design have been directly influenced by American engineering. Concepts such as buttons, toggling, formal data input, configuration settings, and safety against mistakes are but some of the systems that transited from the internal logic and patterns applied to traditional engineering.

International imagery can be heavily pictoric and symbolic. Symbols representing products that have similar designs all over the world are easily interpreted, like pencils, envelopes, lightbulbs, cars, and scissors.

As a rule of thumb, images should have no text rendered in them. This is a basic internationalization rule, and also one that will allow maximum reusability of content. It is noticeably harder to edit an image for appropriate text, except if the image is in vectorial format. For instance, in the case of Scalable Vector Graphics (SVG) and Photoshop Document (PSD) formats, the text layers may be successfully extracted and interpreted by an external application that helps editors and content managers to alter the content appropriately for different versions of the asset. This is quite time-consuming and, in general, not a pleasant experience for either the original content creator or those who will be responsible for its adaptation.

It is generally much more straightforward to handle assets separately, with content split in between text and imagery.

Visual puns in particular are impregnable between different cultures, unless they are of a viral nature (e.g., lolkatz). Using acronyms or onomatopoeias are likely to not work internationally. "Cute" elements also may well not contribute to the overall understandability level of the interface (Fernandes, 1995). Pictures should show the maximum amount of information with the minimum level of detail. Consider how universal design works in the context of devices. An app will have to render a PNG with millions of colors in an understandable way and still ensure that users will have the necessary understanding.

Visual messages do not need to be linked to a language. Icons gain in meaning as they become more akin to an actual physical object relevant to the local culture, but not too much that interpretation is lost. Even metaphors that may seem universal, like the lightbulb for an "eureka" moment, are not actually good representations thereof.

5.8 NEVER-ENDING STORIES

Humans have always been mythmakers.

A short history of myth

Enigmatic German wolves dressed as suspicious grandmothers. Desert desires and courageous thieves in the midst of the Arabian nights. Old men digging their way across mountains in the hardship of Chinese rice fields.

Folk tales are remarkable cultural legacies. They hold the key to the social principles of a culture and reflect perceptions and beliefs of the local people. Their understated (and often euphemized) darkness and animism usually follow a formula and an overarching narrative template. They are sometimes idealistic to a fault, sometimes chillingly creepy (Fig. 5.8.1).

Yet these stories are also remarkably consistent across languages. Snow White, for instance, has minor variations of its basic premise in countries like Armenia. In it, Nourie Hadig (Snow White) is involved in a taut tale involving cursed boys, gypsies, and exploding *saber dashees* (Turkish for "stone of patience"). However, it still uses the same basic premise of an older woman's jealousy and the mistreating of a beautiful young girl.

Snow White is only of one many such tales that are remarkably consistent across cultures. The themes and basic narratives of fairy tales are so similar between different nations and regions that there are a number of international classification systems used to identify the different types. One of the most commonly used systems is the *Aarne—Thompson—Uther classification system*, developed in 2004. This index groups folk tales by

FIGURE 5.8.1
Castles and privileged characters are common archetypes in tales worldwide.

motif and/or tale type, revealing the limited amount of themes used world-wide (Fig. 5.8.2).

From animal tales to forced marriage contracts, most folk tales seek to teach values and principles to the unsuspecting audience, be them altruism, prudence, or persistence. These values remain almost universal, and partly this is due to their origin and our own as a species.

These are the values that cultures live by. As children, the examples in these stories inspire us to "do the right thing," and to do what is "best" in the sense of a commonly accepted behavior in the social context from whence they sprang, and speak to the universal values that bind a common human past.

Fairy and folk tales (the distinction is often hard to pinpoint, even for experts) spring from an oral tradition that dates back over 5000 years. Their origin is enshrouded in the haziness of early history, when the Pan-European civilization was starting to expand to the outer ridges of Asia and Europe, taking with them tales that matured over time.

Because of their common origins and cultural contamination, the structure of the folk tale is an early predecessor to the *dramatic arc*. Greek theater used and popularized this narrative model, and these tales have a clear similarity in the following aspects:

- *Story motif and arc*: There is a dramatic progression towards a dénouement that usually occurs after a series of tests or *crises* the main character is subjected to;
- *Structure*: There is a balanced sequence of events (or acts) matching beginning, middle, and end, although this may be nonlinear in some narratives;
- *Character development*: The hero goes through a personal journey of self-fulfillment, revelation, and ultimately meeting its destiny.

This is a part of the audience's expectations in the West. Most movies and fictional work incorporate this structure, from *Star Wars* to *Iron Man*. Without this tension or conflict, the story is often thought of as dull and lifeless, and fails to engage.

Aarne-Thompson-Uther Classification of Folk Tales

ANIMAL TALES	1-299
Wild Animals	1-99
The Clever Fox (Other Animal)	1-69
Other Wild Animals	70-99
Wild Animals and Domestic Animals	100-149
Wild Animals and Humans	150-199
Domestic Animals	200-219
Other Animals and Objects	220-299
TALES OF MAGIC	300-749
Supernatural Adversaries	300-399
Supernatural or Enchanted Wife (Husband) or Other Relative	400-459
Wife	400-424
Husband	425-449
Brother or Sister	450-459
Supernatural Tasks	460-499
Supernatural Helpers	500-559
Magic Objects	560-649
Supernatural Power or Knowledge	650-699
Other Tales of the Supernatural	700-749
RELIGIOUS TALES	750-849
God Rewards and Punishes	750-779
The Truth Comes to Light	780-799
Heaven	800-809
The Devil	810-826
Other Religious Tales	827-849
REALISTIC TALES	850-999
The Man Marries the Princess	850-869
The Woman Marries the Prince	870-879
Proofs of Fidelity and Innocence	880-899
The Obstinate Wife Learns to Obey	900-909
Good Precepts	910-919
Clever Acts and Words	920-929
Tales of Fate	930-949
Robbers and Murderers	950-969
Other Realistic Tales	970-999
TALES OF THE STUPID OGRE (GIANT, DEVIL)	1000-1199
Labor Contract	1000-1029
Partnership between Man and Ogre	1030-1059
Contest between Man and Ogre	1060-1114
Man Kills (Injures) Ogre	1115-1144
Ogre Frightened by Man	1145-1154
Man Outwits the Devil	1155-1169
Souls Saved from the Devil	1170-1199
ANECDOTES AND JOKES	1200-1999
Stories about a Fool	1200-1349
Stories about Married Couples	1350-1439
The Foolish Wife and Her Husband	1380-1404
The Foolish Husband and His Wife	1405-1429
The Foolish Couple	1430-1439
Stories about a Woman	1440-1524
Looking for a Wife	1450-1474
Jokes about Old Maids	1475-1499
Other Stories about Women	1500-1524
Stories about a Man	1525-1724
The Clever Man	1525-1639
Lucky Accidents	1640-1674
The Stupid Man	1675-1724
Jokes about Clergymen and Religious Figures	1725-1849
The Clergyman is Tricked	1725-1774
Clergyman and Sexton	1775-1799
Other Jokes about Religious Figures	1800-1849
Anecdotes about Other Groups of People	1850-1874
Tall Tales	1875-1999
FORMULA TALES	2000-2399
Cumulative Tales	2000-2100
Chains Based on Numbers, Objects, Animals, or Names	2000-2020
Chains Involving Death	2021-2024
Chains Involving Eating	2025-2028
Chains Involving Other Events	2029-2075
Catch Tales	2200-2299
Other Formula Tales	2300-2399

FIGURE 5.8.2

Aarne-Thompson-Uther Classification of Folk Tales. *Source: http://www.mftd.org/index.php?action=atu. Used with permission from Maarten Janssen.*

The basic template of a common story, or *metanarrative*, encompassing these three factors, has been engrained in our collective unconscious and systematically analyzed by psychologists and sociologists. The most famous work of this kind is arguably *The Hero with a Thousand Faces*, by Joseph Campbell. In it, Campbell basically argues that all stories have been told already, and generations keep retelling the same basic myth: from Jesus to Luke Skywalker, the common hero undergoes a journey of peril, confrontation, and ultimately victory.

This basic myth has been absorbed and reinterpreted by different cultures around the world. However, there are subtle differences in how a story is thought of around the world.

In the West, stories often revolve around the concept of *conflict* and *tension*. The structure of most stories is multistaged. Gustav Freytag, a German playwright, suggested that this three-part dramatic structure can be represented in the form of a pyramid:

- *Beginning (Act I)*: The normal state of affairs is disrupted by a "problem" or an event, which becomes central to the story by the second-act.
- *Middle (Act II)*: The main character is then forced to resolve the situation.
- *Climax (Act III)*: Through a series of perils and difficulties, the hero meets its fate: either by accomplishing a personal or group victory by defeating opposing forces, or (in the case of a tragedy) by being left in a worse position than initially.

The three-act structure can be expanded and subverted, but the basic narrative model is consistent. Think of a classic tragedy like *Romeo and Juliet*, or a more modern narrative like *Still Alice* or *Leaving Las Vegas*. Although the main characters do not have a moment of triumph, the emotional journey they undertake reveals personal truths and the resilience of their own spirits. These tales have similar dramatic frameworks, as their stories are usually individual, with well-defined main characters, and the audience is asked to identify and empathize with them.

Christopher Booker, in his 2004 book *The Seven Basic Plots: Why We Tell Stories*, systematized the bulk of the plots used in Western tales as the following:

- *Overcoming the monster*: The main character is out to destroy an evil force, often equated with the hero's journey. Examples: *Star Wars, The Hunger Games, Dracula, War of the Worlds*.
- *Rags to riches*: A protagonist that is poor or of lesser social standing improves its situation, usually learning the value of humility and self-awareness in the process. Examples: *Cinderella, Great Expectations*.
- *The quest*: The hero undertakes a journey and overcomes obstacles to reach a goal or retrieve an object. Examples: *Iliad, The Lord of the Rings*.
- *Voyage and return*: The character returns from a trip to a foreign land and in the process meets unfathomable dangers. The only reward is the return to the familiarity of its fabled home. Examples: *Odyssey, The Rime of the Ancient Mariner, The Wizard of Oz*.

- *Comedy*: A genre often equated with romance, it is usually structured as a sequence of awkward mistakes and situations. It traditionally implies a social reframing of higher classes or morally superior characters, with an eventual cheerful denouement. Examples: *Much Ado About Nothing, The Taming of the Shrew, Four Weddings and a Funeral, Pretty Woman*.
- *Tragedy*: The main character's flaws or haunting past prompt him or her to engage in a downward spiral that ultimately leads to self-destruction. There is usually a second and slightly removed character that acts as a proxy for the audience and pities the fate of the main character. Examples: *The Great Gatsby, Hamlet, Breaking Bad*.
- *Rebirth*: The main character undergoes a transformation, often after tragic events, which improves them in some way. Examples: *The Snow Queen, A Christmas Carol, Christian Mythology*.

All of these narrative models are innately Western, in that they have in common an easily identifiable main character, and emphasize the individual journey, even when the story has several characters. On the other hand, complex narratives like those designed by Kafka and James Joyce usually present decomposed and subverted versions of these styles.

On the other hand, Chinese, Japanese, and Korean tales have a very different narrative approach. One of the classic narrative structures, *Kishōtenketsu* (起承転結), distinguishes itself by having a slightly different structure with four distinct moments:

- Introduction: The characters and story are set and established;
- Development: Relationships deepen, the first signs of change loom;
- Twist: A new character or a change of settings is introduced that seems to have no relation to the previous two stages;
- Reconciliation: Both the initial characters or setting and the twist are framed together and tie both strands together.

This type of narrative does not warrant a tension or conflict, either internal or external, as the core of the story. There might be confrontation, difficulties, and stand-offs, but the tale is more about the convergence of two distinct backdrops into one consistent ending. *Kishōtenketsu* is about the *connections and relations of situations, rather than the one person who can make a difference*.

Another distinctive aspect of traditional Japanese lore is the frequent reluctance to *distinguish between good and evil*. Characters are often portrayed in a struggle with the spirit world, represented by nature's elements and various mythical creatures. The narrative is ultimately one of surprise and self-identification, rather than a cautionary tale or one that can be taken as an example.

Outside of the odd landmark novel like or the quirky action/horror movie, Asian narratives are seldom popular in the East. However, Western-style narratives are becoming more popular in China and Japan, and the model is very familiar nowadays thanks to radio, television, and online sources.

Region	Morality	Characters	Structure
Asia	Good and evil are not easily discernible and are sometimes two faces of the same coin	Emphasis on character ensemble rather than an individual hero, nature is often anthropomorphized	Rise-fall and fall-rise with a twist. Often past deeds are met with consequence later in the tale. Rebirth as a means to overcome present challenges
Europe	Good and evil are easily identifiable	Main character is easily identifiable and empathetic	Hero's journey, dramatic-tragic. Rebirth is often seen as a victory
North America	Good and evil are easily identifiable	Main character is easily identifiable and empathetic	Hero's journey, quests
South America	Good and evil are usually identifiable	Main character is diverse and representative of his or her community	Hero's journey, quests, dramatic-tragedy
Middle-East	Good and evil are easily identifiable. Religion plays a major role	Flawed characters are met with reckoning justice, and acting virtuously is rewarded	Heavily performative and often musical
Africa	Moral tales emphasize integrity and resilience	Character can change dramatically in the same story	Emphasis on retelling and adaptation

This style of storytelling is inevitably different from African and Middle-Eastern storytelling models. African storytelling is similar to the Western model in that its style is primarily educational and moral, but adds a complex layer of performance. Proverbs and stories based on oral tales originated centuries ago are common, and play a more dominant role in modern storytelling than what is common in the Europe–US narratives. Old truths live on and play an active role in everyday life. However, similarly, rarely is there a concept of "authoritative" versions: the tale lives on and is reinterpreted with each new telling.

As with Indian myths, Central Asian storytelling is often laced with music. Unlike African tales, most stories are heavily prescribed and have a limited room for improvisation or adaptation. The most traditional form of storytelling is the *dastan*, a type of Turkic epic that constitutes a complex part of Central Asian literature and influenced literature and folk tales in the region. It is often set in verse and celebrates battles and victories of the local peoples against invaders.

Middle-Eastern storytelling is often characterized by a layered and complex plotline, and may employ different registers and genres in the same tale. It is not unusual that a single tale includes multiple plotlines and incorporates elements of tragedy, comedy, and satire.

PART III
About Face

CHAPTER 6

Cutting Copy

ABSTRACT

Everything we interact with generates a specific emotion suited to reinforcement or repression. Regardless of culture, users are emotionally affected by the register and tone of the content. In an age of diminishing attention spans, textual content must be impactful, concise, and available in the local language. There are basic principles that improve the grittiness of mundane user experience and can guide the redaction and production of content geared for a global audience. This chapter discusses some of those strategies.

Keywords: Copy; resuability; dialect; translation; transcreation; localization; content; machine translation; search engines

6.1 CLARITY AND REUSABILITY

> She had always wanted words, she loved them; grew up on them. Words gave her clarity, brought reason, shape.
>
> **Michael Ondaatje**

That dusty copy of *The Catcher in the Rye*. That self-help book that kept you afloat during hard times. The battered-down, rustic paperback of *Tom Sawyer* with torn pages read in elementary school years. That child-rearing magazine you subscribed to when planning for a new child.

Universal UX Design. DOI: http://dx.doi.org/10.1016/B978-0-12-802407-2.00006-X

Books, like all things we hold dear, can have substance and emotional content. People hold on to them because it means something. May be the book provided an helpful answer to a dilemma. May be the book accompanied them on an exotic journey.

But the book always serves as an emotional anchor for personal experiences and insights. The text in the book does not matter as much as the experiences surrounding it and what was learned from it.

Written content in websites follows a similar principle. Websites do not benefit from texture or physicality, and only have around 10 seconds to stimulate the user's attention. A novel usually requires a little more time than that.

Most importantly, for all the talk of content as business assets and emotional triggers in websites, it is extremely common to forget one simple fact: people do not love websites.

Websites are not artefacts like books, which can be held on to for emotional reasons. Their nature is transient and dynamic, and can quickly be taken down or fade with time.

In the case of social media, users can love the interaction with other people that the website allows. Or they might enjoy the trips they can book through a search website. But, unless they created it themselves, a website is not something to treasure. A website is not special in and of itself.

The content in the website, however, can be. It can teach the user, it can charm them. It can be creative and daring, or supportive and outreaching.

Localization does not start with the first translated language: it starts with the source. Knowing your audience and styling your content is just the beginning in a long journey towards a better user experience, but one that can make your content feel like a directed, cared-for labor of love, and not a patched-up set of snooze-inducing business and technical clichés.

As Audre Lorde once stated about the power of the word, "[it] is not only dream and vision; it is the skeleton architecture of our lives. It lays the foundations for a future of change, a bridge across our fears of what has never been before." As the connective tissue of our present into the wired future, language and communication are the pump lines of our own substance as a species, and these pathways will overcome the test of time wherever it may be put.

Language is the human essence. It weaves and bobs our existences, lacing it with meaning and the power of connection. By far, language is the most essential human skill, whether it is spoken, written, or mimed. Language as communication has unbridled power and a paucity of isolation, allowing us to transcend our own shells and comfortable spaces.

6.2   REFINING AFFINITY AND TONE

"Pedro," I asked the poet numerous times. "What do you think he was telling you?"

"I never understood a word, Pablo, but when I listened to him I always had the feeling, the certainty that I understood him. And when I spoke, I was always sure he understood me as well."

Pablo Neruda, I confess I lived memories

Everything we interact with generates a specific emotion suited to reinforcement or repression. Regardless of culture, users are emotionally affected by the register and tone of the text. There are four "R" principles that improve the grittiness of mundane user experience and guide usability:

- Responsiveness: Provide feedback and ensure that the functionality is in accordance with the user's actions.
- Respect: Guide your users without being patronizing or smug about it (e.g., artificially escalating error messages and providing adequate feedback for user actions).
- Relatable: The voice and register used in the text have been shown to create empathy or reduce the relatability of a given text.
- Relevance: The information expected by the user should be in line with user goals, therefore avoiding excessive and redundant information.

The Adestra Email Subject Lines 2012 study found that consumers are 33.4% less likely to open a message that had their name in the subject line and 53% less likely to click through the contents. This is one of the reasons why clarity in messaging is so important. I recently read the ultimate upselling strategy in a conference description: "we offer you a free workshop for the price of your ticket." When is paid for actually free? Words can be used to obscure and obfuscate, not just in their intent, but also in their very length.

If you are familiar with Reddit's lingo (or indeed any forum, particularly of a technical nature), you know that verbosity and propensity are usually dismissed with despondent disinterest, peppered with sarcasm. Most users take a similar stance when using a website or software application that is too fond of text for its own good.

It is not just laziness that drives most users to avoid interacting with overlong texts. In evolutionary terms, although oral language evolved over 2 million years, the first written symbols date from only 3500 BC, and the first alphabetic records date from 1000 BC. During our cognitive evolution, language became a natural skill, but writing appeared long after our basic brain structures were already in place. Therefore unlike oral language acquisition, reading and writing are not innate skills in infants and have to be learned.

FIGURE 6.2.1
The first characters etched in stone were part of what would become the Proto-Sinaitic script, the basis of all modern scripts. They are dated from a period ranging from the mid-19th century to mid-16th century BCE (Fig. 6.2.1).

Since literacy is individually variable, and users typically want to avoid as much effort as possible, clarity is key for user acceptance and retention. A localized version of a product can emphasize functionality by upholding the following criteria in the master locale:

- Use consistent, simple, and task-focused terminology.
- Use plain language (in advanced workflows, this can entail implementing Simplified English).
- Idiomatic expressions should be conceptualized and consistent (e.g., interjections, expressions, proverbs should be tagged as such and used in a consistent context).
- Avoid incomprehensible technical jargon.
- Avoid excessive wordiness. Use primarily short sentences with only one or two phrases.
- Avoid repetitive text and branding on the same window (e.g., having the company name on logos and in-context messages in the same screen).
- Use capitalization to clearly structure your on-screen content (e.g., use title case in the main title, but only sentence case for subtitles).

Keep in mind that reading on-screen is more wearisome on the eyes and takes almost twice as long as reading on paper. Therefore text density also plays a role in providing visual comfort for reading. Depending on the resolution, short lines with a maximum of 80 characters are a good rule of thumb.

6.3   DIALECTS AND VARIATIONS

Languages are as fluid as the cultures that spawn them, and they are never as standardized and formal as dictionaries and grammar books would have us

believe. Accents and idiomatic expressions shift with just a few miles separation, but languages also fracture and diverge according to groups, regional
position, and local dynamic. Dialects are representations of this difference,
and the separation between America and the United Kingdom exemplifies this
distance, with examples like "waste basket" and "rubbish bin" coloring the difference. Any serious product or service aiming at success in either territory
would benefit from having a specific linguistic version for both territories, as
there is no universal "English" variation.

An example that is more consensual is Spanish, both European and the Latin
American variants. Although the language has some regionalisms between the dif-
ferent countries, there is generally no immediate prejudice against reading
Spanish as written and read in Spain. The same is not true of Brazilian Portuguese.
Dialects that have slight changes in grammar and use of pronouns are often
equated with a general form of the language rather than individual dialects.

6.4   BUILDING A GLOBAL CONTENT STRATEGY

Web content is bent on immediacy and conciseness, and with so many
options in the market, common knowledge stipulates it has to be "punchy"
and "to the point." It has to be "structured" and include all the "relevant
search engine optimization (SEO) keywords."

Content, however, must not simply be content, it must *have* content. It has to
matter to the audience. It can even teach them during the process.

Localized content is even more critical, because of the necessities and changing
habits of international audiences.

Therefore content must take into account three basic factors:

1. Who are we talking to?
2. What do we want to tell them?
3. How can we make this relevant to their experience?

Nowadays, localization offices find themselves dabbling more and more in
copy. Copywriting, particularly for international websites, is where source content lives and grows.

And often companies fail to understand that localization does not start with
the first translated language: it starts with the source.

Knowing your audience and styling your content is just the beginning in a
long journey towards a better user experience, but one that can make your
content feel like a directed, cared-for labor of love, and not a patched-up set
of snooze-inducing business and technical clichés.

A localized website into Japanese has its own particular needs, and the modern necessities of tight timelines and decentralized work often do not allow
for a sufficiently agile approach to content.

So, how can we sort an approach to the content that maximizes translatability while still maintaining relevance?

- Talk to in-country offices.
- Arrange for user meetings and meet-ups.
- Check your forums.
- Consult your marketing department on what the customer response is in certain territories.
- Experiment with A/B testing.

Traits like "personality" and "charm" do not have to be the nemesis to "translatability" and "consistent." As Bruce Lee stated, it is not about the increase, but about the decrease. Get rid of the unessentials and, underneath the varnishing of wording, the message will resonate and shine through.

6.5   TRANSLATION AND TRANSCREATION

In translation studies, the debate has been ranging for decades, if not centuries: should translation attempt to be as literal as possible in order to emulate the style of the original or should it try to emulate the effect that the author intended on the audience? Should it mime the content or try to achieve an overall amplified effect similar to the original?

In localization, given the cultural instantiation between the target cultures, and the need to establish an emotional connection with the user with minimal external contextualization, translation is a principle that translation should be as effect oriented.

When a user interacts with a given UI scheme, the concepts and flow of the layout, control disposition and internal logic are subjacent to the user's own goals. The user wants to accomplish a task or a set of tasks with minimal interference from dodgy and inconsistent control placement or avant-garde artistry.

There is a cognitive threshold for how much information can be assimilated simultaneously on both a visual and perceptual level. Most users will have a hard time reading on-screen, which is naturally more tiring and takes almost twice as long as reading on the paper.

6.5.1   Keep the Flow: Spice Up the Show

Elements should be consistent enough that user goals are continuous and no compartmented jaded interruptions arise. UX design is based on principle of seamless, continuous interaction patterns that present something new to the user in controlled dosages to avoid habituation. Surprising the users with good copy is difficult as the Web is full of good examples of persuasion, from Booking.com to Mailchimp, and even the best copy is not necessarily ensuring a good user experience.

- Establish a simplified English master locale.
- Loss of contextual information—which normally allows translators to consider what they are translating.

- Quick, almost instantaneous turnaround times.
- Much more frequent admin cycles for Project Management (receive—organize—distribute—deliver).
- Loss of interest/motivation from translators.
- Supporting the systems in which content is presented, takes longer than translating itself.

Proper transcreation cannot rely solely on the translator's arbitrary choices and tastes, and should instead be adapted to the desired locale by the use of a style guide and, ideally, consistent terminology usage. Do not ignore the decisive role that this consistency can play in SEO as well.

6.6 INTERNATIONAL SEO

Content discoverability is an operative word in contemporary companies, and practically equates having a high SEO index on the company's websites. Roughly, organic searches are those accomplished intentionally by the user: when you enter a query like "best knife set" in Google, clicking on one of the results is considered an "organic" result.

According to a moz.com survey, over 20% of clicks in the Google search results home page are on the paid results (moz.com), with organic results ranged in the 80% mark. In the United States, over 30% of users click on the first result in the SERP (Search Engine Results Page), with the first three results encompassing almost 60% of all user clicks. The second page of the search results is a lonely and cold place devoid of human attention.

From these facts, it is easy to assume that search ranking is essential for businesses, and many consultancies use this as a prime selling point. However, a good search ranking is not as essential as in the past. In China, where business micropages abound, businesses rely on social network recommendations and reposts in order to generate interest and drive the meta-traffic into their landing pages. Services are increasingly looking at ways of fitting into the particular ecosystem that is WeChat while relying less on the organic search trade.

However, global search and content discoverability remains a critical business function; ensuring that your brand and content can be found online in local markets, and as such, content discoverability goes beyond great localization.

How and where local users find your brand, localized content and on what device type, matters as much as search behavior and intent. Understanding local user search behaviors and intent and ensuring the correct content is used in the right context for each of the types of search traffic usually attached to a public website. In order to properly optimize the SEO quotient of a website, you should be able to quantify and analyze the following:

- Localized keyword research
- Organic search and paid
- Dominant local search engines
- Internal search
- Curation and optimization of the content on your website.

FIGURE 6.6.1
Efficient SEO does not require multiple websites or domains. The same domain, properly localized, can be indexed properly by search engines, even if specialized ccTLD (country code top-level domain) is not used.

The local search engine landscape is a key aspect, as search habits are usually closely related to the engine's own particularities (Fig. 6.6.1).

According to a Webcredible 2015 study, Google is by far the most widely used search engine all over the world by worldwide market share. It is also the most popular search engine in nearly every territory in the world, including Argentina, South Africa, and Thailand. However, there are some key territories that the infamous portal has not managed to win over and obtain the market lion's share:

- China: Baidu is the most widely used search engine with 55% of all queries, followed by Qihoo 360 (28%), which has increased its market share.
- Russia: The multiservice Yandex portal has been a staple for local Internet users with a large market share as of 2015, and Google is making increasing inroads in the local market.
- Hong Kong: Yahoo was for a long time one of the top search providers in the territory, but its influence is diminishing, totaling 24% of searches in 2015.

- Japan: Google dominates the market, and it is even the engine that drives results behind Yahoo Japan, which has a 40% market share.
- South Korea: Native search portals Naver and Daum combined own 97% of the market.
- United States: Google is the most widely used with 72%, but Bing has managed to obtain over 21% of the market in recent times.

China, Russia, and South Korea are part of a handful of select countries where Google has not achieved overpowering dominance over local search engines. What made these countries different and how is the search experience different from elsewhere?

Search engines in these countries focused on local quality content, and spoke to the aesthetic and real-life sensibilities of the Korean users. At a time when Korean page indexing was complex and escaped the limited character encoding of Western websites, local search engines sprouted as a response to the local needs, and established a powerful domineering position over the market that remains largely unchallenged. Three factors influenced this situation directly.

The first factor was language. Indexing the content of different scripts was technically difficult, with Western search engines focusing on Latin alphabets that were carrying languages like English and French.

Second, in a relatively small but extremely intensive online environment, at the turn of the 2000s, there was very little content available to satisfy consumers looking for endemic websites. In Korea, Naver circumvented the situation by emphasizing user-created content in a single integrated service, "Knowledge Search," that allowed users to exchange questions and answers that were then to be ranked according to recommendations. This model was later adopted by the Yahoo! Answers service.

Third, the most successful search engines are not only search engines. Like Google, Naver, Yandex, and Baidu all combine several services, including news, blogs, and mail in the same access portal. They are consolidated solutions to the most basic services users require when accessing the Internet, and provide entry points to users' most commonly used services.

6.7 CONTROLLED LANGUAGE AND MACHINE TRANSLATION

In the modern global business, any mobile app or website is exposed to potential markets numbering in the hundreds of millions, spread across the four corners of the Earth. Cultural and linguistic boundaries are therefore transcended. In order to be as audience-inclusive as possible as well, the language used needs to be simple and accessible, but also familiar.

Organization-wide implementation of Simplified English as the master locale can help you to single-source your content effectively and provide a steady basis for translation and transcreation.

Affordable machine translation has been available commercially for the past few years, and most translation agencies use it in their workflow combined with fuzzy segmentation matching. However, in-house teams can implement their own internal machine translation (MT) server using open-source machine translation engines based on Windows or Amazon Cloud.

Most of these solutions are based on Moses, a statistical machine translation engine that has grown in popularity, which uses the same approach as Google Translate. Once an ambitious project to start a machine translation movement, it has become progressively a reliable engine that complements human-based translation workflows. You can host and service a MT server internally, and leverage translated material that is already available in your documentation to automatically train translation models. The more material you have initially, the better results can be obtained.

If you do not have a large volume of translated material (e.g., less than a million words), you can look at other open-source engines that rely on linguistic rules to process the input. The configuration is hard, but the results might be better for language pairs of highly systemic languages.

The best approach to any form of controlled language is that each lexical entry (root or part-of-speech) has only one possible semantic interpretation in its linguistic domain. The goal with this is to eliminate the need for interactive disambiguation of ambiguous terminology. If you are sourcing the material internally, however, it is possible that upon domain analysis you find hundreds or even thousands of terms that have more than one semantic interpretation, depending on context.

For example, "charge" can be interpreted either as charging an electrical element such as a battery, or pressurizing a gas container such as an ether cylinder.

Ambiguity is the enemy of sound machine translation, making it essential that a streamlined terminology and accurate multiple meanings is essential for accurate machine translation, so we extended the design of the grammar checker to include an interactive disambiguation module. When ambiguous terms are identified, the system asks the author to specify the intended meaning, which is then preserved in the input text using an unobtrusive SGML marker (Mitamura & Nyberg, 1995).

CHAPTER 7
Global Designs

Chapter Outline

ABSTRACT

Although there is negligible genetic disparity between the different people that inhabit the planet, the expression of design varies wildly. From the understated elegance of Japanese architecture to overwrought European Gothic structures, design is as much an expression of culture as it is of time and place. But, for all of its explosive variety, is there an actual universal sense of design? Do humans use essentially the same rules, only with different purposes and sensibilities? Our cognition and intellectual prowess is remarkably similar across cultures, so why are there so many variations on such disparate themes? The essential mechanisms of our mind that make us closer to each other are also the ones that make us closer to the laws of the universe: geometry, patterns, and language. Yet each one of these can be used in a different manner depending on the dominating preferences and tastes of our surroundings. This chapter proposes to analyse these very differences, be it in the input we provide the systems we interact with—or the output.

Keywords: Design; User Interface (UI); User Experience; Golden Ratio; Western design; E-Health systems; smartphones; cognition; internationalization; usability

7.1   CULTURAL AESTHETICS

> The first step to controlling your world is to control your culture. To model and demonstrate the kind of world you demand to live in. To write the books. Make the music. Shoot the films. Paint the art.
>
> **Chuck Palahniuk.**

Although there is negligible genetic disparity between the different people that inhabit the planet, the expression of design varies wildly. From the understated elegance of Japanese architecture to overwrought European Gothic structures, design is as much an expression of culture as it is of time and place. But, for all of its explosive variety, is there an actual universal sense of design? Do humans use essentially the same rules, only with different purposes and sensibilities? Our cognition and intellectual prowess is remarkably similar across cultures, so why are there so many variations on such disparate themes?

To understand the variation of themes, we must understand what they are made of: their basic components and their most essential parts. And this understanding often leads us into the realm of geometry and patterns.

Geometrical regularity has been a pillar of Western design since the outbreak of the Ancients Greeks, a knowledge that was overtaken by the Roman empire. The principles of symmetry and the power of edges and intersections became a dominant discourse in most design work, be it architectural, artistic, industrial, or all of the former.

Mathematical images are prominent in our design aesthetics, and geometry is the regulating defining basis of almost every cultural aesthetic everywhere. The Giza pyramids are one of the most awe-inspiring examples of human design, and its iconic shape and endurance has continued to be a subliminal inspiration for designers throughout history. Triangles force the viewer focus and point toward elements in a futuristic fashion that belies the power of their presence in a design.

Design is not only a matter of laying out pleasing visual aesthetics. In the case of the pyramids, as of landmarks across the globe, design is often infused with a performative aspect, shrouded in ritual and belief. Geometrical concentric drawings called *kolams*, popular in southern India and the Far East, involve a performative ritual whereby the representation is connected to a supernatural view of the world or system of knowledge. One needs not look further than the use of tiles and stained glass in medieval churches, and their inherent association with Christian symbolism, to understand the deep impact of these designs. Geometrical images have always been imbued with deeper meaning, and web design, fundamentally tied to basic principles of typesetting and regularity, reflects this deep and recurring design motif (Fig. 7.1.1).

The influence of these principles is wide-ranging, as certain forms and shapes allow for practical considerations. For instance, triangles, hexagons, and squares are appropriate for stacking and packing. These forms are economical and leave no space in between. On the other hand, natural patterns like branching, or storing, occur in nature, as well as fractals, are one of the most important patterns of design in nature. From the leaves of a tree to the relation between shock waves, the importance of fractals is paramount and one of the most universal design principles across civilizations.

Professor Ron Eglash has devoted a lifetime to understanding the influence of fractals in African architecture and design, and has noted several intriguing uses of fractals in local African populations with little influence The Ba-ila people, a dying tribe found in Zambia, have built villages based on complex fractal patterns, with substructures and dependencies between the various areas of their dwellings. The disposition is circular, with buildings nestled in rings around each other.

The prominence of fractals in African architecture reminds us that technology and sophistication are two separate factors with very little in common. The technology used by these populations would normally be deemed

FIGURE 7.1.1

A *kolam* features designs influenced by geometrical and fractal patterns, and is one of the many cultural representations of universal design principles in a unique and immediately identifiable artefact.

underdeveloped by most Western societies, but they are directly using extremely complex patterns which are a part of the surrounding natural environment in utilitarian manners in a way that avoids straight lines and the "boxed" language of concrete.

This approach is a contrast to the Western preference for regularity and symmetry in detriment of pattern and context. The use of the triptych structure in classical paintings is fundamentally inherited from a sense of balance and aesthetic equilibrium passed on from Classic Antiquity. Greek aesthetics formulated a geometrically-inspired model that relied on proportion and symmetry that is still prevalent in our modern aesthetic outlook.

Webpages, as a modern artefact subjected to the appeal of contemporary taste and interpretation, tend to follow similar organizational and aesthetic patterns. The quality of "harmony" refers to geometrical proportions applicable both to classical works of art to typesetting to web design. Critical attention-grabbing points in the visual framework or the sense of hierarchy between these very elements, like the usage of the "Golden Ratio." The Golden Ratio is an ancient visual device that assigns balance and distribution in a layout according to the Fibonacci sequence, which is obtained by adding the two previous numbers: 0, 1, 1, 2, 3, 5, 8, 13, 21, 34, 55, 89...

The mapping of this sequence will create a regular spiral, and despite the naming being attributed to Leonardo Pisano Bogollo, an Italian mathematician from the 12th century, it was actually a well-known pattern in Indian lore centuries before.

One of the most visible examples of this application is on sites with a heavy emphasis on implicit user tasks, like Twitter and Facebook, with a focus on central content areas and a de-emphasis on peripheral areas.

The question remains, however, whether the application of classical aesthetics in modern design assists or facilitates usability from a practical point of view. Western users have a different perspective on spatial data and information organization, and scan and interpret it differently from Asian cultures. The "Golden Ratio" is not an institutionalized geometric principle in Asian culture and is subjected to various cultural and social constraints (Fig. 7.1.2).

One of the key aspects of this visual interaction is the concentration of information with a left justification, and the use of three columns in the layout itself. In most websites, the use of a tri-parted canvas allows for the following elements to be easily placed and perceived by audiences:

- identity,
- topic,
- exit points.

The identity is most clearly manifested by the website's logo and masthead, which establishes authorship or, most frequently, ownership, and casts dominance over the remaining elements. A website without a clear title or brand is

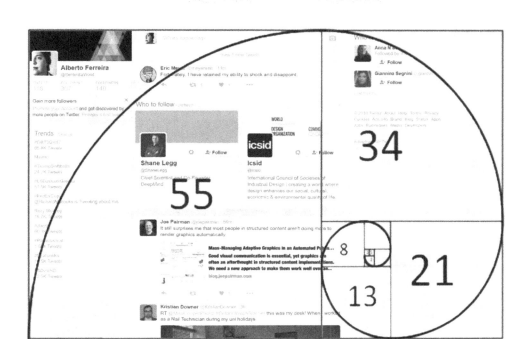

FIGURE 7.1.2

The "Golden Ratio" as applied to the Twitter website. Notice that the proportions are completely dissimilar in its Chinese counterpart, Weibo, where the left bar with the navigation categories and the continuous information sidebar on the right do not follow the same proportions as on its Western counterpart, instead fitting as much on-screen information as possible.

FIGURE 7.1.3
Elements of proportion and space in a grid view.

most easily perceived as confusing, orphaned, or, in the worst possible case, irrelevant. The title is usually set at the top of the page, following conventional typographical principles that date back to the alphabet structure devised by the Phoenicians in the 15th century BCE and the information structure implied therein, whereupon elements relied on the following properties in order to communicate meaning (Fig. 7.1.3):

- weight,
- scale,
- color,
- grouping,
- "silent" or "negative" space.

At their core, websites are structured around an organization most easily perceived through its disposition of vertical columns along the page canvas. A grid model can be applied to its information architecture. The similarity between print and webpage design are striking in the resemblance of most text-heavy websites to their print counterparts, which relied on letter pressing methods for centuries and a paper grid model for the layout work on the page.

7.1.1   Design and Belief

Beliefs are culturally determined both in appearance and popularity. Beliefs condition one's expectations toward achievable and obtainable goals in this life, and play a role in aspirations and interests beyond mere living. For example, many societies in sub-Saharan Africa still perpetuate a belief in animism and the power of natural remedies against larger forces in the universe. Nature is a set of characters that can reflect or illustrate events in one's own life.

This is extendable to Burkina Faso, where Muslim medicine men are extremely prominent and spell craft is prevalent amongst the general population. In the Philippines, belief in supernatural spirits is widespread. Folktales play a major role and education and in shaping the imagination of young children. In Mozambique and Angola, witchcraft and traditional medicine are sponsored and regulated by the Mozambican Department of Health. Even fully industrialized societies like Singapore still carry many superstitions from previous generations.

What is the running thread in these different manifestations of belief? Why are these important to design? Because belief and representation shape symbolism. Symbolism, according to Maggie Macnab, is universal and not a fact, but a common concept. It relies on the representation of basic structures in nature in an iconic form, where shapes in nature are usually engaged in spatial terms. This implies that metaphors and other representations are underlined by symbols of belief: creatures, space, and time. All are encoded in the same form of communication and reflected in different ways from proverbs to visual design.

7.1.2   Semiotics and the Stroop Effect

While criticized in certain quarters, semiotics provides an appealing framework to investigate the weight of culture in UI design. While "the sign can be understood as a correlation of differences" according to Ferdinand de Saussure, contemporary perspectives of semiotics place it closer to the study of culture, and it inevitably has an impact on design. It is for this fundamental reason that one of the key principles of design, visual affordance, is often not enough when learning how to organize knowledge and standard practices of usage. Artefact design is often reliant on cultural assumptions: the impact of metaphors, aesthetic choices, imagery, and information structure directly have an impact on the interpretation of a technologically mediated interface.

However, measuring and quantifying this impact, particularly on a cross-cultural basis, demands a sturdy conceptual framework, to which the concept of User Experience is often attached to. It has become a ubiquitous term in contemporary software engineering, reflecting the "person's perceptions and responses that result from the use or anticipated use of a product, system or service" (as per the definition in the ISO standard). Its emphasis on the emotional persuasion of the user, then, prompts the question on what constitutes a desirable representation medium for different cultural backgrounds.

For instance, Japanese and Chinese websites are often criticized by Western designers as being too busy and dense, therefore conditioning usability and unclear information architecture. However, internationally localized websites are routinely redesigned and adapted to local expectations, often without proper usability testing, prompting the question: are localized websites taking into account user expectations at all? The fact that Chinese and Japanese UI design differs so much from prevailing design tendencies in both America. Europe is deeply connected with political and commercial reasons, namely the fiendishly transient nature of the market, as well as a demand for feature and information abundance at the expense of abundance. Whereas the minimalistic stance of Western UI design promotes accessibility and privileges repetitive task methodology through clear placement of affordances and conditioning expectations, Chinese and Japanese mobile markets focus on the value of anonymity and density.

This attitude is, however, changing. Popular websites such as QZone already feature a minimalistic interface, which conforms to the common Western design standards, but this change is still not prevalent in websites such as Weixin and, most importantly, in the UI of its applications, which use manga-inspired emoticons extensively (Fig. 7.1.4).

Social networks are one of the richest semiotic systems in HCI: regulated by social organization structures that act as metaphors of actual social interactions, with continuous content delivery systems acting as object-world environments co-created by the channeling user. This form of engagement is further expanded in Toshi Takahashi's theory of audience engagement, which encompasses seven modes:

- information-seeking activity,
- connectivity,
- "world-creation,"
- parasocial interaction,
- utility,
- interpretation,
- participation.

This conceptual framework should be explored in the context of culture, encompassing the organized and socially enforced system of signs, expectations, and indoctrinated aesthetics that users are embedded in.

FIGURE 7.1.4
The official QZone website is in line with the latest Chinese trends: simple, one-page layout that focuses on pushing a mobile service rather than providing more information on the service to the unsuspecting user.

The impact of culturally-specific semiotics in User Experience is relevant in the appeal and comfort that a specific website or product holds for users. Clarisse Sieckenius de Souza's pioneering study of semiotics in the context of computer-mediated communication published in 2005, demonstrates that the sign system encoded in a UI is an exchange between designer and user mediated by technology. Semiotic engineering has been increasingly viewed as a valid methodology in the analysis of the information structure underlying user interfaces. The field has since produced relevant studies in the matter, including Shaleph O'Neill's perspective on the ways that semiotic models can be applied to interactive media.

Semiotics are relevant to User Experience as it often finds itself construed as a multidisciplinary field aimed at optimizing a product design and delivery in a way that optimizes the emotional receptivity of the audience. This includes taking into account the user's moral values, aesthetic sense, emotional outset, cultural stance, preferred ergonomics, and usability preferences. User Experience is, then, a combination of all of these elements into one single unified node: how we connect with the world and with others as the digital divide erodes barriers of communication modes.

7.2 INDIGENOUS USER INTERFACES

She had studied the universe all her life, but had overlooked its clearest message: For small creatures such as we the vastness is bearable only through love.

Carl Sagan, *Contact*.

Empathy aids us to establish a perspective of the other, to understand what the implications and especially the motivations are behind the actions of the users. Why is the checkout cart abandoned midway? Why are they drawn to certain areas of the service? What are they looking for? Why are they visiting the website in the first place?

Behavior modeling does not have to be a huge taxing endeavor. Often times the simple cues and guides are the best ways to trigger a change. Contemporary technology usage is heavily utilitarian and remarkably superficial. The complexity and sophistication of an app or website has absolutely nothing to do with the actual experience of the user. A bad connection is enough to downgrade the overall perception and ultimately the reputation of a product or company.

There is only a short window to stimulate a user's interest and curiosity. This is one of the reasons that have led the OASIS open standards consortium to start an initiative for delivering personalized user experiences online. This standard reflects the customization of content and layout for planned audiences, and marks an initiative that extends to the various projects taking place in areas of the globe where the experience of data and web design necessarily needs to be curtailed and adapted to the local needs and perceptions of technology.

One example is the Mukurtu project (mukurtu.org), a community development initiative, started in Australia by the Warumungu Aboriginal community. It has produced a web-based content-management system and a set of ethical processes for tailoring guidelines for archiving and sharing information via the CMS.

The aim of the project is to provide indigenous community groups with digital resources for cultural heritage preservation as well as providing the means to do this work in accordance with community values. The project leaders recognized, from the outset, that archival work is value-laden and that information systems often have built-in assumptions about access and representation that can threaten the core goals of cultural heritage preservation work. Where communities' ability to represent themselves—via descriptions and images of artifacts, places, and people—become threatened, so do core human values of individual and collective sovereignty.

Other projects, like the one led by Kasper Rodil and other researchers (2014), focused on co-design with indigenous groups, particularly with the Herero community in Namibia, in order to study the categorization and interpretation of concepts that the members of the community displayed when classifying objects. This method was primarily based on location and layout rather than causality, which is the main identified method in Westerners.

User-centered design is not a straightforward process that can be applicable necessarily to other cultures without some form of cultural interference. Smith, Dunckley, French, Minocha, and Chang (2004) suggest that user-centered design might be influenced by the Western culture's "view that users as individuals have a democratic right to be involved in the development of software," whereas other cultures may have a very different conception of the implications of design.

These differences are relevant in the wider context of globalization and outsourcing. This is a common practice, with a visible effect on the relationship between European and American companies and Indian or Latin-American UX agencies, respectively. This outsourcing is often driven by financial factors, and design and development, but research services are seldom used. Sergio Nouvel, co-principal of Continuum, argues that "there's a whole lot of front-end and UI design work done in Latin America, especially the graphic/HTML work, because a native English speaker is required to produce UI copy with the nuances and the right tone."

Producing content is a focal point that requires familiarity with the local culture. Sergio emphasizes the importance of local specialists with knowledge that are aware of the cultural distinctions: "one of our Peruvian clients worked with IDEO before us, and one of their main complaints was that, despite the high quality work, the American consultants were not able to capture the subtleties of Peruvian culture, and decided to prioritize local consultants for future projects."

The search for short-term financial saving pushes American and European companies to outsource work to emerging economies with equally trained and specialized professionals, like Argentina and Uruguay. This has an impact on the development of local talent, but it also has an impact on other countries. Brazil, for instance, is developing a sizable web-design workforce with a sizable chunk working directly for local branches of large companies in the country. Companies still face tremendous challenges when entering the continent via Brazil, as they have to establish different offices in other Spanish-speaking countries due to the language barrier in the continent.

7.2.1 Galapagos and Sushi: Japanese Web Design

Amongst the conundrums of UI design, the Japanese indulgence in apparently ugly interfaces is intriguing to Westerners. Most Japanese websites gleefully escape the paradigm of simplicity and specialization that colors most Western websites, or even most modern Asian websites such as Nicovideo and Ameba.

Driven by their own internal consumer and design trends, website design in Japan became a discipline with its own background and quirks. The direct result of specialization via the Galápagos syndrome, web design in Japan is a fascinating insight into how isolation is opposite to homogenization.

The adoption of HTML5 and other technologies was slower in the country due to legacy and tradition, in a country that is imminently creative but bound by hardened social and professional ties. One of the reasons for the apparent abundance of content in Japanese websites is the perception that a site that hides information from the user is enclosing itself deliberately, which reduces trust and openness. This visual "horror vacui" manifested itself in overly busy sites (to Western eyes), but has since been minimized, particularly in the international versions of Japanese brands.

This stands in stark contrast to the Japanese concept of "ma," a concept that entailed the use of negative space and implicit relations. Instead of expressing something literally, "ma" ( ) encouraged the use of gaps and intervals in order to allow the viewer to build their own mental depiction of a design and envisage the consequence.

Seeing as Apple took more than a page from Japanese minimalistic design, the reasons why digital web design in particular remained steeped in tradition is related with the functional attitude toward web technology.

7.3 GENDER AND UX

I would rather trust a woman's instinct than a man's reason.

Stanley Baldwin.

Gender is encoded subtly in many elements of our everyday lives. From color to shapes, femininity and masculinity are frequently alluded to in everyday observations, yet seldom recognized consciously. "That's a macho thing." "That car is a bit girly." "This is a manly pocket watch." As sexist stereotypes, the use of such generalizations is under questioning and reframing in the general media and the voice of the public. The binary opposition is slowly giving way to more rounded descriptions with other options in registration forms and personal profiles pages.

Gender is largely a cultural construct, but it can also reflect personal, physiological, and psychological stances about personal identity. Gender is not only genetic, but an essential component of social role, and personal identity and expression.

Its relevance in UX design is manifest in the need to design in an inclusive manner that reaches out to most users in increasingly polyvalent and heterogeneous societies. Imbuing your site with masculine imagery, or appealing to a feminine aesthetic, may fly in the face of an audience that includes transgender and nonbinary users. This does not imply that the design needs to be stale and devoid of any sexualized elements, but it does necessitate user testing and a deep reflection on the deeper motifs and strategy behind this digital presence.

Assuming that the audience has a particular set of physical attributes, or using the wrong gender implication in the copy, can alienate the audience and negate concepts of self in a way that is both damaging to the individual and the brand proposition. This is especially essential when writing in Latin languages and others that have gender encoded as part of the subject. The use of the male form is prevalent throughout these languages, with no neutral form and forcing the use of masculine pronouns as the standard. This is in line with the audience's expectations, but should be used with care in order to avoid disparaging other audiences (Fig. 7.3.1).

In Western design, the distinction between masculine and feminine (and the blurred lines between them) still persists as a method to critique and frame purpose, identity, and visual appearance. It is easy to justify a design choice as a reframed self-as-user bias, and UX, like other technical fields, can suffer from an overly masculine sensibility. Part of this is related to the stereotypes that can seep in through the designer's attempts to create a new and engaging experience. Nicola Marsden, professor at the IT department of Heilbronn University, found this to be consistently true in the way e-commerce German newsletters address their audience:

> In signing up to shop on their websites, about half of them did not ask for any title. The other half of the online stores usually gave me the choice between "Herr" (Mr.) and "Frau." Frau is equivalent to both "Ms." and "Mrs." [...] Of the sites that asked for a title, one-third placed the female title first and two-thirds have the male title first—

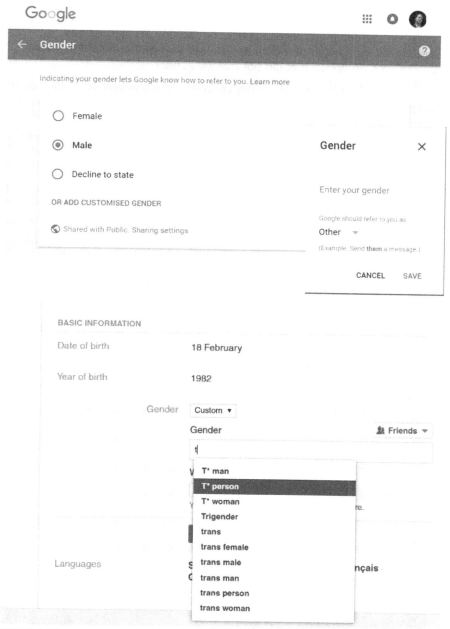

FIGURE 7.3.1

Google has introduced the possibility to introduce a custom gender to its profile pages. This follows an industry trend to allow for nonbinary gender descripts in social media network, as the Facebook page also shows. By allowing the users to choose their own gender, the acknowledgment of a fluidity of identity is infused in the basic user registration profile.

even though in Germany, like the U.S., most ecommerce revenue comes from women. Nearly all of these websites allowed me to make a selection regarding the gendered title, but around 20 percent had already set the gender at a default—almost always the male title—and they offered no option that did not include gender.

Recommendation: When implementing controls for an interface, do not incorporate gender in the name titles. Avoid encoding gender in the title. The use of "transgender" or other as an additional option to "man" or "woman" is strongly discouraged, as it can contribute to marginalizing these communities as alternatives to the mainstream binary. Be consistent in your choices across markets (Fig. 7.3.2).

"Gendered interfaces" have been theorized extensively in feminist research, but they are a real-life concern in increasingly diverse societies, namely because of the following factors:

a. *Men process information differently from women.* Simon Baron-Cohen's Extreme Male Theory of Autism proposed that the neurological

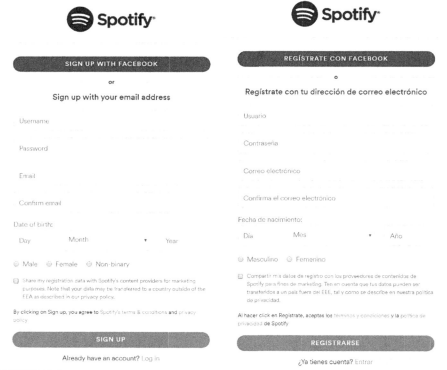

FIGURE 7.3.2
Although Spotify was one of the first companies to include a nonbinary choice in its form after pressure from the mxactivist community, this only extended initially to the United Kingdom, United States, and Australia, with this option remaining elusive to other markets.

difference between men and women made both genders develop different cognitive styles. While male babies would be more prone to pay attention to movement and spatial layout, female babies would be more interested in social stimuli like faces and voices. These tendencies would eventually develop into preferences for *systemizing*, in the case of men, and *empathizing*, in the case of women. Baron-Cohen proposes that the male brain can be essentially located at different spots of the autistic spectrum, and more extreme cases of systemizing would be reflected in clinical cases of autism. Only 20–25% of the autistic population is female.

b. *Men interact socially in a different manner than women.* A 2013 study demonstrated that males have on average a higher friend count on Facebook than women across most countries. Research at the social media giant also consistently showed that women receive more comments and acknowledgments from their social network. Women also tended to post more status updates with messages concerning thankfulness, family fun, and birthday wishes than men.

c. *Men use the Internet differently.* A 2004 Pew Internet survey showed that men are most likely to go online to get general and political news, make reservations, and check sports scores. Women were most likely to search for health, support group and social media sites, and obtain spiritual and religious information. (The same report also highlighted that African-Americans were more active than white people in searching for school or job information, and in listening and downloading music.)

Different concepts on how to apply these principles effectively in the context of UX design exist. One of them is the GenderMag method, which aims at finding gender-inclusiveness issues, led by Margaret Burnett, Professor of Computer Science at Oregon State University, and incorporating academics and researchers from Cambridge University, Microsoft, and City University London. The inspection framework is aimed at highlighting gender-inclusiveness issues in software design and development, according to persona facets like *motivation, information processing styles, computer self-efficacy, risk aversion,* and *tinkering.*

The greatest value of this empirical method is to introduce realistic and observable metrics that can guide designers toward a greater awareness regarding the masculine and feminine aspects of their designs—and their impacts on audiences.

7.3.1 Gender Disparity in the UX Industry

Design is not traditionally seen as a field where the gender disparity is a major issue, but the starkness of numbers shed a dark light on the subject. Design schools are generally populated with fairly similar ratios of men and women. Half the doctorates in science and engineering in the United States are awarded to women. However, the active community of professional UX and industrial designers is predominantly male in both the United States and the United Kingdom, and women take up only 5% of engineering teaching positions at a postgraduate level in the United States.

The popular UX blog A List Apart launched in 2009 a poll about readership gender. 82.6% of the respondents were male web designers. When asked whether there was any gender bias in the field, 66.5% of the participants answered "definitely not."

Stereotypes and strained relationships in the working place are also part of the prejudiced bias against women in scientific fields. Tim Hunt, a distinct Nobel laureate, was compelled to resign his post at University College London after remarking publicly at the World Conference of Science Journalists in Seoul, South Korea: "Let me tell you about my trouble with girls... Three things happen when they are in the lab... You fall in love with them, they fall in love with you, and when you criticize them, they cry." (The Guardian, 2015).

Apart from difficult relationships in the working place, technical fields show a distinct predominance of male presence versus female, and this is and this unbalance has been addressed in several studies. However, there have been recent remarkable strides in achieving a greater equilibrium between the sexes, particularly in digital media. One of these projects is Chicas Poderosas, an initiative started by Mariana Santos, an ICFJ Knight International Journalism Fellow and a former member of the interactive team at The Guardian UK newspaper. What she saw in her daily experience with media teams and in other offices prompted her to start an initiative that would give "voice to the underrepresented stories and women" and help women climb up the ladder of "leadership, management and entrepreneurship." Other projects to give voice to audiences that had previously been denied a voice in the production and direction of the design industry are the Design for Women Foundation in Africa and International Women's Media Foundation (IWMF).

Research suggests that, predominantly, technology design is biased in favor of groups similar to the designer (Jonge & Schraner, 2010), and women may be at a disadvantage when using propositions designed mostly by men. "The appropriation of technology by men, and the exclusion of women from many of the domains deemed technical, are processes that leave their mark in the very design of tasks..." They argue that technology has resulted in "the construction of men as strong, manually able and technologically endowed, and women as physically and technically impotent" (MacKenzie & Wajcman, 1999: p. 25) (Fig. 7.3.3).

According to the U.S. Bureau of Labor Statistics, women make up only a third of the web development force, but these numbers are much smaller elsewhere in the world. However, the situation is changing. According to the United Nations World's Women 2010 report:

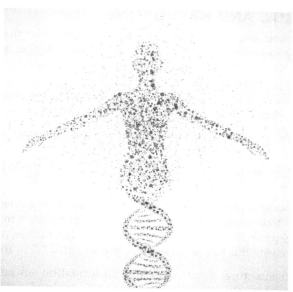

FIGURE 7.3.3
Technology is engendered by practice, but there is no biased prerogative on its universality. It is up to designers to work with universal variables rather than in-built limitations.

Nevertheless, with fewer female designers in tech, it is only inevitable that design as a discipline suffers an unwanted bias in accordance with the dominant group: men. The matter of gender diversity is relevant to design, both technical- and service-wise, not only because of the social value of the audience in question, but also because of the accessibility and suitability of the design in disciplines ranging from gardening to urban planning.

For instance, the American Planning Association and Cornell University's Women's Planning Forum denounced the fact that most urban settings are male-oriented in a 2014 survey with more than 600 planners. Some of the main difficulties highlighted included the unsafe condition offered by poorly lit parking lots and public transportation, as well as the difficulty in maneuvering strollers in sidewalks and public buildings. Moving around comfortably and safely in public transportation is a very different experience depending which group you are on, and a relaxed ride home can easily be filled with apprehension and fear if you happen to be on the wrong side of the gender or racial fence. Depending on gender and race, security and infrastructural planning and design may not answer these differences fully. Designing for gender poses specific inclusion challenges and, in a post-feminist society where different experiences and perspectives are not only respected but a crucial part of the social matrix of societies worldwide (Gill, 2007), fostering diversity in your audience is not an option, but a necessary effort that is at the very crux of the UX field.

7.4 SCRIPTS AND KEYBOARDS

In his 2013 dissertation, Santiago Ruano Rincon argued that there is a case to be made for the use of cultural factors in user interface design, after an experiment with the Nasa Indians in deep Colombia. In it, Santiago accounted for the influence of writing systems, literacy, and aesthetic perception in the drafting of software user requirements. The work followed on the footsteps of previous research, which had stumbled primarily because of two aspects:

1. the native computer users were unaware of desktop as an interface metaphor
2. the Nasa language was not fully supported by keyboards available in Colombia.

This is not an isolated case where a minority language being directly limited by the mainstream technology. In 2015, an Irish woman by the name of Caoimhe Ní Chathail was prevented from corresponding with her mobile phone provider through their website due to the presence of the accented "í" in the name.

In terms of infrastructure, there is usually no limitation on language implementation in most major OS (Windows, Mac OS, Android, and iOS). Several conditions must be fulfilled in order for a language to become available as both an input and output language, namely:

- The language tag should be defined in the BCF 47 series of documents by the Internet Engineering Task Force,
- A language character encoding (such as the ones included in Unicode) must be available in order to allow alphabets and other language characters to be rendered digitally.

Nearly every language in the world is accommodated for in the list of available languages. Android 5.0.1 includes over 600 locales, amongst variations of Uzbek, Moroccan Tamazight, Bafia (Cameroon), and Langi (Tanzania). Compatibility with scripts is an essential part of any app or website. The minimal expectation is to be able to render the language intended for that territory correctly, e.g., correct script, punctuation, and spacing. Another huge internationalization necessity is the support for the regional settings, like currency, date, and address formats.

The most frequently used types of scripts are:

- Roman,
- Kanji,
- Cyrilic,
- Arabic,
- Kana,
- Devanagri,
- Korean,
- Bengali,
- Thai,
- Telugu,

- Burmese,
- Greek,
- Hebrew.

A script look is very powerful in terms of product identity. The size of the scripts also matters, as both large and small systems can take up a significant amount of space in the design layout. Chinese, for instance, has a significant amount of characters which do not fit into the same conventional spacing used by the Roman character sets. This is one of the reasons why Chinese UI normally appear stilted to Western eyes, even when using Western alphabets. The Chinese character inset is a few pixels wider than the Roman script, and its layout is necessarily larger.

Asian systems can also count in the tens of thousands of symbols, like with Chinese and Japanese, compared to alphabets such as the English, which counts only 26 characters. The combination of different writing systems is also a problem in these languages, where the use of different writing systems in the same text block can generate an unbalance in the kerning.

As in the Internet, countries can have several official languages. Communities can live side-by-side and have a completely different idiom. Nowhere is this truer than in Africa, by far the most multicultural and multifaceted continent on the planet. This is where the current holder of the world record in official languages lives: Zimbabwe has a total of 16 official languages, approved by the Zimbabwean parliament. According to Wikipedia, the languages are: Chewa, Chibarwe, English, Kalanga, Koisan, Nambya, Ndau, Ndebele, Shangani, Shona, sign language, Sotho, Tonga, Tswana, Venda, and Xhos. Sign language is one of the official languages, and its status is recognized in over 30 countries around the world as a social language.

This prompts several adaptations that a responsive layout will need to address in order to maintain order and weight in the typeset.

The direction of the script is essential to understand the impact of a different web script on the overall layout and design. The direction can be bidirectional (bidi) or unidirectional. The former poses the most problems in terms of internationalization, as the direction of the script can be compromised by the frameworks used. Arabic is one of the most complex scripts to use in design because of its bidirectionality, and also its ability to switch directions for numbers and special words within the same sentence.

Apart from bidirectionality, you also have to consider the impact of the string axis. Japanese is normally written vertically, whereas web concessions have normally laid out the characters horizontally. Most Japanese expect web text to be horizontally laid out.

Right-to-left languages represent a challenge to most web designers who want to achieve a consistent design whilst thinking of international audiences. The interface is normally mirrored, with the strings roughly implemented in the same relative positions.

Insertion points should also be relative to the direction of the word.

Bidirectional languages will change the insertion point according to the relative position on the word. Similarly, the text orientation plays a role and is culturally determined: many countries prefer the flow of the text on a book spine, for instance, to be from the bottom to the top. The United States prefer top to bottom. However, any trademarked names need to be in the original language: law is (for the most part) language-neutral (Fig. 7.4.1–Fig. 7.4.4).

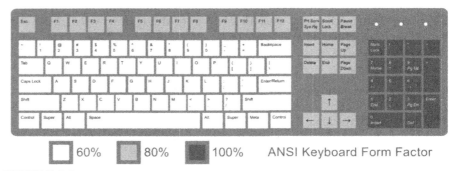

FIGURE 7.4.1

ANSI keyboard layout for US-based locales, which can also be presented in more compact formats excluding the keys present in the grayed out areas. *Source: Wikipedia.org.*

FIGURE 7.4.2

The AZERTY keyboard layout is based on the Latin alphabet, with local variations in France and Belgium. The most popular layout in German-speaking countries uses an alternative layout with QWERTZ and diacritical characters. *Source: Wikipedia.org.*

FIGURE 7.4.3

The Russian (or JCUKEN) keyboard layout as used by default in Windows. Most keyboards include the Latin characters in addition to the Cyrillic correspondent on the face of the keys. *Source: Wikipedia.org.*

FIGURE 7.4.4

Japanese, like Chinese and Korean, requires an IME which allows the user to input thousands of characters without the need to have one-to-one key mapping. The keyboard allows the user to enter Rōmaji (Latin) characters in order to make up more complex characters like kanji. *Source: Wikipedia.org.*

7.4.1 Arabic Script

Arabic is one of the most distinctive and oldest languages in the world, but its relevance to the web design world is still stifled by inadequate standards and lack of local development. Its fine calligraphic qualities and attention to detail earmark the script as one of the most beautiful in the world.

However, compared with Roman scripts, Arabic has a far more restricted font library available in the web design world. Its right-to-left direction, extended use of ligatures and cursive nature render the script's typefaces particularly difficult to handle as standardized fonts. The ascension of Unicode has assisted in the creation of more compatible desktop fonts, but the situation is still unfair to ambitious web designers who want to leverage the calligraphic script in their websites.

Contemporary Arabic script is indebted to the popular Kufic style, now over a thousand years old. The Kufic calligraphic style has a revered historical relevance, as it is the script used in the earliest known copies of the Qur'an. European imitations of the script have come to associate it closely to the Arabic language in the West, and pseudo-Kufic adorns several landmarks in southern France and the Iberian Peninsula. The historical implications are vast and far-reaching.

Arabic scripts have two basic text styles that influence its presentation:

- Naskh,
- Kufi.

Common Unicode system fonts like Ariel, Verdana, and especially Tahoma were until recently routinely used as *de facto* choices in Arabic design and typesetting, but browsers and the increased adoption of web fonts has made Arabic fonts more accessible and easier to use in Web development. There are several fonts commercially available, but their legibility and typesetting difficulty can compromise usage in mobile devices.

Since 2014, Google has started to make available additional Arabic web fonts to web designers. Other fonts have started as an open collaborative project by hobbyists and designers, like Amiri. The font "is a revival of the beautiful type-face pioneered in early 20th century by Bulaq Press in Cairo, also known as Amiria Press, after which the font is named," as the designer, Khaled Hosny, explains. "It is one of the few metal typefaces that were used in typesetting the Koran, making it a good source for a digital typeface to be used in typesetting Koranic verses" (Hosny, 2016).

The amount of glyphs available in these types are increasing, making it easier for designers to integrate them in their designs (Figs. 7.4.5 and 7.4.6).

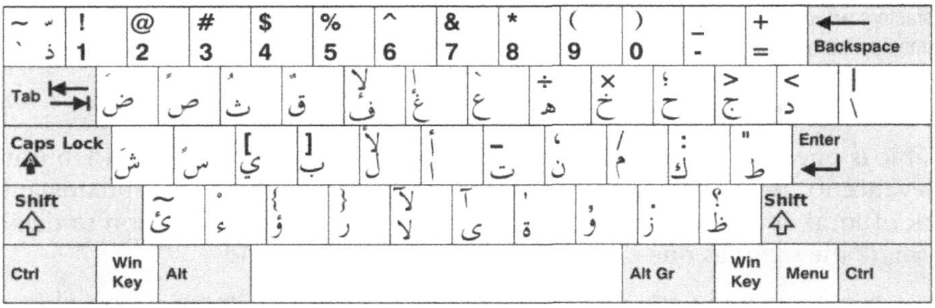

FIGURE 7.4.5

The Arabic keyboard layout is an evolution from the layout for the original Arabic typewriter, developed by a Syrian, Selim Shibli Haddad, in 1899. The Windows version differs slightly from the Mac version. Transliteration from Latin characters is offered in most standard word processors, but, notably, the Mac version of Microsoft Word has not been compatible with right-to-left script, leaving Arabic Mac users to look for alternative solutions. Several solutions are available for covers and stickers that can overlay Arabic characters on the physical keyboard. *Source: Wikipedia.org.*

FIGURE 7.4.6

An Apple Mac with an Arabic keyboard. These keyboard also contain Latin characters, which are necessary for URL and e-mail addresses. The first instance of the Arabic layout dates from 1899; today, it is used by over 400 million users.

7.4.2 Lessons From the Field: Minority Languages

Some movements are in place in order to push for the acceptance of minority languages, particularly in mobile technology. The Interaction Design for Indian Needs Lab at the Indian Institute of Technology in Bombay is research-ing and designing solutions for literacy and education. "Our focus is on using design to solve problems and creating social impact," stated the group. The group has a community focus and is a good example of how local digital research can be leveraged with limited means. It actively collaborates with masters and PhD students, along with the interns that join them every year, in the pursuit of better digital solutions for local populations, free of concerns over technology and corporate sponsorship. The group is currently developing Swarachakra, an Android gesture keyboard app for touchscreens, which has been released for 12 Indian languages, including Hindi, Marathi, Telugu, and Punjabi. The apps are open source and depend on the contribu-tion of volunteers. The group has also been developing fonts for other lan-guages as well.

7.5 INTERNATIONALIZATION REQUIREMENTS

Cyberspace. A consensual hallucination experienced daily by billions of legitimate operators, in every nation.

William Gibson.

Internationalization issues abound in most UI implementations, despite the contemporary availability of frameworks that minimize or even completely offload developers from its perils, like the Ninja Web Framework (a Java library) or i18next (for JavaScript). The fact that an app can be released and updated in over a hundred countries simultaneously has put different pres-sures on developers, who have a wider audience provide on-the-fly feedback on localization issues. On the other hand, the checklist to get through when localizing a product for the first time has become wider: translate the App Store market description, update app screenshots, translate strings and docu-mentation, privacy policy, websites, blogs, establish local social media marketing...

Different environments have different requirements, however. Android has in-built internationalization frameworks in the form of resource qualifiers, where each locale can have a specific strings XML file. Like most mobile operating systems, the locale depends on the user-configured system language. A similar mechanism is employed by iOS apps, where the internationalization depends on the environ-ment compatibility, and string files made available.

On the Web, the omnipresence of internationalization frameworks is reliant on the browser's compatibility with encoding standards like Unicode and UTF-8 for HTML and JavaScript, allowing any pages to open correctly in their native language without character corruption as long as the character set con-figuration is harmonized.

However, this does not minimize internationalization issues which can occur both with native and desktop apps, and can be categorized in a number of ways (Shneiderman, 1998; Fernandes, 1995):

- characters, numerals, special characters, and diacritical,
- left-to-right versus right-to-left versus vertical input and reading,
- date and time formats,
- numeric and currency formats,
- weights and measures,
- telephone numbers and addresses,
- names and titles,
- social-security, national identification, and passport numbers,
- capitalization and punctuation.

According to Del Galdo and Nielsen (1996), internationalization issues can be broadly split into:

- Comprehensibility: A computer interface that is capable of displaying the user's native language, character set, and notations, such as currency symbols.
- Usability: A computer interface that is understandable and usable in the user's native language.
- Desirability: A system that is able to produce systems that accommodate users' cultural characteristics.

7.5.1 Sorting Issues

Different accented characters might be sorted differently in languages. A may be followed by ä, á, but where would ã go?

Among the many conventions enunciated in Japanese traditional and cultural, the sorting order is one such example of variable arbitrariness. The language harbors various sort orders such as the "poem" order, which lists an arbitrary sorting delineated by a traditional poem.

7.5.2 Controls

Checkboxes are sometimes difficult to decipher for cultures that use the symbol to cross out the choices they do not desire, e.g., Switzerland, Korea. Radio buttons are always preferable. One other example of the shoddy usability provided by the symbol is the red cross versus checkmark conundrum that befalls many a design, and the toggling between both choices.

7.5.3 Currencies and Number Handling

On your latest trip to Russia, getting a bank extract from an ATM might have seemed a bit off. For an instant, your bank account may have fooled you into believing you had been scammed by a local hacker. Assuming you had no WiFi connection in a remarkably cold country, and that you actually took the risk of hanging around Moscovite streets in an attempt to collect a meaning-less piece of information.

Nevertheless, for the sake of argument, the position of the point and the comma internationally is one of the most common causes of frustration amongst avid bank statement reviewers. Russia uses the point to separate the digits of the thousands and space for the decimals.

7.5.4 Calendars

Time is relative, we learn. But even more than relative, there are several ver-sions of its measurement ruling the daily lives and habits of people all over the world. Although the Gregorian calendar is used by mostly Western coun-tries, and in the process has reached other corners of the world as an authori-tative reference for international dealings. However, there are other calendars that are references for millions:

- Arabic lunar calendar,
- Jewish calendar,
- Iranian calendar,
- Japanese imperial calendar.

Apart from different holidays and week/month measurements, the calendars differ greatly in application. The Japanese imperial calendar is still applicable to traditional businesses that regulate their time based on the Emperor year of reign. Normally, the Gregorian calendar is used by Japanese businesses that communicate frequently with the West, but the old timescale is still honored in certain quadrants of the society.

Some of the implementation faux pas of this type of calendar include an old implementation of Lotus 1-2-3 where the Emperor reign year had an option to be reset, which did not fall favorably with the notion of the Emperor's immortality. The company quickly removed the feature.

Holidays and their applications should also hold the regional preferences and politics in mind. Keeping calendars in mind might impact usability with the assumptions put forward by geotracking and regional IPs. Dates themselves are also prone to the same variety of representation both in full and short forms. Week days have different spellings and their abbreviation differs depending on space requirements, times, and layouts.

Time formatting is equally distinctive, with North America using the ante/post meridian (a.m. and p.m.) standard. 24-hour clocks are normally used in Europe, a standard that the American military also adheres to.

This is an exception that North America adheres to, but is by no means the only one. The most distinctive idiosyncratic choice in this domain is the unit of measure, with the pounds and stones of the imperial system still causing disruption in many international shipping routines. The metric system, how-ever, prevails over most of the world's economies.

7.5.5 Postal Addresses

The traditional landline telephone is quickly becoming an outdated artifact in 4G-converted countries, but it is still the main means of emergency calls in remote areas, and an essential tool of voice communication all over the world. Phone numbers and their conventions, however, are still as variable as the countries in which they are available. The use of area codes is restricted to only a few territories, as well as prefixes for certain numbers. Most countries use a single string of digits, and even when the additional previous digits are a part of the overall number, the different representations are mostly for local recognition only and there is limited difference in the actual number itself.

Other conventions include ANSI for US flowcharts and DIN standards for German.

Color specification standards also differ, such as Pantone, CMYK, and Toyo, and should be held in account.

Paper sizes differ between different territories, with the traditional Letter format of 8 1/2 by 11 in. A4 is the most popular paper size in Europe and Japan.

7.6 CROSS-CULTURAL USABILITY

Philipp Bachmann (2013) suggested six basic patterns for cross-cultural usability:

Multicoded instruction. By encoding the same message in various ways in the interface, the cognitive load on the user is minimized and the possibility of a loss in information. One example of how to overcome the difference in attention and interpretation is the use of a simultaneously visible pictogram and a text label in any interactive label on an interface.

Message catalog: The application or website should use a lookup function in order to retrieve the same message in different languages, depending on the user's configuration and the intended locale. By allowing the application to have the same message handle represented in various languages, potential internationalization issues can be minimized, which also includes time zones, number formatting, and other culturally-specific units.

Culturally and environmentally neutral persistence: The design should not depend on any one locale in order to perform conversions from, instead sticking with a standardized form. For example, using coordinated universal time (UTC) as the standard internal time for the code, and converting it using the local settings of the operating system for end-user representation.

Culture and environment-aware persistence: Design for and be aware of the local value as well as the internal neutral value. Store units in nonculture specific models so that they can be easily retrieved and converted when necessary by the front-end. The design should be aware of the locale and the units used, like currencies, in order to reuse them in the future when necessary.

Input example: If the design expects data input from the user, text fields with in-line validation can be used in order to provide information like phone numbers, dates, location, etc. Instead of providing additional information via pop-ups and explanatory text next to the control, provide examples of the intended input in the textbox itself. When possible, suggest statistically probable values based on the user's previous preferences, or data that can serve as example, e.g., next week as dates for flights.

Hierarchy driven by target culture: Phone numbers, addresses, and dates are all variable in structure around the world. American usage privileges the month preceding the day, e.g., MM/DD/YY, whereas the European standard usage is DD/MM/YY. Similarly, the state is often a prevalent field in online forms, legacy of the American standard form, but few other countries around the world require this in address records.

7.6.1 Conventional Usability Issues

Wayfinding. Problems in website navigation are usually equated with the process of using contextual information to navigate to a selected destination. In the context of user interface design, it is most visible as the visual cues provided to the user in order to guide it to a specific functionality or process (e.g., Wizards) or monitoring its position in a given stage of the interface flow (e.g., breadcrumbs). In these cases, a visual indication usually helps the user to keep the flow in mind. Breadcrumbs are the most suitable to this type of context, as they can help route monitoring, particularly when a wayfinding mistake has been made and backtracking is necessary.

Error classification and escalation of user actions. According to the conventionally standard classification introduced by Donald Norman, there are two basic types of errors: slips and mistakes. Slips are usually errors of execution where the user goes through a set of automatic and unconscious processes and misses a common step or does not execute an action as intended due to motor or cognitive distractions (e.g., unintentionally clicking on the wrong button because it is too close to the intended button).

Mistakes are sometimes referred to as errors of intention or errors of planning, and occur when an intention is inappropriate. For example, a mistake occurs when a user is shown a warning and selects the wrong settings to try to fix it. It is a conscious process of decision-making that is biased according to currently available information and expectations. Another example is that the user is biased to select only from visible options and avoid more complex processes that involve navigating dialogs to go through a process. In cases where the user is warned with an "error" in the guise of a warning, cognitive dissonance can be created.

Unbalance in screen real-estate usage. Screen real-estate is, according to UsabilityFirst, "the amount of space available on a display for an application to provide output."

Typically, its proper use is directly related to the information conveyed in the dialog, the aesthetics, and the context. Maximizing effective use of screen real estate is one of the most difficult design challenges: excessive information may be poorly organized or confusing, so effective screen layouts must be used with appropriate use of white space. Another principle of usability that is of particular interest to static areas is the memory load over user actions. Users have to learn and remember the navigation flow of the UI to reach for the required functionality.

Optimally, especially in applications with a limited feature scope, any functionality should be reached within one click, or a key combination stroke. The sidebar can be refactored into a toolbar or status bar where the available actions are permanently presented to the user. A horizontal bar is preferable because it reduces the area of the dialog used to present options and hotspots and uses this space more effectively.

Gulf of expectations and evaluation in information structure. The gulf of execution is a quantified distance between a user's intentions and expectations and what is actually possible to do with the interface. According to Norman, it is the difference between the intentions of the users and what the system allows them to do or how well the system supports those actions. The gulf of evaluation, on the other hand, is related to the user's ability to diagnose what the UI process actually implies in terms of steps: from interface to interpretation and to evaluation. In other words, the gulf of evaluation is directly related to how easy it is for the user to get information on the current status and feedback on its actions. This separation between action and information areas increases the interaction cost since the information areas and the action points are spread across different panes of the vertical tabs.

Inconsistent use of controls. Consistency, both functional and aesthetic, enables users to efficiently transfer knowledge, learn new processes more quickly, and grow trust in the design of any given system. Functional consistency refers to consistency of meaning and action (e.g., a traffic light that shows a yellow light before going to red). Functional consistency improves usability and learnability by enabling people to leverage existing knowledge about how the design functions. Aesthetic consistency refers to consistency of style and appearance (e.g., a company logo that uses a consistent font, color, and graphic). Aesthetic consistency enhances recognition, communicates membership, and sets emotional expectations.

Low signal-to-noise ratio in dialog information. In the context of UI design, the signal-to-noise ratio is relevant to the conciseness and directness of the information presented to the user. Extraneous elements (noise) degrade the form and quality of information relevant to the user (signal). Maximizing signal means clearly communicating information with minimal degradation. Signal degradation occurs when information is presented inefficiently: unclear writing, inappropriate graphs, or ambiguous icons and labels. Signal clarity is improved through simple and concise presentation of information.

System status is not permanently available. In technical settings, the system status is critical to proper operation: from a forklift to a cell phone, the general status of the device or entity should be both clearly visible and clear to the user. The same happens in UI, especially for security software. The usability of a system is improved when its status and methods of use are clearly visible.

Feature implementation dissemination. Simplicity is one of the prime examples achieved when everyone can easily understand and use the design, regardless of experience, literacy, or concentration level. It is one of the basic principles of UI design and it is a powerful ally against feature creep: unnecessary complexity should be avoided and consistency becomes of prime value as it decreases interaction cost. Consistency and control centralization can be better be achieved by reusing patterns and control sets.

Inefficient use of control metaphors. The use of controls as metaphors is represented universally in UI layouts, from the traffic light window controls in the Mac OSX to the use of the trash as a metaphor. Generally, metaphors trigger in the user a sense of familiarity and allow it to associate a system functionality or structure with another real-life concept or object known by the user (Fig. 7.6.1).

Color is also a component of this metaphor system. It allows highlighting or attracting attention to specific elements of the UI, as well as signal status in an effective way. Saturated colors (pure hues) naturally attract attention as they are perceived as more vivid and dynamic to the human eye. However, intense use of saturated colors can also cause fatigue to the user.

The use of a switch as a metaphor is much more efficient when the switch itself uses the symbolism to its potential. The absence of color for highlighting status in switches makes it harder to determine its status. The use of two text labels next to the control introduces complexity unnecessarily as the control status is being clarified with additional text instead of using the control itself as a representation of the metaphor. The switch used for signaling on/off does not necessarily have to be a neutral color native switch and could instead use a bitmap that uses red and green, or an illustration to show its current state.

One example is the folder icon, with it yellowish color suggesting the idea of a filing folder for everyday use to Western users. However, this particular office

FIGURE 7.6.1
A common desktop metaphor: the trash can.

artefact is not popular in Asian countries, like for example, China. Chinese folders are characterized by their thick rectangular brown paper without tabs, seemingly cardboard-like in appearance. For Chinese users, the Western folder icon has no immediate association to an everyday folder and this association is not a clear association.

Duplicate configuration logic. Discrete design based on elementarity implies smart decisions on building functionality models in an application. This is directly related to the Occam's Razor principle, which in itself is a solid adaptation of the simplicity paradigm and equates that entities should not be multiplied without necessity. Functional equivalence is only to be duplicated in cases where concrete usability studies and metrics justify it. This is also a prime directive for effective information architecture: pin it, lock it, reuse it.

CASE STUDY
Developing a Western Brand in China

Agency: IT Consultis

Client: Sunglass Hut

When: 2014–2015

Methods: Behavioural, Attitudinal, Quantitative, Qualitative, Exploratory, Generative, Evaluative

Type: Design process

China is a hotbed of feverish consumerism, but Western brands often struggle for success and even acceptance in the distinctly insular marketplace. IT Consultis sought to curb this on a project to establish the new Sunglass Hut Chinese site. The stylish brand has adorned the tanned faces of many a movie star in idyllic marinas throughout Europe and America, but Asia remained an elusive world.

The challenge for IT Consultis was to build a brand new web presence that stood out in an increasingly crowded marketplace. The first step was to assess the actual distinctions and differences that the particular local version of the website demanded. A full site audit was performed in order to check its appropriateness and resonance with the Chinese audience. Every page in the main user journeys was reviewed by a local team, as well as the sitemap and main navigation categories. Essential components for social media were integrated in the website structure:

- A custom Weibo feed in the footer of the website to gain traffic and to drive users to become a follower of the brand.
- The WeChat QR code was placed directly in the menu side bar in order to allow users to follow the brand on WeChat at any point during their navigation.

As a fashion retailer, the popularity of Sunglass Hut in the USA is unparalleled, but it remained largely unknown to Chinese consumers. However, there is an eager audience for luxury brands, many of which are represented in the portfolio. The visibility of these companies was leveraged in order to increase the overall brand awareness. Brands like Armani, Burberry or Miu Miu were given a personalized touch by creating dedicated pages for each one of them, allowing users to get more information on a single-stop point for their products in the official Sunglass Hut website.

Dedicated brand pages also benefitted SEO, as the content could be specialized and optimized accordingly for each brand. All elements of the website (pictures and content) were built with a view to being indexed by search engines, enabling a much-needed boost to the search engine presence of the brand new website.

Performance was also a consideration. The assets and code of the entire website were revised and optimized in order to facilitate access for Chinese users with slower connections. The new website was built to be locally hosted for connection reasons, and local APIs and lazy loading were implemented in order to allow for a smoother page navigation and loading.

The website also received a dedicated mobile version exclusively for deployment on smartphone browsing. This allowed for a better integration with WeChat, improving the odds of success by having a dedicated version of the site for the most popular social media network in China.

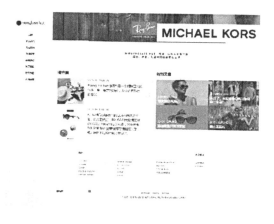

7.7 VIRTUAL REALITIES

Deep in the human unconscious is a pervasive need for a logical
universe that makes sense. But the real universe is always one step
beyond logic.

Frank Herbert

Computer and communication scientist Marc Weiser suggested in 1991 that "in
the 21st century the technology revolution will move into the everyday, the
small and the invisible." Often appointed as the father of ubiquitous computing, this Xerox Parc visionary pointed the way to technology assuming an omnipresent, increasingly supporting and discrete role, reducing conscious user
interaction and aiding the user instead of hindering or patronizing his actions.

This is the paradigm behind ubiquitous computing, a set of technologies that
can help redefine technical communication.

As the term indicates, *ubiquitous technology* is upon us everywhere: in airports,
art galleries, public spaces, and even the comfort of our own homes. The term
loosely refers to the "calm technology," as baptized by Marc Weiser, where
information processing and user interaction happen in the background or sur-
reptitiously in peripheral systems, and are not constricted to button-pressing
on a keyboard.

As a recent advancement in computing, there is still some wide-eyed wariness
over the concept of ubiquitous technology and its implications on privacy,
habits, and machine decision-making. However, its ultimate ambitions are still
only suggested in our current technological setting, even as we see the first
signs of its standardization.

From the Internet of Things to hands-free interfaces, game consoles, media
computers and mobile devices are being taken by storm by alternative interfaces that render computing less obtrusive and interaction more intuitive.

The future of interaction will eschew button-pressing keyboards and pads, and
instead rely on tactile and direct sensing interfaces. Our communication with our
devices is already cross-modal, mixing visual and audio. When we set our phone
to vibrate mode instead of using an audible ringtone, it is using a haptic mode to
communicate with us. Promising research from Tactus Technology allows the creation of physical buttons on a flat smartphone screen, literally allowing users to
change the way an object can feel. The REVEL project, developed at Disney
Research, aims at integrating different textures onto everyday objects.

Despite its potential, haptic research still accounts for less than one percent of
all multisensory research. Haptic feedback carries many advantages, like the
ability to use body language as an information carrier. Over 95% of our communication is established through our body language: to use only verbal or
written input with a machine implies a tremendous waste of contextual information, including the urgency of our goals (e.g., whether we are in a hurry)
and the social context (e.g., whether we have company).

Ubiquitous computing is also the perfect vehicle for transmitting information without distracting the recipient. Too often, users' attention is distracted by other tasks, alerts or the inconveniences of having to access information physically, losing the sense of flow when doing something. When searching for information on Google, it is easy to get sidestepped by tabs, ads, chats, and environmental distractions. Our attention is split across a multitude of levels, all vying for our intervention. Ubiquitous computing sidesteps this with an adaptive approach that can deliver the right information at the right time— and to the right people.

7.7.1 Content Delivery and Communication

Technical communication is evolving, not only in its delivery, but also in the nature of what is delivered. Instruction manuals are slowly being replaced with assisted guidance, where instructions are placed in-context when the user tries to interact with an equipment.

Ubiquitous technologies allow us to look at content as a set subjected to responsive conditions, which can be grabbed, cropped, recombined and reused. Intelligent content using XML data models like DITA, or Linked Data formats like RDF or JSON-LD, can group and deliver shreds of content using a semantic model that enables highly adaptive and granular delivery of content. An example of this semantic indexing is Google's massive Knowledge Graph, which displays relevant information about a search already on the results page.

Dynamic content does not equal a factored version of static content, but instead a rich tapestry of text and visual assets that are assembled with a rich structure. In a world that is ruled by the ebbs and tides of social media, big data and machine processing are not the bogeyman of yesteryear: they are tools with which to understand and process content as an organic network of structures.

As such, the delivery of content in this ambient intelligence can vary wildly. In the following sections I will highlight its main applications.

7.7.2 Context-Awareness

Everyday, millions of Bluetooth and WiFi modules are produced around the world and built into smartphones, computers, cars, vending machines, kiosks, and other digital products. These modules are the size of a pin and can accommodate the highest possible broadband speeds available.

Ubiquitous computing is often envisioned as the natural step in taking advantage of this miniaturization trend. It proposes a seamless context-aware approach to information and services regardless of whether the user is on the move or located in a specially equipped environment, like an airport or

FIGURE 7.7.1
"Smarthouses" represent some of the leading current environments for ubiquitous computing.

hospital. The success of this technology relies, however, on the adequacy and relevance of the content generated and delivered to the user and on the place, time, and profile that the user is supplied with.

Motion and proximity sensors, as well as satellite connections, allow our phones to provide contextual, relevant information depending on location, time and even our own motion. Context-aware systems can respond naturally to user activity. The usability of ubiquitous computing relies to a large degree on its adaptivity: a sensor that is triggered by the user's presence should be smart enough to trigger the right action and "mute" itself should the user indicate that no action is required (Fig. 7.7.1).

7.7.3   Voice-Recognition Environments

Walking into your living room after a long day at work, you are concerned with the plans for the evening: that well-deserved ticket to the star-studded arena show could not come at a better time. But your tickets are not yet printed. You speak to the open air: "Computer, print the tickets for tonight's concert. Also check a store nearby that sells leather jackets."

Voice-activated technology is intimately associated with golden-age science fiction and Star Trek galaxy-surfing, but its actual benefits as a cross-modal interaction method is becoming a research priority. On a consumer level, there are already projects like the Ubi, an always-on ambient voice computer that can sit behind your couch and respond to vocal request, giving the means to browse the Internet only with the sound of your voice, without any need for a screen. When asked, the system can deliver and read the weather forecast, calculations, instruction manuals, warning leaflets, and any other content accessible through the Web.

This attempt to introduce discrete voice-recognition systems already features prominently in consoles like the Xbox and the iPhone and Android platforms through Siri and other speech recognition and synthesis software. Although imperfect, the technology works remarkably well in closed quarters and points the way to a future where keying in information will be an option and not a necessity.

7.7.4 Guidance

One of the best examples of ubiquitous computing with transparent purposing are the guidance and interaction systems that are starting to populate public facilities like museums and gardens. With the growth of the digital market, traditional brick-and-mortar institutions are increasingly compelled to find new solutions to engage communities. Part of the solution is precisely to take advantage of the digital arena. For example, the Cleveland Museum of Art's Gallery One (http://www.clevelandart.org/gallery-one) cleverly combines an augmented reality app called ArtLens with in situ interactive displays.

These services are not only multidevice, but also multilingual. The Ueno Zoo Ubiquitous Guide Service, in Japan, allows users to gain information about animals by using a small iPhone-like device on code tags in the Ueno Zoological Gardens. Similarly, the Hama-rikyuu Gardens service allows explanations in multiple languages regarding the history of the gardens in the Tokyo Metropolitan Park.

7.7.5 Real-Time Localization

Software giants are also wary of the role ubiquitous localization can play in today's international market. One of the most successful examples of this technology, Word Lens, offered a glimpse into real-time localization by allowing common users to see translated signs and lettering instead of the content they display in reality. The technology is based on a set of optical recognition frameworks and graphical display methodologies that allow it to emulate a specific type font just seamless enough to provide a practical augmented reality overlay feature to users that complements and offers an useful glimpse of possible mass applications of the otherwise cumbersome and usability-inept device. Acquired in 2014 by Google, the technology behind Word Lens is now being integrated in the Google Translate services.

One of the reasons behind the growing popularity of these apps is the ubiquitous nature of mobile devices: despite the variation in size, specifications, and service providers, cell phones and tablets remain the primary disseminators of "calm technology," offering contextual information and tools that are increasingly relevant to our geographical position and everyday activities. On the other hand, devices like Google Glass have not yet reached a point of maturity to allow their mass adoption as standard everyday devices, primarily due to being heavy and cumbersome to wear and because of the stigma associated to social interaction (Fig. 7.7.2).

FIGURE 7.7.2
Word Lens augmented reality technology enabled smartphone users to translate any sign on their camera to a selected language. The has since been integrated in Google Translate in 2015.

Real-time interpretation without human intervention is also now becoming a reality, as a result of the integration of voice recognition and synthesis, and automated translation. The new functionality, soon to be included in Skype Translator, can translate a spoken utterance almost immediately into the language of the person on the other end of the line. This technology can be easily transposed to an auditorium with simultaneous translation or to virtual classrooms around the world.

7.7.6   E-Health

Mobile technology is becoming more important than ever in keeping track of health and general wellbeing. The explosion in running and fitness tracking apps like Endomondo and Runtastic shows the growing role of the handheld device as a personal and adaptable trainer, with far more precise metrics and records than a human coach could possibly track.

Health is one of the most critical and practical applications of ubiquitous computing. It is estimated that, in 2010, over one-third of Europe's population has had at least one chronic disease, and this number is increasing. With aging populations and receding health budgets, e-health provides a critical method for using mobile technology to replace traditional paper diagnosis forms and stimulates awareness of the importance of quality of life.

The greatest advantage of mobile technology is that it is almost permanently available to the patient. Projects like MONARCA, which focuses on bipolar disorders, used the phone sensors as well as wearable technology in order to trace the process of the patient's mental state throughout the day.

Other systems like autonomic management of ubiquitous e-Health systems (AMUSE) are based on on-body sensors that can interact with ubiquitous environments. This is useful, for example, in hospitals where the environment is recording the body temperature, breathing rate, and other vitals of patients as they move around freely, unencumbered by monitoring equipment.

As Geoffrey Miller states in his essay, The Smartphone Psychology Manifesto, "smartphones could transform psychology even more profoundly than PCs and brain imaging did." And indeed the same applies to the wider field of medicine.

7.7.7   E-Learning and E-Training

The mobile technologies involved in ubiquitous computing allow users to empower their learning by being free to access online learning platforms anytime and anywhere. Online MOOCs (Massive Open Online Courses) and other platforms are available for users who want to accommodate the learning experience by module or course to their own availability.

Learning technology, however, is a bourgeoning field that accommodates other modes of learning. The effectiveness of lectures and tests can be limiting for students, and more effective learning strategies will translate into better results.

Projects like Mindtool-Assisted In-Field Learning (MAIL), developed at the National University of Taiwan, rely on a combination of digital technology and fieldwork. When learning in-field, students can use a specialized app in their phones, which provides information on the images that are captured by the camera. This type of blended learning works well in training contexts, where the user is expected to undergo a series of tasks and execute them correctly with the help of documentation delivered through an app.

Ubiquitous learning allows students to move across learning contexts and stimulates learning in nonconventional contexts, mixing both real-world situations and digital support like augmented reality. This implies a rethinking of the traditional curriculum that programs like LOGOS (Knowledge-on-demand for ubiquitous learning) and workshops like Digiskills attempted to prototype on an institutional level.

In the corporate setting, u-learning and training represent an opportunity to reduce long-term costs, since the average training cost of an employee in the USA is around $1500. The past decade has seen a constant increase of studies on Virtual Learning Environments (VLE) and their applicability as ubiquitous learning environments to train prospective agents, officers, and employees.

However, the great potential of ubiquitous e-learning in a fully-formed discipline that combines a community of learners, real-world interaction, and a task-based evaluative framework, is yet to be fully unlocked.

CASE STUDY
MDInteractivo
MDInteractivo, JWT Puerto Rico/Gatorade

MDInteractivo Gatorade produces sports beverage and food products based on performance data, and works with celebrity athletes.

In 2010, Gatorade wanted to sponsor the Central American and American Games, due to its widespread audience and popularity, but this position was already occupied by Powerade, a competitor. The challenge for Gatorade was to create the impression of an association with the Games without paying for official sponsorship, to benefit from its popularity amongst athletes and sports fans, and to foster an image of innovation.

Instead, Gatorade sponsored NBA player Jose Barea, one of Puerto Rico's most popular athletes, who was the country's most likely candidate for winning a gold medal, and had been selected for the prestigious act of carrying the flag during the Opening Ceremony of the Games. Due to the lack of official game sponsorship, Gatorade could not directly use The Games' grounds, logo or name. So, in pursuit of innovation, they drew on technology to find their way in, and measured Barea's heartbeat, respiration, temperature, activity, and even heartbeats and emotions, through a chest strap. They broadcast these intimate statistics live over the internet and television, including mobile apps, which meant that they reached fans directly, who could experience carrying the flag, and winning a gold medal win directly with him. This was transmitted to over 300,000 households through television, and over 60,000 people on the web and mobile sites: a large proportion of Puerto Rico's 4 million population.

The campaign was a huge success, despite not involving the usual large sponsorship budget. It inspired a new, ubiquitously-used nickname, "The Heart of Puerto Rico" for Barea, and was honored with PepsiCo's "Smile for Excellence Award," the most prestigious accolade that the region had received. The official sponsor, Powerade, may have been able to pay for its logos to be featured in the event, but through creative thinking and clever use of technology, Gatorade was able to tap into the emotions of the country, to resounding success.

CHAPTER 8

A Thousand Pictures

ABSTRACT

As a common form of nonverbal communication, gestures are simultaneously universal and yet culturally determined. We communicate information to nearby observers by our mere poise and our expressions. Our gestures can immediately tell our state of mind, our perception, and our reaction. However, gestures are also naturally dependent on energy, context, and application. Although their physicality is appealingly universal, it was also one of the key detractors to their adoption as a standard interaction method. Hardware constraints and designing for understanding constitute the greatest challenges of UX design, and achieving a concerted international design strategy requires a layered approach.

Keywords: Touchscreen; gesture; scanning pattern; color scheme; design; user experience

8.1   GESTURES AND INPUTS

Between an action and reaction, between a gesture and its consequences, everybody agrees that there is an exact relationship, but not necessarily a proportionate one.

Filippo Bologna.

As a common form of nonverbal communication, gestures are simultaneously universal and yet culturally determined. We communicate information to nearby observers by our mere poise and our expressions. Our gestures can immediately tell our state of mind, our perception, and our reaction.

Universal UX Design. DOI: http://dx.doi.org/10.1016/B978-0-12-802407-2.00008-3

However, gestures are also naturally dependent on energy, context, and application. Although their physicality is naturally bound to the ergonomic factors of our bodies, they are also inherently personal and highly variable, which represented for many years one of the key detractors to their adoption as a standard interaction method. Even after they became an industry standard, several researchers (Baudel et al., 1993; Norman, 2010) argued that gestural interface design and touchscreens were a resounding bad idea for everyday devices:

- Interactions would always be inaccurate, due to the variability in pressure, finger size, and expected acceleration,
- Users would quickly get tired of pressing and sliding on a flat surface.

However, in just a few short years, touchscreens have become the norm across the world. The interactions allowed by touchscreens are intuitive and represent affordances common to the physical world, such as pressing a button or pushing something out of the way by sliding. These and other gestures have become ubiquitous and gestures a necessary part of interaction. Is there any measurable difference in the way that different cultures use gestures with their mobile devices?

Largely, yes. A UX Fellows Study in 2013 (Goto & Wörmann, 2013) examined an international sample of participants on making gestures and commands. It is found that everyday gestures are surprisingly similar between countries. For example, the gestures of telling somebody to be quiet and making a phone call were found to be the same across all 18 countries studied. Even the sign for writing an email, despite having become a common technology only in the past 20 years, was the same in 16 out of 18 countries. The study also found that signaling 'OK' is usually made in 1 of 2 ways: European countries (except Italy) raise a thumb, whereas Russia, Australia, and East Asia put their index finger and thumb into a circle (Fig. 8.1.1).

All the countries included in the study also counted from two to five on their fingers in a near-identical manner. However, counting from one to three brought up slight differences: most countries used three fingers for this, though participants from Argentina, Germany, France, and Italy mostly used a thumb and two fingers.

The study also found that across cultures, many people are influenced by touchscreen technology, and use "swiping" motions as a result. This was mostly observed in participants from Australia, Spain, Finland, France, Mexico, the Netherlands, and the United Kingdom. These motions were used most frequently when dealing with computer menus, and when navigating forwards or backwards. Whether participants "swiped" from left to right or from right to left was determined by their country.

One of the most basic commands, turning a device on and off, in fact did not correlate strongly within each country, and was determined on an individual basis. The study observed that this usually involved idiosyncratic gestures that incorporated sound, such as clapping hands and snapping fingers, as if devices could not "see" the users, and had to be "woken" from "sleep."

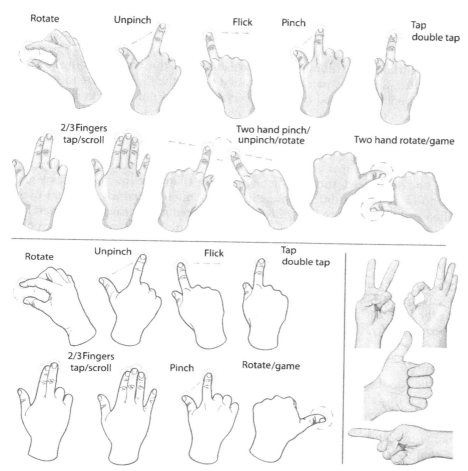

FIGURE 8.1.1
Touchscreen devices have developed a new gestural language which include: from left to right, the single-tap, double-tap, long tap, tap and hold, two-finger tap and double-tap, long two-finger tap and hold, and swipe and rotation with one and two fingers.

Study participants found it reasonably easy to make a gesture to skip to the next or previous chapter, however less than half of the countries included chose the same one. Some countries, including Belgium, China, Spain, Finland, Mexico, and the United Kingdom, used swiping gestures for this, again influenced by touchscreen interfaces, whilst others, including Argentina, Australia, Canada, Germany, Italy, and Korea, chose a new semantic gesture.

In order to restart a paused film, most participants used the same gesture they had used for stopping or pausing the film. Interestingly, participants also found it difficult to identify unique gestures for getting information about the current program, with the same gesture often used for both commands.

At the beginning of the study, participants were told that their gestures did not need to accord to an internally consistent logic, nevertheless, many attempted to do this throughout, and when performing the opposite of a command, such as turning the volume down instead of up, the corresponding gesture was inverted. Similarly, participants tended to use the same gesture to restart a film that they had paused it with. However, this did not apply to switching a TV on versus turning it off, for which participants often chose different types of gestures. Because these gestures were more abstract, they were rated among the most difficult, and subscribed the least to cultural trends.

A majority of participants stated that for each function, only certain gestures should be recognized, such as when selecting a chapter, allowing the same gestures to be reused in different functions. This offered a conclusion that users wished to have a reduced cognitive load, by needing to learn and remember less gestures. Users also stated that possible gestures were limited by the positions in which they might watch TV, which would restrict their physical movements.

The study concluded that two distinctions in gesture can be drawn: those that directly draw upon relationships in reality, such as raising an arm to raise volume; and those that have a more metaphorical connection, based in language or iconography, such as indicating a roof to prompt returning to the homepage.

In terms of neighboring countries, the study found few similarities. For example, participants in the United Kingdom indicated different difficulty ratings to those from France, and this difference was also observed between China and Korea.

Finally, the study determined that there was usually a difference determined by country in whether a participant found it easier to think of everyday gestures: for participants from Turkey, Mexico, Finland, Canada, Belgium, Spain, and the Netherlands, everyday gestures were much easier than abstract gestures to conceptualize. Those in China, Russia, the United States, Italy, and the United Kingdom, on the other hand, found it comparatively difficult to think of both everyday and abstract gestures.

Older audiences tend to have different patterns, particularly in relation to the position of the elements on the screen. A study on older Portuguese adults (Leitão, 2012) showed clear preferences in terms of the position of elements and optimal position on screen:

- Tap gestures: works better with targets larger than 0.55 in. (14 mm).
- Swipe gestures: more accurate with targets larger than 0.68 in. (17.5 mm).

The same study found that the orientation of the swipe gesture did not make an impact on the usability level, but that the optimal areas for tapping were the **center, right side, and bottom right corner** of the average smartphone display.

8.2 COGNITION AND CUES

To achieve, you need thought. You have to know what you are doing and that's real power.

Ayn Rand.

Cross-cultural research must also address the process of acculturation, namely when populations are exposed to other cultures. In the case of immigration, the local culture can absorb the cultural shock waves of a mass migration, but it is largely the individuals who migrate who are influenced by the target culture in terms of beliefs, language, and habits (Suinn, Ahuna, & Khoo, 1992). Several acculturation scales exist, like the Suinn-Lew Asian Self Identity Acculturation (SL-ASIA), which consists of a multiple-choice survey with 21 questions and, while on a holistic perspective, this may account for differences of behavior and perception between communities, it presents an insight into fundamental mechanisms of interpretation and information processing across the human brain (Fig 8.2.1).

Think about how you scan visual information. Scanning patterns consist of the path our eyes take when looking at something, like a picture or a book. Westerners usually start from the top left of the screen and then proceed to drift to the next line of available text on the left. When these gaze paths are marked on a screen, they create a distinct F-shaped pattern that reveals a distinct behavioral trait: the further away an element (picture or text) is from top left half of the screen, the less attention it gets from the user. What about cases when there is nothing on the left corner, like a homepage with just a big blue button (usually to register or download an app) in the middle? Does the gaze path change there? Yes, but because the user usually start from the top left where they enter the URL of the page, the results can be biased as well. The gaze path in eye-tracking studies also stands in stark contrast between cultures. An early study (Hotchkiss, 2007) found that Chinese users tended to pay attention to a lot more contextual elements in a layout than Westerners, who were more focused and granular when scanning a page. They jumped from title to title in a quick scan before getting into the details of the page. There was also evidence that our reading habits play a role. When compared to the left-to-right gaze direction of European and North American users, those who read from right to left, as in the Arabic languages, have been identified as preferentially scanning pictures in the same direction. Japanese, conversely, scan a picture from top to bottom following the same pattern as the writing system (Goodnow & Levine, 1973).

This tendency is related to more than just the overall direction of scripts. Hebrew uses left to right strokes for single letters, even though the direction of the script is right to left. In analyzing a picture, a Hebrew speaker is more likely to scan it from left to right. There is some correlation between the motor skills and a tendency to replicate certain patterns in writing for drawing, e.g., in drawing a circle. Comparative studies between Japanese and American adults show that American adults tend to draw circles in a counterclockwise direction whereas Japanese adults tend to draw them in a clockwise direction.

FIGURE 8.2.1
In addition to the wars waged in the late 19th century, there was an effort by the then young American government to indoctrinate Native Americans with the cultural values and habits (even down to the attire) brought into the continent by Europeans.

Depth perception is also one of the main factors in visual interpretation. Our brain only collects visual information in two-dimensional form, as the stimuli provided by our eyes is purely deciphered and does not match the actual reality of things front of us (Hoffman, 1998). This has inspired many a philosopher to go into serious bouts of alcoholism, but it remains one of the conundrums of cognitive science. The images our eyes seem to capture are purely a fabrication of our brain's interpretation. In other words, our brain is tricking us into believing a particularly subjective form of reality. One of the most evident displays of this is our inability to describe colors and even, occasionally, to agree on what a given color looks like. As in most of our perceptions, culture plays a dominating role in determining what we understand visually. There is some stability in cross-cultural studies about the naming of basic colors, as the extensive World Color Survey (WCS) has shown (Kay & Regier, 2003; Lindsey & Brown, 2006; Regier, Kay, & Cook, 2005).

Education and exposure to three-dimensional pictures can dramatically improve visual perception of visual illusions, like the devil's tuning fork (Vaughn, 2010: p. 83). In this sort of visual illusion, people with less educational and training opportunities often regard the picture as two-dimensional and not particularly complex or difficult to interpret. There is also evidence to suggest that tricky visual illusions often confuse educated Western viewers more than those coming from rural areas or other cultural contexts. Urban dwellers are more prone to horizontal visual illusions then vertical ones, particularly those related to an escape point (Fig 8.2.1).

This is also related to the forms and shapes that we are raised with as children. Our exposure to straight angles and boxed outlines from the earliest moments of our existence, for the most part, tends to dominate our expectations of design perceptions, cues, and affordances.

This is the premise behind the "carpentered world" hypothesis put forth by Segall, Campbell, and Herskovits (1966), who suggested that our exposure to a world that is primarily square and straight tends to overcome our adjustments in interpreting nonrectangular figures as geometrical variations of rectangles scene from an angle. Living in rectangular spaces, with the bulk of architecture based on straight lines, has influenced our perceptual set. This is the way we see the world and anticipate its visual rules to manifest themselves: the sum of our perceptual expectations. This controls the bulk of our interpretations of shape, color, and visual qualities.

Studies suggest (Bar et al., 2006; Reber et al., 2004) that people generally *feel better with curved shapes*, leading to positive feelings, whereas hard edges to shapes create a sense of negativity. *We also prefer simple shapes.* The density of elements in a layout may vary, but the threshold on acceptability is largely up to the individual. However, there is a clear impact of two key factors:

- Parsimony: the complexity of the individual elements used in a layout.
- Orderliness: the way in which these elements are organized.

In short, the density of a web design is not as important as the structure and internal layout of its information architecture, and the elements themselves should be as consistent and simple as possible.

8.3 TYPESETTING AND TYPOGRAPHY

Typography may be defined as the art of rightly disposing printed materials in accordance with specific purpose: of so arranging letters, distributing the space, and controlling the type as to aid to the maximum the reader's comprehension of the text... Therefore, the disposition of printing material which, whatever the intention, has the effect of coming between the author and the reader is wrong.

Stanley Morrison, First Principles of Typography.

Beautiful and intricate, the Japanese language is one of the most difficult languages to typeset, as its character set includes over 6000 characters. Before word processors came into force, most Japanese texts were written by hand and the layout seldom conformed to a standard or obeyed formal guidelines. Typesetting later became a wider issue when software word processors were introduced. Software such as WordPerfect helped to introduce the concept of the computer as a typewriter, but by the very nature of its logographic organization, hierarchy and order were difficult factors to have in account during the typesetting.

Japanese writing featured rows and columns of 20 characters in a grid, with the orientation from top to bottom and right to left. The ruled writing-pad was, however, never used in a productive setting, and the typewriter paradigm eventually became ubiquitous in word processing in office and home work.

Japanese has since become one of hundreds of languages supported by software, with its intricacies and unique writing system perfectly represented in both desktop and mobile devices, including its layout. Typesetting relies on more than sequential placement of characters, as the Japanese furigana, for instance, relies on the integration of small characters which are meant as pronunciation aids. This annotation is common in children's books, particularly for lesser-known kanji characters.

Like children's books, which rely heavily on attention-seeking cues and must adopt a strategy of brevity and clarity, a good UX-oriented interface should use typography smartly. Text placement, layout and typographical arrangement are essential parts of the equation. Weight and scale are just two of the aspects that should be privileged.

Large titles with striking typography are easily remembered due to the quick impression they perform on short-term memory, and the increasing size of the text used in websites in recent years, along with its increasing conciseness, are reminders of the digital emphasis on legibility and accessibility, reconciling the ergonomic and literacy factors that often distinguish audiences.

The way the text is printed on-screen carries deep semantic implications for its meaning. Common fonts used in modern Western scripts are mostly based on sans-serif fonts. Serifs (aesthetic projections of letters meant to underscore their limits) were progressively eliminated from characters in order to save ink on printing. Also, sans-serif characters are easier to read in pages where there is a large density of text. Text design, such as the choice of font, can influence the user's interpretation directly. For example, Irish pubs worth their salt might have a sign with a Celtic font. This has cultural implications and is meant to provide a sense of familiarity. The same can be applied to websites with a strong cultural appeal.

When adapting a UX pattern into other languages, particular attention should be paid to the following items:

- Avoid widows and orphans. Widows are single words at the end of lines, while orphans are single lines of a paragraph at the top of a column. These break text flow and compromise a harmonious look and feel.
- Ensure kerning, tracking, and leading are aesthetically sound. Regardless of the target script, ensure that kerning (the distance between characters) and leading (distance between lines) remains consistent in different target cultures. Right-to-left scripts such as Arabic or special pictographic languages such as Chinese often require leading adjustment as text density can increase dramatically.
- Avoid centered text. Because of its variable margins, centered text gives a feeling of discontinuity.
- Use grids as aids for localized layouts. A webpage or a desktop application layout can have an arrangement and layout adaptation facilitated by using a grid to visualize margins and limits in a clearer way.

Large titles with striking typography are easily remembered due to the quick impression they perform on short-term memory, and the increasing size of the text used in websites in recent years, along with its increasing conciseness, are reminders of the digital emphasis on legibility and accessibility, reconciling the ergonomic and literacy factors that often distinguish audiences.

At its core, websites are structured around an organization most easily perceived through its disposition of vertical columns along the page canvas. A grid model can be applied to its information architecture. The similarity between print and webpage design are striking in the resemblance of most text-heavy websites to their print counterparts, which relied on letter pressing methods for centuries and a paper grid model for the layout work on the page.

Text is a part of a complete visual system that allows users to interact with an information system directly through codified linguistic signs. Text allows users to retrieve and access information, and directly represents the most accessible entry point to the interaction model offered by the user interface.

European typesetting industry promoted the need for it. Paper production methods were far from optimized, meaning that paragraph alignment was not just a mere formality, but a necessity in order to make the best possible use of the text area.

A pictographic language like Chinese or Japanese is not limited in hyphenation by syllables, and a break can be introduced at nearly any point in the text. A hyphen is not necessarily used. Arabic does not allow word hyphenation. Roman script, on the other hand, can be easily underlined and made bold. Japanese scripts, however, use *amikake*, where the word is surrounded with a background rectangle. Bullets are placed above the character itself (*wakiten*) (Fig. 8.3.1).

Decisions regarding color in typography are critical. Colored type appears smaller to the human eye than the same type in black. This is important to consider when designing user interfaces. One must also consider the "smear" effect on typography in displays, based on the color chosen and interaction with colors around it. Additionally, quality and calibration of displays impact characteristics of color online.

Official typefaces are over 600 years old, and the reliance on them cannot be overstated in contemporary web design. Typefaces were unleashed onto the world to represent a certain set of values and aesthetic concerns, and their

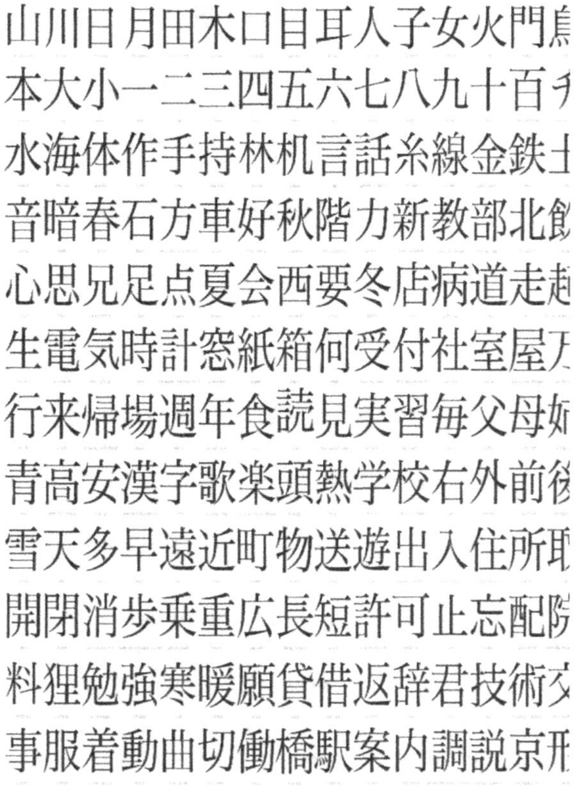

山川日月田木口目耳人子女火門鳥
本大小一二三四五六七八九十百千
水海体作手持林机言話糸線金鉄土
音暗春石方車好秋階力新教部北館
心思兄足点夏会西要冬店病道走起
生電気時計窓紙箱何受付社室屋天
行来帰場週年食読見実習毎父母姉
青高安漢字歌楽頭熱学校右外前後
雪天多早遠近町物送遊出入住所耳
開閉消歩乗重広長短許可止忘配防
料狸勉強寒暖願貸借返辞君技術文
事服着動曲切働橋駅案内調説京開

FIGURE 8.3.1

Set of Japanese kanji.

value is deep and intrinsic when representing cultures. Think about how quickly you can identify a "celtic" design for an Irish pub, an "oriental" design for a Chinese restaurant, or the cold linear sharp edges of a "Swiss" type. Then wonder how these typefaces actually carry a cultural meaning and association, despite what seems to be an arbitrary association.

Sometimes typefaces fall flat on their face (pun intended). Comic Sans is one such example. Often heralded as the fall of Western civilization and notorious for being one of the few fonts with its own hate website ("Ban Comic Sans"), the typeface created by Vincent Connare in 1994 was originally intended to be used in one of the most advanced front-ends in the Windows universe, Microsoft Bob. Eventually, Comic Sans was not used in what came to be recognized by PC World as one of the worst tech products in history (http://www.pcworld.com/article/125772/worst_products_ever.html), but its legend only grew with time. Its initial release in Windows 95 marked the beginning of a long journey that saw it become one of the most reviled typefaces in the world.

Part of the hatred came from its ubiquity. Comic Sans was considered an extremely accessible and playful font and the advent of mass computing in the 1990s meant that the appealing typeface was soon adopted by a swelling wave of home users who thought its playfulness could enliven anything from birthday cards to real estate agent adverts. It didn't help matters that there was a reduced number of fonts available, and most of them were Serif fonts, a solemn style geared towards readability (like Times New Roman).

Consider the difference between Comic Sans and Times New Roman, and your receptivity towards each other. Apart from any previously acquired bias, Comic Sans is mainly unpleasant not of its inherent informality, but due to the disproportionate visual weight of the lettering. Each character is unbalanced, using the same stroke width through each segment. This characteristic makes Comic Sans an unmodulated font, and a visual mess that is hard to read in smaller font sizes and can make any text look like an inelegant screeching piece of juvenile graffiti. The distance between the characters (kerning) is also nonsymmetrical, a jarring difference from other fonts like Helvetica and Arial.

This combination of visual issues contrast with the classic sense of proportion and balance sported by typesetting standards. These were largely inherited from the ones used by Middle Age scribes and, later, passed into the earliest printing presses. Our visceral reaction to Comic Sans is mainly a subconscious reaction to a visual aesthetic that clashes with that aesthetic, one that counters our intuition of what constitutes "attractive" type for reading.

8.4 COLOR SCHEMES

Colors, like features, follow the changes of the emotions.

Pablo Picasso.

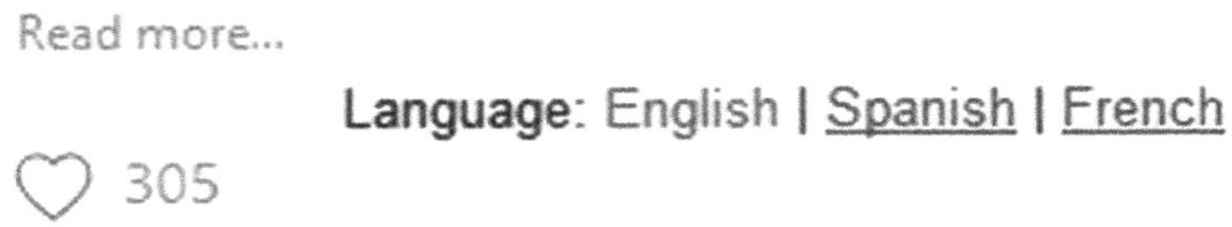

FIGURE 8.4.1
Black is not the dominant color for body text on the Web, with various shades of gray harming legibility. Past conventions like blue (gray in print versions) for hyperlinking are also subsiding as flat design favors homogeneous palettes and the use of blue (gray in print versions) is unsavory with text of a gray inkling.

The deception of perception is the ultimate factor of variability in everyday life. We tend to assume that our perception covers all five senses in an equal and universal manner, and nowhere is that more evident than in color. Colors do not look the same to everybody, and the difference is often jarring and confusing.

> We live in a global world, so when in Rome... Remember that different colors have different connotations within various cultures, religions, professions, etc. For example, in the United States on February 14th, red means love, but in Korea, red means death, and in China, red is used in weddings and symbolizes good luck and fortune. In many other countries, red means revolution. To a competitor, red means first place, and to an accountant, red means a negative balance. To a motorist, red means stop, and in emergencies, a red cross means medical help. (Jacko, ed., 2012: p. 335)

This includes text coloring. As stated by the Institute for Color Research, we establish our opinions about a "person, environment, or item within 90 seconds of initial viewing, and between 62% and 90% is based on color alone".

Color is dependent on context, location, size, and visual acuity (Fig 8.4.1). In his book *The Interaction of Color*, Josef Albers lays out the basic principles of using color effectively, and labels the key factors in its changing perception:

> *In addition to quantity, form, and recurrence, wider aspects exert still more changing influences. These are:*
>
> - *changed and changing light—and, even worse, several simultaneous lights;*
> - *reflection of lights and of colors;*
> - *direction and sequence of reading;*
> - *presentation in varying materials;*
> - *constant or altering juxtaposition of related and unrelated objects.*
>
> With these and other visual displacements, it should not be a surprise that the sympathetic effect of the original "ideal" color combination often appears changed, lost, and reversed (Albers, 2006: 42).

Albers lays out one of the key principles of using color in interaction: that it should be seen in context. Color compositions can be laid out in accordance with tested circumstances and actual user observations, in order to refine the visibility and legibility of all elements during an actual user session. Many mobile devices already have dynamic brightness adjustment preintegrated as a way to counter changing circumstances of usage in dark or well-lit areas. However, these also have a direct effect on the hue and chromaticity. This is especially relevant as different screens have different calibrations, depending on their hardware and intended audience. However, there are standards like the ISO 15076-1:2010, aimed at image technology color management, which provide an authoritative reference for color in software.

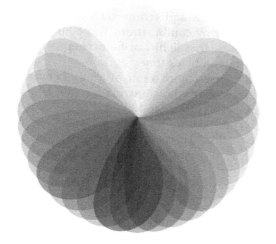

The deeper challenge with color, however, resides in its usage in changing circumstances. The colors that a commuter sees when using his iPhone over a long trek in a subway are not the same seen on the same screen in the comfort of an halogen-flooded kitchen. Apart from the environmental distinctions, the user itself may be in different conditions psychologically: fatigue and expectation make a huge difference to the vividness and perception of color.

This is not immediately apparent to most, however, because color is primarily psychological and less-than-optimal color perception is naturally compensated by our brain. If the cones in our eyes are not capturing enough information to render the correct color of an object in the darkness (e.g., in a cellar or at night), our brain triggers compensatory mechanisms that allow for color constancy.

Age also compromises color sensitivity. Older audiences have problems discerning blue and darker hues, and, for these people, colors often need to be more vivid in order to make more of a visual impact. Regardless of sensorial ability, there are also cognitive conditions hardwired that can even disable the ability to perceive color. Color-blindness affects especially male population (around 8%), and particularly in the inability to distinguish red from green.

Our learning of color is the product of three distinct processes: (1) empirically, we learn from the environment how to distinguish and identify them in a practical manner; (2) culturally, we learn about the representations of color and its various meanings; and (3) cognitively, we are predisposed to certain perception bias and reactions due to our particular physiology and nervous systems (Belpaeme & Bleys, 2005; Dowman, 2007; Jameson, 2005; Komarova, Jameson, & Narens, 2007). But, outside of our own perception, is there a fundamental agreement on how color is seen and described? Color theory is based on this premise. For the purposes of categorization and distinction, colors are fundamentally split into three groups:

- *Primary colors:* Red, blue, and yellow are the basic shades that can originate any other color by combination. These fundamental colors are the three additive colors that light can be decomposed into. An equal mix of all three generates a black tone.
- *Secondary colors:* These colors result of a mix between two primary colors. The three secondary colors are: orange (red and yellow), violet (red and blue), and green (yellow and blue).
- *Tertiary colors:* These colors result of a mix between one primary and one secondary color. There is a large variation of possible colors, including amber or marigold (mix of yellow and orange), saffron or vermilion (red and orange), magenta (red–purple), violet (blue–purple), teal or turquoise (blue–green), and chartreuse/lime green (yellow–green).

Colors have significant cultural meanings that vary around the world, and have important implications for web design. Ken Rohrer (2010) has noted the way in which colors represent various "…feelings, people, [and] countries", determined by culture. He offers the following examples of the relation between colors and certain symbolic themes:

- Happiness: Red
- Helpful: Gray
- Marriage: White, pink (as in the West)
- Wealth: Blue, gold and purple

And colors themselves can have multiple meanings:

- Black: Sorrow, evil
- Green: Eternity, family, harmony, health, peace, posterity
- White: Children, helpful people, marriage, mourning, peace, purity, travel
- Gold: Strength, wealth

He described the way in which this can be used by companies: those wanting to promote an environmentally friendly image tend to use green in their branding, for example. Similarly, car insurance firms sometimes "…charge more for red cars because some of the owners of red cars are more aggressive or take more risks." (Rohrer, 2010).

It is important to note that these symbolisms can be radically different between cultures: blue, e.g., represents calmness or authority in Europe, truth in Arabic cultures, and villainy for Japan (Pettersson, 2002). The variation in color symbolism even extends to genders, as the color pink is associated with females in the West, whereas it is extremely popular with both genders in Japan.

Bear (2010) also theorizes color as being able to offer symbolism and meaning through nonverbal communication, which can even have physical effects, such as the color red raising blood pressure. She also emphasizes the significance of the "…relationship of adjacent, harmonizing, contrasting, and complementary colors," which can also impact the perception of color: the more contrasting the colors, the more likely they are to be noticed. Complementary colors, on "opposite side of the color wheel," are more effective than similar ones. Bear also offers the meanings behind certain color groups:

- Cool Colors—calming: Blue, green, turquoise, silver;
- Warm Colors—exciting: Red, pink, yellow, gold, orange;
- Neutral Colors—unifying: Brown, beige, ivory, gray, black, white.

Color is subjective and immeasurable, as people see colors differently. However, it usually provoke similar emotional responses within single cultural groups. Combining colors can affect their meanings: red, e.g., has negative associations in the West, but it has more positive associations when combined with green, representing Christmas, or with red, representing Valentine's Day.

Language also impacts cultural color associations, as Mario De Bortoli and Jesús Maroto (2001) have determined, through drawing on Benjamin Whorf's "Linguistic Relativity Hypothesis" (1956). For example, in Zimbabwe, people do not perceive the difference between red and orange, because the Shona language does not distinguish a difference. They also explore the impact factors such as gender, age, and climate on color perception, and concluded that women preferred softer colors, while men prefer brighter ones; that children prefer "…strong, warm and intense colors", as oppose to the "subdued" colors that are "more attractive" to older people; and that the sunnier the climate, the warmer the colors that tend to be preferred.

In the case of web design, brighter colors are most effective in attracting the user's eye (Beaird, 2007). Pettersson (2002) has shown that, when comparing colors of equal intensity, white, yellow, and green are the most visible, whereas red, blue and violet are the least visible.

The variety of color arrangements and the cross-cultural psychology implications are of primary concern when creating a design, and the difference between elements and a wise use of contrast should pave the way to an appropriate design (Table 8.4.1).

Table 8.4.1	Colors and Associated Meanings in Different Cultures (Bortoli & Maroto, 2001)
North America (US and Canada)	
Red	Excitement, warning, sex, passion, adultery, safety rescue, hot, spicy
Yellow	Visibility, cautionary, happy, sunny, cowardice
Blue	Trustworthy, official business, philosophy, soothing
Green	Environmental, outdoorsy, masculinity, freshness, healthy, envy, jealousy, inexperience
Orange	Visibility, refreshing, danger
Purple	Nobility, bravery, law, excess
Pink	Feminity, childhood, fun, sweetness, homosexuality
Brown	Dullness, boring, fertile, strength, unprocessed, poverty
Gold	Money, wealth luminosity
Black	Death, evil, sin, nothingness, business, adult, formal, sexy
White	Clean, pure, elegant, antiseptic
Silver	Sleek, classy, modern
Gray	Humility, grief, depression, strength, wisdom
Latin America	
Mexico	
Red	Sunny, religion, compass, vibrancy, intensity, death
Yellow	Sun
Blue	Mourning, trust, tranquility
Green	Vegetation
Gold	Wealth, church adornments
Black	Mourning, religion, respect, death
White	Pure, clean, peasant
South America	
Argentina	
Silver	Gauchos, craftsmanship
Red	Craftsmanship
Blue	Sky, freedom, infinity, blessing, ocean
Yellow	Wealth, religion, ceremony, visibility
White	Light, cool, purity, accomplishment, aspiration
Brazil	
Red	Visibility, Vibrancy
Purple	Mourning
Green	Environment
Orange	Environment
Brown	Nature
Black	Sophistication, authority, mourning, religion, formality
Western Europe	

(Continued)

Table 8.4.1 **Colors and Associated Meanings in Different Cultures (Bortoli & Maroto, 2001) (Continued)**

Black	Mourning, formality, death, evil, elegance, sophistication
White	Pure, clean, good, empty, bleak, neutral, antiseptic, surrender
Gray	Architecture, ambiguity, wisdom, experience
Silver	Masculinity, technology, expensive, craftsmanship
Red	Sexy, love, romance, vigor, optimism, strength, caution
Yellow	Visibility, hazard, quality
Blue	Sky, fidelity, serenity, truth, reliability, responsibility, emotion
Green	Nature, fertility, confidence, jealousy, inexperienced
Orange	Visibility, cheap, loud
Brown	Masculinity, earth
Purple	Nobility, luxury, power, vanity
Pink	Delicate, flirtation, femininity, sensitivity, soothing
Gold	Mysticism, luxury, wealth, excessive
England, Scotland, Wales and Ireland	
Red	Power, authority, government, visibility, temper
Yellow	Visibility, rubber

8.5 ICONOGRAPHY AND IMAGERY

In order to grow your audience, you must betray their expectations.

Hayao Miyazaki.

Emotions create physical reactions in our bodies. As the sympathetic nervous system excites your organism to react to a specific stimuli, the parasympathetic inhibits and normalizes this response when needed. This provided evidence for neuroscientists and researchers to associate physical reaction with emotional stimulation. Our bodies literally react according to what we feel.

The distinction between images with a strong emotional content and neutral effect on the users can be measured with a number of techniques. The most popular model of emotional space is composed of two basic dimensions: *valence* and *arousal*. *Arousal* loosely determines the intensity of the emotion and is closely related to physiological body reactions. *Valence*, on the other hand, determines the "intrinsic attractiveness or aversiveness" (Frijda, 1986: p. 207) of an emotion, meaning the desire with which it is pursued.

One of the most powerful stimulation devices for emotions is the visual medium. We are permanently stimulated by our vision, and around 40% of our brain is devoted to the processing of visual information. The visuals we come into contact with can make a lasting impression: how then can visual content be chosen in a way that stimulates perception and interest? And how does it translate in a way that can cross-cultural expectations?

On a formal level, humans share similar cognitive mechanisms and our cognitive subsystems for visual perception are largely similar across populations. The emotion displayed by facial expressions is an universally common factor. Darwin suggested the idea in 1872, after successfully conducting a small pioneering experiment with a single-blind study on several pictures taken by the French physician Guillaume-Benjamin-Amand Duchenne during his attempts to correlate certain groups of muscles with facial expression. Darwin successfully showed that emotion was universal, and that idea was perpetrated fully in his theory of evolution, which suggested that emotion was not only innate, but directly correlated with evolutionary adaptation.

Unlike the theory of evolution, the idea of universal facial expressions was challenged by social scientists for decades, believing it to be merely a by-product of cultural framing (Ekman, Friesen, & Ellsworth, 1972). It was only in 1962 that reputed psychologist Silvan Tomkins again established the link between human emotion and facial expression. A series of cross-cultural "universality studies" ensued in the 1970s, with psychologists Paul Ekman, Wallace Friesen, and Carroll Izard proving that facial expressions like smiling and disgust were used consistently across cultures and did not depend on education and social factors.

While it took centuries to prove scientifically that the seven basic human emotions (anger, contempt, disgust, fear, joy, sadness, and surprise) are indeed applicable to societies across the world, they depend largely on context. And this is where the need for a grounded approach resides.

Concrete imagery that either shows a human face in context or generates an immediate emotional response is more effective in long-term memory. Academic projects like the International Affective Picture System (IAPS), which includes a standard group of images for large standardized groups, point the way to a more normative approach of content testing, but how much of this imagery is actually universal? (Fig. 8.5.1).

If you draw a person on a piece of paper, odds are that, no matter how sophisticated your design is, it will be easy for somebody else to identify it as a person. However, your perception of that image is a trained one.

Your concept of how a person looks like as a result of experience and personal preferences.

FIGURE 8.5.1

Cultural iconography can be geographically linked to a particular area, but the symbolism can resonate clearly in other contexts as well.

According to the Swiss psychologist Jean Piaget, who pioneered an influential cognitive development model, development of sensory perception is the result of education and upbringing, which links existing cognitive structures to a set of symbols and imagery surrounding and nurturing it in the social context that you are brought up on (Piaget, 1952). Although globalization, media diffusion, and the Internet have allowed cultures to have access to content from all over the world, we are learning as users to accustom ourselves to images and realities completely alien to our own, as well as the aesthetic and formal preferences that come with it. There is no such thing as a universal aesthetic that is necessarily inherent to all cultures. For example, in a study developed by Deregowski et al. (1972), members of the Mekan tribe revealed severe difficulties to correctly identify detailed pictures of animals that they saw on an everyday basis.

We are led by the visual meanings of things. We can recognize a tool, an asset, a warning, by recognizing how it looks and the way it is shown to us. The use of visual metaphors in user interfaces is becoming narrower: despite the experimentation in certain fields, designers are mostly using textual content and standard metaphors like a button or a switch in order to get their message across. This is not coincidental with the growing international nature of most products. Traditionally, textual content was a priority even in street signs. American streets feature an assortment of signs with varying messages concerning parking, traffic rules, and points of interest. This jungle of physical pop-ups is bound to be informative, but also overloads the perception of the average pedestrian and driver. There is less of an implicit message in these situations: the Anglo-American world tends to prefer verbose descriptions of rules, featuring even in crossings with the "Don't Walk" sign.

While pretty to look at, most complex interfaces with heavy use of graphics are typically more confusing than impressive when actually used in a productive setting. Consistency and simplicity pave the way for a smooth locale-independent source that can be then implemented in other locales. The modern return to basics with an emphasis on typography and minimalistic, sparse backgrounds and layouts is not a passing fad: adaptation into different devices and cross-platform rendering is made much easier with this arrangement.

While text can be used effectively in guiding the user towards specific points of interest, let users figure out the score by using visual cues and inference points. Users can interpret subtleties of speech more clearly if they are not buried under a torrent of text. For instance, when suggesting that a user introduced a password incorrectly and that the password is case-sensitive, it is redundant to tell the user explicitly to check the Caps Lock key. A much more user-friendly way to resolve this is to provide a pop-up while writing the password that notifies the user that the key is active.

There is a number of international standards that regulate and promote pictograms that can be used as a guidance for safety and technical contexts. ISO is the most active regulation body in this regard (Fig. 8.5.2), with the following standards being the most relevant:

- The ISO 3864 series of standards which specify design requirements, including shapes and colors, for safety signs.
- The ISO/IEC 80416 series of standards which specify basic principles for graphical symbols for use on equipment.
- ISO 7000, Graphical symbols for use on equipment—Registered symbols.
- ISO 7001, Graphical symbols—Public information symbols.
- ISO 7010, Graphical symbols—Safety colors and safety signs—Registered safety signs.
- ISO 17724, Graphical symbols—Vocabulary.
- ISO 20712-1, Water safety signs and beach safety flags—Part 1 : Specifications for water safety signs used inworkplaces and public areas.
- ISO 20712-2,Water safety signs and beach safety flags—Part 2 : Specifications for beach safety flags—Color, shape, meaning, and performance
- ISO 20712-3, Water safety signs and beach safety flags—Part 3 : Guidance for use
- ISO 22727, Graphical symbols—Creation and design of public information symbols—Requirements
- ISO/IEC Guide 74, Graphical symbols—Technical guidelines for the consideration of consumers' needs.

FIGURE 8.5.2
International pictograms set as defined by ISO standards.

CASE STUDY

Culture: Dotting the I's

Adapting a global site into an international experience with depth and appeal is not an easy task. Quantifying cultural factors in particular can be a daunting proposition. Using the Hofstede cultural model, Mannheim/Berlin based design studio "The Geekettez" successfully implemented cultural dimensions as the first step towards a new digital strategy plan.

The client had received feedback from the international offices that the landing pages were not appealing to the local markets. Some features expected by the local markets were not available on the international landing pages. In order to harmonize the situation, the company decided to create country-specific pages, offering a shared base of content modules and components. These could be combined differently on the local websites in order to allow greater freedom in the international designs.

This container system allowed the designers to curb the expense of building specific regional websites. Stefanie Kegel, co-founder of The Geekettez Gbr, promoted the flexibility of the approach, where "different content [can be placed] within predefined and designed containers, which can be switched on and off." These modules were contained in a TYPO3 database system, and consisted of a combination of JavaScript and HTML.

Agency: The Geekettez Gbr

Client: Brain Appeal GmbH, Internet Agency, Mannheim, GER: Coding TYPO 3 and Hosting

When: 2014

Deliverables: Analytics (Google check/audit, optimizing, action plan)
Benchmarking
Cultural Research
Content Strategy
Mockup Sketches
Visual Design

Methods: Behavioural, Attitudinal, Quantitative, Qualitative, Evaluative

Type: Expert review
Design process

The existing country-specific landing pages were analyzed according to variables based on Geert Hofstede's hypothesis of cultural dimensions. Dimensions like power distance, especially individualism versus collectivism, masculinity versus femininity, uncertainty and avoidance, were used to make choices on imagery and content related to cognition and behavior.

Based on this research framework, The Geekettez produced a report which included examples of do's and don'ts for each country, as well as best practice examples. The research was topped off with a referral on how content modules should be displayed for the individual countries.

Next, a Google Analytics analysis took place in order to align the recommendations with the company's brief, especially their business goals and visions, their strengths and Unique Selling Points, as well as their ambitions for their communication framework. These recommendations formed the basis for a concept paper on the company's digital content strategy.

Some of the recommendations for collectivistic cultures included:

- the use of imagery relevant to communities and groups;
- iconography depicting a sustainability and collective responsibility message;
- the use of color according to the local meaning interpretation, especially warmer colors like red and yellow, which have very different meanings depending on the target market.

FURTHER LINKS

www.thegeekettez.com.

The Geekettez, Intercultural Aspects of Interface Design, http://www.thegeekettez.com/intercultural-aspects-interface-design/, 2014.

The navigation and color scheme retained the familiarity of the company's original web presence, but was refreshed and updated in order to allow greater flexibility of presentation.

Collectivistic photos and a sense of familiarity was used in order to make the brand seem friendlier in the Asian websites.

8.6 RESOLUTIONS AND DEVICES

Cyberspace. A consensual hallucination experienced daily by billions of legitimate operators, in every nation.

William Gibson.

Devices around the world share a limited range of screen sizes, and Apple devices are typically much more standardized than Android devices. Emerging markets tend to have fewer PPI (pixels per inch), and even when the screen size is bigger, the image quality tends to suffer. The trend for optimization implies that Full HD has become the standard for mid-range phones, whereas qHD (exemplified by Samsung S7 and HTC 10) is increasing in acceptance and popularity (Fig. 8.6.1).

Although the App Store dominates worldwide app revenue with 58%, the overall number of app installs is higher in Google Play, with over 60% of install volume and 36% of revenue in 2015.

As the largest smartphone market in the world, the Chinese market is still maturing. Apple steers the market as the iPhone gathered momentum in China since its introduction, and quickly became associated with a sign of status and a popular choice due to its minimalist aesthetic in the social eye.

However, home-grown brands like Huawei and Xiaomi have also grown considerably in the market and dominate large segments of the market. Apple remains a consistent presence in the country, particularly in tier 1 cities like Beijing and Shanghai, and has traditionally been perceived as a high-end phone with a lifestyle association. In a strategic move, Apple has targeted "Chinese premium smartphone consumers," according to James Gong, vice president of Nielsen China.

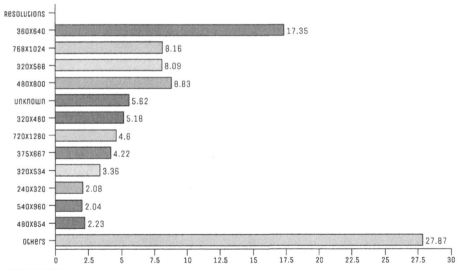

FIGURE 8.6.1

The most widely used web resolutions used worldwide. 360x640 remains the most popular resolution, used by devices like Nokia N97 and Sony Ericsson U8i. These devices are largely dated and discontinued, and a variety of higher resolutions is on the rise. *Source: statcounter.com, May–July 2015.*

FIGURE 8.6.2

Adjusting for mobile responsive breakpoints involves being aware of the screen requirements for the devices used by your audience.

However, the competitive market has pushed high-end phones like the Xiaomi Mi 5, which includes a 5.15 in. full HD and high-ranking aspects, to the top positions as some of the most popular phones in the country. As the middle class proliferates throughout the country, and purchasing power increases, the 560-million strong mobile user base is pushing for higher-quality mobile devices, and the protectionist policies of the country help to drive domestic brands to the pole positions, even when their international standing is minimal (Fig. 8.6.2).

However, there are still an abundance of lower-end models, primarily Android phones, which make up over 50% of the total Chinese smartphone market. Samsung is a major player in the lower rungs of the market.

Apple's dominance, however, is much more visible in Japan, where it commands nearly half the mobile market. Home brands like Sony and Sharp share popularity segments, with Samsung trailing, even as it pushes the outer limits of mobile technology with its Galaxy devices and integration with Gear VR and smartwatch technology. Japanese mobile technology is almost exclusively focused on high-end models, as it pioneered many ubiquitous features in the earlier days of mobile: e-money, camera, music, car navigation. Low-end smartphones are not a sizable market in the country, with the average family income exceeding US$57,000.

One of the main reasons for Apple's domination in the market is the partner-ship with local phone operators, with phone contracts allowing the devices to be sold at a more reasonable price than Samsung or Sony's high-end devices. Coupled with smart marketing, this allowed the iPhone to become the most

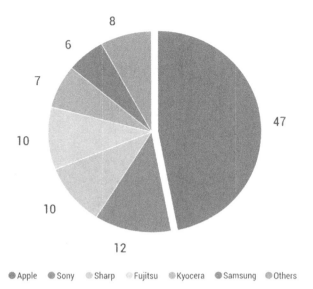

FIGURE 8.6.3
The smartphone market in Japan is dominated by Apple, whereas domestic brands like Sony and Sharp barely scrape a sizable chunk of the market. *Source: statista.com.*

used mobile device in Japan and the Japanese app market to become the largest in the world in 2013 in combined Android and iOS sales. As the feature phones in the country were amongst the most advanced in the world, smartphones took several years to catch on, but over 75% of the mobile users in the country owned a smartphone by 2015. Desktop ownership rate is in a downward trend since 2009, with laptops and tablets becoming the most popular devices for work and entertainment at home (Fig. 8.6.3).

Japan also leads the amount of mobile e-commerce transactions and conversions, along with South Korea and the United Kingdom, arguably the largest mobile economies. However, in terms of growth and expansion, Africa is still at the forefront of cell phone expansion.

8.7 PERSONAS AND CHARACTERS

All the world's a stage and most of us are desperately unrehearsed.

Seán O'Casey.

Personas are a tool that allow end-user qualities and characteristics to be recognized, addressed, and incorporated into the design process. They allow design teams to focus on the various users of a given product, and to ensure that the product meets their needs.

Personas take the form of conceptualized versions of the people that a company estimates are using its products. Even though they are effectively abstract, they are given detailed descriptions, and given a story through which they can be visualized. The most crucial element of all is to define the goals of each persona, which allows design to cater for them.

Creating personas has long been a staple within marketing processes, where they are based on statistical averages and demographics, in order to build a successful marketing campaign that appeals to the audience in their targeted area.

However, in software design, personas are used for different purposes, and through different means. Here, the aim is to produce a product that suits users' needs. Instead of being based on numbers, personas in software design consider the types of people who would use the product in the 'real world', on a conceptual basis, and imagine the functions that they would require. Software can then be developed in order to meet these requirements. This often involves balancing the various needs of different users: some, e.g., prefer more complicated menus, with many options available, while others prefer a simpler, streamlined approach. Personas enable design to cater for those who will be using it.

Typically, personas should be shared across are created for each project. Usually, they should be recreated for each project, though in certain contexts, the same can be reused if addressing the same user base. From these personas, 1−3 are selected as primary personas, whom the design is based upon most directly.

Bear in mind that each persona is a fictional character: while they might share characteristics with people we know in reality, they should not be based directly upon any one real person, in order to build a picture of the most representative users and generate the most effective results in terms of team guidance (Fig. 8.7.1).

Each persona should be given a name and a picture (e.g., from a magazine or search engine), to allow everybody working on the project to be in sync. They should each have a detailed description, with their physical traits, likes and dislikes, in addition to their desires, goals, and needs. The most effective way to work with personas is to be familiar with them, on an everyday basis: one way of achieving this is through putting up posters with their core details on the office wall.

It is important to note that different members of a team interpret personas differently, according to varying expectations. Because personas are used across teams, and correlate to constructions created by UX designers and product managers, they are not comprehensive enough to cover every detail of a real customer, and can involve assumptions. For example, if a persona uses their cell phone on the subway, teams would assume the user to be able to use its cell phone effectively and achieve its goals in transit, and would picture them in an urban setting with strong reception.

The perceptions of the perceiver make a big impact upon these narrative elements of the persona. Nielsen (2010) showed the way in which

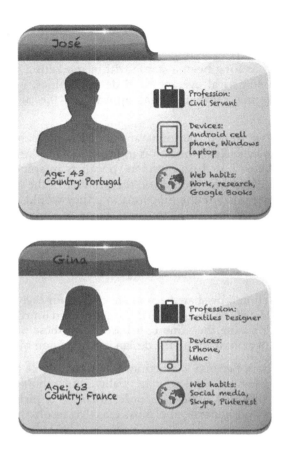

FIGURE 8.7.1
Personas should include definite dimensions and standardized discrete data. The storytelling element is also important: personas should be believable.

personas are perceived differently by people from different countries, and that this also applies to the customer experience. Customer experience maps can be used to map this. They allow layers of information to be built up, such as indicating which activities are relevant to each persona. This can also incorporate research findings by country, and activities specific to different markets, which highlights the similarities and differences between them. Through doing so, any areas that need more localization attention can be flagged, allowing design and development budget and time to be allocated to them.

Segmenting the customer journey with actual data from users is key to a firm strategy, and performing user research is crucial to develop a perception of their actual habits, expectations, and requirements. Research can take the form of ethnographic studies, user interviews, focus groups, or international surveys on the qualitative side, but more than not, with established businesses, you will have to leverage the *quantitative data* your analytics and traffic statistics are providing.

Start by analyzing the geographical information of your business traffic:

- What markets are primarily active on the transactional pages?
- Where in the countries are actual clients coming from?
- Is the abandonment rate high? If so, why?

Usability issues, socio-demographic, user habits all come into play here and assumptions should be challenged and reframed. Internal references from sales and marketing might be a useful operator to add dimensions to your personas. Specifically, for international brands, it is important to be aware of what different clients and users do in different markets.

Even if you do have demographic data, do not rely on it exclusively, and do not assume qualitative dimensions from data traffic alone. While it is very easy for a brand to argue that the current profile of their customers is the be-all and end-all of user knowledge, it is important to understand the user's definition of success and how these markets will evolve in the future. Again, the possibility of starting a conversation with the user will result in a structured list of insights that will help you build an accurate portrayal of your primary and secondary personas.

International personas should also accommodate for the differing channels (mobile, desktop, tablet, online—offline) used by the different profiles, as well as the local habits. The local culture, as well as the technology range, will make a huge difference in the decisions you make for your designs.

Personas should supersede the empty categorization of stereotypes. You may perceive that part of your user base is composed of "millennials", but there is a need to analyze what the underlying motivations are. Values like "environment-friendly" and "technology-savvy" are seldom worthwhile epithets.

8.7.1 Gamification

Different gamification strategies apply to different cultures. The benefits of achievement and competition are viewed differently across cultures. For example, Scandinavians with a more equalitarian and interpersonal social structure do not view openly competitive behavior as an end in and of itself.

Gamification is the application of game-oriented principles in nongame contexts (Deterding et al., 2011) and its appropriation by a number of contexts has expanded its reach into productivity, corporate work, finances, and community building. The value impressed upon gamification strategies varies with the actual values in practice in the cultural mindset.

Sometimes the product is appropriated by a specific group for a different purpose then the intended original market just hijacking is very common and physical products such as the Doc Martens, which were initially designs for

British police officers and later taken over by Guinness and punks who integrated it into their own subculture of subversion and rebellion.

8.7.2 Case Study: Decisions on Subscriptions

A project with a leading newspaper aimed at understanding how readers used the games section to solve puzzles, as well as their preferences and expectations regarding this type of game.

20 individual semistructured interviews were held with readers from different backgrounds:

- 5 × digital subscribers
- 4 × nondigital subscribers
- 6 × casual readers
- 5 × general nonreaders

The expectations were to understand how the readers were engaging with these games, and the type of activities that most interested them. In order to collect this information, the interviews approached mainly their opinions, attitudes, preferences, past experiences, and other expectations with general games and puzzles like Sudoku, including those provided by the challenges in the newspaper.

The personas were developed from the analysis of these interviews, with 5 distinct personas emerging from the possible audience. The age of the persona influenced their tendency to engage with and stay with the game, seeing as younger audiences tend to play on multiple devices, at various points throughout the day, and engage with different types of games, ranging from competitive arcade to multiplayer strategy.

The older personas also had more time available and were more reticent to engage in games with complex rules, and preferred to have different options for their gaming.

Personas also reflected the likelihood of engaging with the newspaper gaming, clearly reflecting an increase in interest as age increased for the average persona.

Conclusion: Spirits in a Digital World

As a race, human beings were always caught between the double-edge of survival and prosperity. We were assaulted by the winds of Winter and attacked by natural predators and, as largely physically inferior beings, we had to fight with the one weapon we have: our minds. We designed better tools to survive and developed means to perpetrate our knowledge down the generations. The rise of the scientific method allowed us to focus on facts instead of assumptions, and brought our knowledge out of the shadow of belief. However, as human beings, it is inevitable that we are molded by our environment and transformed by circumstances. Our very existence is the result of genetic accident, ensuring that each one of us is uniquely featured with different heights, appearances, and physiological distinctions. Difference is not a choice, and its impact on billions of lives worldwide earns a serious recognition from those that are developing solutions for the lives of those who may depend on them for comfort and even survival.

We are still at the onset of a long journey. To achieve the ability to personalize solutions for the individual, as opposed to the masses, we require deeper tools of thought, and more detailed methods of data collection and application. The mysteries of the human mind will likely continue to elude us for a long time, but the most important part of universal design lies in ourselves and is perfectly within immediate reach: we need to care. Care for others like we would care for ourselves. Care for a creation in order to ensure its purpose in the world has value. Design is not about selling a commodity, or repackaging an idea or concept: it is about providing the means to interact with the world and make our life in it easier and more practical. All that is designed, digital or not, should fulfill a role in somebody's life.

The world's most complex design problems can be reduced to a simple dictum: finding the least harmful and most rewarding way to satisfy a human need. The path to this ultimate objective will involve using technology to unlock the potential of human interaction and learning. An old dictum says that we are always learning. The more we learn about the world, the more we learn about ourselves, and only through empathy and awareness we can overcome the challenges that too often we pose ourselves as a race—challenges like war and poverty, or age and death. The ultimate path to this objective includes unlocking the potential of our own cognitive processes by allowing us to learn constantly by simply interacting. An old dictum says that we are always learning; technology will help us enforce that at last.

Before we challenge mortality, however, we must master the realities that we are currently building in the digital realm, virtual and otherwise. In the 1960s Marshall McLuhan foresaw that the world would be reduced to a global village. We are embedded in a sea of digital systems, where every connection is linked by information and data. We are designing a progressively smarter reality, but the core of our experience is the human. As we design environments by applying smarter and deeper solutions, so we design ourselves. The applications of technology become wider and clearer, challenging cultural and social stasis. In a world progressively troubled by political turmoil and social unrest, technology can be the great unifier, and design the discipline to cross beyond the brink of tolerance.

The world of tomorrow is a promising one, no matter what the present holds. Let us celebrate the differences that bind us by recognizing the premise that we all are different—and yet profoundly similar. In an age where the specter of endless conflict looms over many complex parts of the world, and fundamentalism threatens the last vestiges of empathy, it is essential to realize that which is common between us. Regardless of religion or creed, our canvas of the world is subject to the same common principles of design, perception, and cognition. Different perspectives may have different strokes, but the paint brush is largely the same. These similarities are essential in making us human, empowered by ingenuity to make the lives of those impacted by our practice easier and more fruitful. Technology is by its very definition dehumanizing. Standardization and functional design are an integral part of modern industrial practice. In a global economy, this makes sense, saving costs and reducing time to market. But these metrics are secondary in the face of human variation and creativity, and that is what universal design promotes: a space for discussing the requirements of those groups that often reside at the periphery of the world economy. Regardless of whether groups are challenged by ergonomics, cross-cultural issues, linguistic issues—or simply unable to experience technology in a way that enriches both the larger economy of their countries and the citizens. This is the heart of design. This is the heart of being human.

References

7 Habits of China online shoppers. Accessible at <www.chinainternetwatch.com/17471/online-shopper-habits/> Accessed June 2016.

Aaker, J. L. (2006). Delineating culture. *Journal of Consumer Psychology*, *16*(4), 343−347.

Aaker, J. L., & Lee, A. Y. (2001). "I" seek pleasures and "we" avoid pains: The role of self-regulatory goals in information processing and persuasion. *Journal of Consumer Research*, *28*(1), 33−49.

Aaker, J. L., & Maheswaran, D. (1997). The effect of cultural orientation on persuasion. *Journal of Consumer Research*, *24*(3), 315−328.

Aaker, J. L., & Sengupta, J. (2000). Additivity versus attenuation: The role of culture in the resolution of information incongruity. *Journal of Consumer Psychology*, *9*(2), 67−82.

Ahire, S., et al. (2015). Interaction design for Indian needs lab, IIT Bombay. *Interactions*, *22*, 14−17 . Available at <http://interactions.acm.org/archive/view/september-october-2015/interaction-design-for-indian-needs-lab-iit-bombay>.

Albers-Miller, N. D., & Stafford, M. R. (1999). An international analysis of emotional and rational appeals in services vs goods advertising. *The Journal of Consumer Marketing*, *16*(1), 42.

Ambady, N., & Bharucha, J. (2009). Culture and the brain. *Current Directions in Psychological Science*, *18*(6), 342−346.

Ames, D., & Fiske, S. (2010). Cultural neuroscience. *Asian Journal of Social Psychology*, *13*(2), 72−83.

Andrew, R. (1991). *Strange weather: Culture, science, and technology in the age of limits* (p. 3). London; New York, NY: Verso.

Arce, R. (2011). 7-El escenario costarricense para el empresario web-InterGraphicDESIGNS. *Youtube*. Accessed at <https://www.youtube.com/watch?v=vHdihZ9B47w> .

Arnheim, R. (1974). *Art and visual perception: A psychology of the creative eye*. Los Angeles, CA: University of California Press*Art and visual perception: A psychology of the creative eye*. Los Angeles, CA: University of California Press.

Arnold, D. J., & Quelch, J. A. (1998). New strategies in emerging markets. *Sloan Management Review*, *40*(1), 7−20.

Aronoff, J. (2006). How we recognize angry and happy emotion in people, places, and things. *Cross-Cultural Research*, *40*(1), 83−105.

Ayabe-Kanamura, S., Schicker, I., Laska, M., Hudson, R., Distel, H., Kobayakawa, T., & Saito, S. (1998). Differences in perception of everyday odors: A Japanese-German cross-cultural study. *Chemical Senses*, *23*(1), 31−38.

Bacon, F. (1909−14). *The new Atlantis. Part 2. The Harvard classics* (Vol. IIINew York, NY: P.F. Collier & Son.

Bar, M., & Neta, M. (2006). Humans prefer curved visual objects. *Psychological Science*, *17*(8), 645−648.

Bar, M., Neta, M., & Linz, H. (2006). Very first impressions. *Emotion*, *6*(2), 269−278.

Barboza, D. (January 20, 2014). A popular Chinese social networking app blazes its own path. *The New York Times*. <http://www.nytimes.com/2014/01/21/technology/a-chinese-social-network-blazes-its-own-path.html?_r=2> Viewed 09.06.14.

Barbrook, R., & Cameron, A. *The Californian ideology*. <http://www.imaginaryfutures.net/2007/04/17/the-californian-ideology-2/> Accessed 24.03.13.

Baudel, T., & Beaudouin-Lafon, M. (1993). Charade: Remote control of objects using free-hand gestures. *Communications of the ACM*, *36*(7), 28−35.

Baumeister, R. F., Tice, D. M., & Hutton, D. G. (1989). Self-presentational motivations and personality differences in self-esteem. *Journal of Personality, 57*(2), 547−579.

BayCHI. (2005). *User research strategies: What works, and what does not work.* Retrieved December 15, 2015, from <www.baychi.org/calendar/20051011>.

Beaird, J. (2007). *The principles of beautiful web design.* SitePoint.

Bear, J. H. (2015). Color *symbolism: What different colors mean to us.* About Tech. <http://desktop-pub.about.com/cs/color/a/symbolism.htm> Accessed October 2016.

Belk, R. W. (2000). Wolf brands in sheep's clothings: Global appropriation of the local. In J. Pavitt (Ed.), *Brand New* (pp. 68−69). Princeton, NJ: Princeton University Press.

Bell, D. (1976). *The cultural contradictions of capitalism.* New York, NY: Basic Books.

Berry, J. W. (2005). Acculturation: Living successfully in two cultures. *International Journal of Intercultural Relations, 29,* 697−712.

Beu, A., Honold, P., & Yuan, X. (2000). How to build up an infrastructure for intercultural usability engineering. *The International Journal of Human-Computer Interaction, 12*(3&4), 347−358.

Bieber, M., Englebart, D., Puruta, R., Hitlz, S., Noll, J., Preece, J., et al. (2002). Toward virtual community knowledge evolution. *Journal of Management Information Systems, 18*(4), 11−35.

Bochner, S. (1994). Cross-cultural differences in the self concept: A test of Hofstede's individualism/collectivism distinction. *Journal of Cross-Cultural Psychology, 25*(2), 273−283.

Bordwell, D. (1997). *Narration in the fiction film.* London: Routledge.

Bornstein, M. H. (1973). Color vision and color naming: A psychophysiological hypothesis of cultural difference. *Psychological Bulletin, 80*(1973), 425−445.

Bortoli, M. D., & Maroto, J. (2001). Translating colours in web site localisation. In *Proceedings of the European languages and the implementation of communication and information technologies (Elicit) conference.* University of Paisley.

Bouissac, P. (Ed.), (1998). *Encyclopedia of semiotics* New York, NY: Oxford University Press.

Bovee, C. L., & Arens, W. F. (1989). *Contemporary advertising* (3rd ed.). Irwin: Homewood, IL.

Bradshaw, J. (2007). *Punk: A directory of modern subversive culture.* Lulu.com.

Brewer, M. B., & Gardner, W. L. (1996). Who is this "We"? Levels of collective identity and self-representations. *Journal of Personality and Social Psychology, 71*(1), 83−93.

Briley, D. A., Morris, M. W., & Simonson, I. (2005). Cultural chameleons: Biculturals, conformity motives, and decision making. *Journal of Consumer Psychology, 15*(4), 351−362.

Brockner, J., & Chen, Y. R. (1996). The moderating roles of self-esteem and self-construal in reaction to a threat to self: Evidence from the People's Republic of China and the United States. *Journal of Personality and Social Psychology, 71*(3), 603−615.

Bruner, J. S. (1957). On perceptual readiness. *Psychological Review, 64*(2), 123−152.

Carlsson, C. (2008). *Nowtopia: How pirate programmers, outlaw bicyclists, and vacant-lot gardeners are inventing the future today!.* Stirling: AK Press.

Castells, M. (2007). Communication, power and counter-power in the Network Society. *International Journal of Communication, 1,* 238−266.

Cateora, P. R., Mary, C. G., & John, L. G. (2013). *International marketing* (16th ed.). New York, NY: McGraw-Hill Irwin.

Chaiken, S. (1980). Heuristic versus systematic information processing and the use of source versus message cues in persuasion. *Journal of Personality and Social Psychology, 39*(5), 752−766.

Chartrand, T., & Bargh, J. (1999). The chameleon effect: The perception-behavior link and social interaction. *Journal of Personality and Social Psychology, 76*(6), 893−910.

Chipflip. (2009). *Demoscene theory with Doctor Botz | CHIPFLIP.* <http://chipflip.wordpress.com/2009/11/01/demoscene-theory-with-doctor-botz/> Accessed 17.03.13.

Chiu, L. H. (1972). A cross-cultural comparison of cognitive styles in Chinese and American children. *International Journal of Psychology, 7*(4), 235−242.

Cho, B., Kwon, U., Gentry, J. W., Jun, S., & Kropp, F. (1999). Cultural values reflected in theme and execution: A comparative study of US and Korean television commercials. *Journal of Advertising, 28*(4), 59−73.

Choi, I., & Nisbett, R. E. (1998). Situational salience and cultural differences in the correspondence bias and actor-observer bias. *Personality and Social Psychology Bulletin, 24*(9), 949–960.

Choi, I., Nisbett, R. E., & Norenzayan, A. (1999). Causal attribution across cultures: Variation and universality. *Psychological Bulletin, 125*(1), 47–53.

Chua, H. F., Boland, J. E., & Nisbett, R. E. (2005). Cultural variation in eye movements during scene perception. *Proceedings of the National Academy of Sciences of the United States of America, 102*(35), 12629–12633.

Cohen, D., & Gunz, A. (2002). As seen by the other: Perspectives on the self in the memories and emotional perceptions of Easterners and Westerners. *Psychological Science, 13*(1), 55–59.

Combs, A. W., & Snygg, D. (1959). *Individual Behavior: A Perceptual Approach to Behavior.* New York, NY: Harper.

Connolly, J. (1996). Problems in designing the user interface for systems supporting international human-human communication. In E. Del Galdo, & J. Nielsen (Eds.), *International user interfaces* (pp. 20–40). New York, NY: John Wiley & Sons.

Conway, M. A., Wang, Q., Hanyu, K., & Haque, S. (2005). A cross-cultural investigation of autobiographical memory. *Journal of Cross-Cultural Psychology, 36*(6), 739–749.

Council of Europe Committee of Ministers. (2001). *Resolution ResAP (2001)1 on the introduction of the principles of universal design into the curricula of all occupations working on the built environment.* Adopted by the Committee of Ministers on 15 February 2001, at the 742nd meeting of the Ministers Deputies. <http://www.accessibletourism.org/resources/resap_2007_3e_achieving-full-participation-through-universal-design.pdf>.

Craig, C. S., & Douglas, S. P. (2006). Beyond national culture: Implications of cultural dynamics for consumer research. *International Marketing Review, 23*(3), 322–342.

Curtis, M. E., & Bharucha, J. J. (2009). Memory and musical expectation for tones in cultural context. *Music Perception, 26*(4), 365–375.

Danesi, M., & Perron, P. (1999). *Analyzing cultures: An introduction and handbook.* Bloomington, IN: Indiana University Press.

Davis, D. A. (2000). A revolution in consumption. In D. S. Davis (Ed.), *The consumer revolution in urban China* ((pp. 1–22). Berkeley and Los Angeles, CA: University of California Press.

Davis, D. A., & Sensenbrenner, J. S. (2000). In D. A. Davis (Ed.), *Commercializing childhood: Parental purchases for Shanghai's only child* (pp. 25–53). Berkeley and Los Angeles, CA: University of California Press.

Day, V. & Evers, V. (1999). Questionnaire development for multicultural data collection". In E. del Galdo & G. Prahbu (Eds.), *Proceedings of the international workshop on internationalization of products and systems, Rochester, 20–22 May 1999.*

De Mooij, M. K. (2009). *Global marketing and advertising: Understanding cultural paradoxes.* Newbury Park, CA: Sage.

De Ruyter, K., Van Birgelen, M., & Wetzels, M. (1998). Consumer ethnocentrism in international services marketing. *International Business Review, 7,* 185–202.

Demers, J. (2006). *Steal this music: How intellectual property law affects musical creativity.* London: The University of Georgia Press.

Deregowski, et al. (1972). Pictorial recognition in a remote Ethiopian population. *Perception, 1,* 417–425.

Dray, S., & Mrazek, D. (1996). A day in the life: Studying context across cultures. In E. Del Galdo, & J. Nielsen (Eds.), *International user interfaces* (pp. 242–256). New York, NY: John Wiley & Sons.

Driscoll, K., & Diaz, J. (2009). Endless loop: A brief history of chiptunes. *Transformative Works and Cultures, 2.* http://dox.doi.org/10.3983.

Earley, P. C., & Erez, M. (1997). *The transplanted executive: Why you need to understand how workers in other countries see the world differently.* New York, NY: Oxford University Press.

Eco, U. (1986). *Semiotics and the philosophy of language.* Bloomington, IN: Indiana University Press.

Ekman, P., & Friesen, W. V. (1971). Constants across cultures in the face and emotion. *Journal of Personality and Social Psychology, 17*(2), 124–129.

Ekman, P., Friesen, W. V., & Ellsworth, P. (1972). *Emotion in the human face: Guidelines for research and an integration of findings.* New York, NY: Pergamon Press.

Emmerson, S. (Ed.), (2000). *Music, electronic media, and culture* Aldershot; Burlington: Ashgate.

Engelen, A., & Brettel, M. (2011). Assessing cross-cultural marketing theory and research. *Journal of Business Research, 64*(5), 516–523.

Etzioni, A. (2000). Creating good communities and good societies. *Contemporary Sociology, 29*(1), 188–195.

Evers, V. (1998). Cross-cultural understanding of metaphors in interface design. In C. Ess & F. Sudweeks (Eds.), *Attitudes toward technology and communication, London, 1–3 August 1998.*

Evers, V., & Day, D. (1997). The role of culture in interface acceptance. In S. Howard, J. Hammond, & G. Lindgaard (Eds.), *Human Computer Interaction: INTERACT'97* (pp. 260–267). Sydney: Chapman and Hall.

Evers, V., Kukulska-Hulme, A., & Jones, A. (1999). Cross-cultural understanding of interface design: A cross-cultural analysis of icon recognition. In E. del Galdo, & G. Prahbu (Eds.), *Proceedings of the international workshop on internationalization of products and systems, Rochester, 20–22 May 1999.*

Feldwick, P. (1996). What is your brand equity anyway, and how do you measure it? *Journal of the Market Research Society, 38*(2), 85–104.

Fernandes, T. (1995). *Global interface design.* San Diego, CA: Academic Press.

Frijda, N. H. (1986). *The emotions.* London: Cambridge University Press.

Frith, S. (1998). *Performing rites: On the value of popular music.* London: Harvard University Press.

Fry, P. S., & Ghosh, R. (1980). Attribution of success and failure: Comparisons of cultural differences between Asian and Caucasian children. *Journal of Cross-Cultural Psychology, 11*(3), 343–346.

Fryberg, S. A., & Markus, H. R. (2003). On being American Indian: Current and possible selves. *Self and Identity, 2*(4), 325–344.

Gage, J. (1993). *Color and culture: Practice and meaning from antiquity to abstraction.* Boston, MA: Bulfinch Press.

del Galdo, E. M. (1996). Culture and design. In E. Del Galdo, & J. Nielsen (Eds.), *International user interfaces.* New York, NY: John Wiley & Sons.

Ghosh, S. & Joshi, A. (2013). Exploration of multimodal input interaction based on goals. In *APCHI '13 Proceedings of the 11th Asia Pacific conference on computer human interaction* (pp. 83–92).

Goodnow, J. J., & Levine, R. A. (1973). "The grammar of action": Sequence and syntax in children's copying. *Cognitive Psychology, 1973*(4), 82–98.

Goriunova, O. (2012). *Art platforms and cultural production on the Internet, . Routledge research in cultural and media studies* (Vol. 35New York, NY: Routledge.

Greenwald, A. G., & Banaji, M. R. (1995). Implicit social cognition: Attitudes, self-esteem, and stereotypes. *Psychological Reviews, 102*, 4–27.

Gutchess, A. H., Welsh, R. C., Boduroğlu, A., & Park, D. C. (2006). Cultural differences in neural function associated with object processing. *Cognitive, Affective, & Behavioral Neuroscience, 6*(2), 102–109.

Hall, E. T. (1976). *Beyond culture.* Anchor: Oxford.

Hall, E. T., & Hall, M. R. (1990). *Understanding cultural differences.* Yarmouth, ME: Intercultural Press.

Hall, S., & Jefferson, T. (Eds.), (1976). *Resistance through rituals: Youth subcultures in post-war Britain* London: Routledge.

Han, S. P., & Shavitt, S. (1994). Persuasion and culture: Advertising appeals in individualistic and collectivistic societies. *Journal of Experimental Social Psychology, 30*, 326–350.

Hardin, C. L. (1989). Could white be green? *Mind, 390*, 285–288.

Hardin, C. L. (1993). *Color for philosophers: Unweaving the rainbow (expanded edition).* Hackett: Indianapolis, IN.

Hartson, H. R., Castillo, J. C., Kelso, J., Kamler, J., & Neale, W. C. (1996). Remote evaluation: The network as an extension of the usability laboratory. In *Proceedings of the conference on human factors in computing systems* (pp. 228–235).

Heine, S. J., Lehman, D. R., Markus, H. R., & Kitayama, S. (1999). Is there a universal need for positive self-regard? *Psychological Review, 106*(4), 766–794.

Hertzum, M., & Jacobsen, N. E. (2001). The evaluator effect: A chilling fact about usability evaluation methods. *International Journal of Human-Computer Interactions, 13*(4), 421–443.

Hirschman, E. C. (1986). The effect of verbal and pictorial advertising stimuli in aesthetic, utilitarian and familiarity perceptions. *Journal of Advertising, 15*(2), 27–34.

Ho, D. Y. (1976). On the concept of face. *American Journal of Sociology, 81*(4–6), 867–884.

Hofstede, G. (1980). *Culture's consequences: International differences in work-related values*. Beverly Hills, CA: Sage Publications.

Hofstede, G. (1991). *Cultures and organizations*. New York, NY: McGraw-Hill.

Hofstede, G. (1997). *Cultures and organizations: Software of the mind, intercultural cooperation and its importance for survival*. New York, NY: McGraw-Hill.

Hofstede, G. (2001). *Culture's consequences: Comparing values, behaviors, institutions, and organizations across nations*. Newbury Park, CA: Sage.

Hoft, N. (1996). Developing a culture model. In E. Del Galdo, & J. Nielsen (Eds.), *International user interfaces* (pp. 41–73). New York, NY: John Wiley & Sons.

Hofstede, G., & Bond, M. H. (1984). Hofstede's cultural dimensions: An independent validation using Rokeach's Value Survey. *Journal of Cross-Cultural Psychology, 15*(4), 417–433.

Hofstede, G., & Bond, M. H. (1988). The Confucius connection: From cultural roots to economic growth. *Organizational Dynamics, 16*(4), 4–21.

Holmes, T. (2008). *Electronic and experimental music: Technology, music, and culture* (3rd ed.). New York, NY: Routledge.

Holyoak, K. J., & Gordon, P. C. (1983). Social reference points. *Journal of Personality and Social Psychology, 44*(5), 881–887.

Honold, P. (2000). Culture and context: An empirical study for the development of a framework for the elicitation of cultural influence in product usage. *International Journal of Human-Computer Interaction, 12*((3 & 4), 327–345.

Howlett, V. (1996). *Visual interface design for Windows*. New York, NY: Wiley Computer Publishing, John Wiley & Sons, Inc.

Hsu, F. L. (1981). *American and Chinese: Passage to differences*. Honolulu, HW: University of Hawaii Press.

Huo, Y. R., & Randall, D. (1991). Exploring subcultural differences in Hofstede's Value Survey: The case of the Chinese. *Asia Pacific Journal of Management, 8*(2), 159–173.

Iser, W. (2000). The reading process: A phenomenological approach. In N. Wood (Ed.), *Modern criticism and theory: A reader* (pp. 188–205). Harlow: Pearson Education.

ISO (2001). *ISO/IEC 9126-Software engineering—Product quality—Part 1: Quality model*. Geneva: International Organization for Standardization.

ISO 9241-210:2010—*Ergonomics of human-system interaction—Part 210: Human-centred design for interactive systems*. <http://www.iso.org/iso/catalogue_detail.htm?csnumber=52075> Viewed 09.06.14.

Ito, M., & Nakakoji, K. (1996). Impact of culture on user interface design. In E. Del Galdo, & J. Nielsen (Eds.), *International user interfaces* (pp. 105–126). New York, NY: John Wiley & Sons.

Izard, C. E. (1971). *The face of emotion*. New York, NY: Appleton-Century-Crofts.

Ji, L. J., Peng, K., & Nisbett, R. E. (2000). Culture, control, and perception of relationships in the environment. *Journal of Personality and Social Psychology, 78*(5), 943–955.

Ji, L. J., Zhang, Z., & Nisbett, R. E. (2004). Is it culture, or is it language? Examination of language effects in cross-cultural research on categorization. *Journal of Personality and Social Psychology, 87*(1), 57–65.

Kastanakis, M. N., & Balabanis, G. (2012). Between the mass and the class: Antecedents of the "bandwagon" luxury consumption behavior. *Journal of Business Research, 65*(10), 1399–1407.

Kim, H., & Markus, H. R. (1999). Deviance or uniqueness, harmony or conformity? A cultural analysis. *Journal of Personality and Social Psychology, 77*(4), 785–800.

Kitayama, S. (1992). Some thoughts on the cognitive-psychodynamic self from a cultural perspective. *Psychological Inquiry, 3*(1), 41–44.

Kitayama, S., Duffy, S., Kawamura, T., & Larsen, J. T. (2003). Perceiving an object and its context in different cultures: A cultural look at new look. *Psychological Science, 14*(3), 201–206.

Kitayama, S., Markus, H. R., Matsumoto, H., & Norasakkunkit, V. (1997). Individual and collective processes in the construction of the self: Self-enhancement in the United States and self-criticism in Japan. *Journal of Personality and Social Psychology, 72*(6), 1245–1267.

Kitayama, S., & Uchida, Y. (2003). Explicit self-criticism and implicit self-regard: Evaluating self and friend in two cultures. *Journal of Experimental Social Psychology, 39*(5), 476–482.

Kline, J. M. (2005). *Ethics for international business: Decision making in a global political economy.* London: Routledge.

Knapp, M. L., & Hall, J. A. (2009). *Nonverbal communication in human interaction* (7th ed.). Boston, MA: Wadsworth.

Kotler, P., & Armstrong, G. (1999). *Principles of marketing* (8th ed.). Upper Saddle River, NJ: Prentice Hall.

Kroeber, A. L., & Kluckhohn, C. (1952). *Culture: A critical review of concepts and definitions. Peabody museum of American archeology and ethnology* (Vol. 47Harvard University.

Kroeber, A. L., & Kluckhohn, C. (1953). *Culture: A critical review of concepts and definitions* (p. 3). New York, NY: Vintage.

Lalwani, A. K., Johnson, T., & Shavitt, S. (2006). What is the relation between cultural orientation and socially desirable responding? *Journal of Personality and Social Psychology, 90*(1), 165–178.

Lee, F., Hallahan, M., & Herzog, T. (1996). Explaining real-life events: How culture and domain shape attributions. *Personality and Social Psychology Bulletin, 7*(22), 732–741.

Lee, R. M., Noh, C.-Y., Yoo, H., & Doh, H.-S. (2007). The psychology of diaspora experiences: Intergroup contact, perceived discrimination, and the ethnic identity of Koreans in China. *Cultural Diversity and Ethnic Minority Psychology, 13*(2), 115–124.

Levin, D. T., Momen, N., Drivdahl, S. B., & Simons, D. J. (2000). Change blindness blindness: The metacognitive error of overestimating change-detection ability. *Visual Cognition, 7*(1–3), 397–412.

Levy, B., & Langer, E. (1994). Aging free from negative stereotypes: Successful memory in China among the American deaf. *Journal of Personality and Social Psychology, 66*(6), 989–997.

Lim, E. A. C., & Ang, S. H. (2008). Hedonic vs. utilitarian consumption: A cross-cultural perspective based on cultural conditioning. *Journal of Business Research, 61*(3), 225–232.

Luo, Y. (2000). *Partnering with Chinese firms: Lessons for international managers.* Aldershot, Hants, England; Burlington, VT: Ashgate.

Luong, T., Lok, J., Lok, S., & Driscoll, K. (1995). *Internationalization: Developing software for global markets.* New York, NY: John Wiley & Sons.

Lysloff, R. T. A., & Gay, L. C. (Eds.), (2003). Music and technoculture. *Music/culture* Middletown, CT: Wesleyan University Press.

Macrae, N. C., & Bodehausen, G. V. (2001). Social cognition: Categorical person perception. *British Journal of Psychology, 92*, 239–255.

Maddux, W. W., & Yuki, M. (2006). The "ripple effect": Cultural differences in perceptions of the consequences of events. *Personality and Social Psychology Bulletin, 32*(5), 669–683.

Marcus, A. (1996). Icon and symbol design issues for graphical user interfaces. In E. Del Galdo, & J. Nielsen (Eds.), *International user interfaces* (pp. 257–270). New York, NY: John Wiley & Sons.

Marcus, A. (2006). Culture: Wanted? Alive or dead? *Journal of Usability Studies, 1*(2), 62–63.

Marcus, A., & Gould, E. M. (2000). Cultural dimensions and global web user-interface design. *Interactions, 7*, 32–46.

Markus, H. R., & Kitayama, S. (1991). Culture and the self: Implications for cognition, emotion, and motivation. *Psychological Review, 98*(2), 224–253.

Markus, H. R., & Kitayama, S. (2010). Cultures and selves. *Perspectives on Psychological Science, 5*(4), 420–430.

Markus, H. R., Kitayama, S., & Heiman, R. J. (1996). Culture and "basic" psychological principles. In E. Higgins, & A. W. Kruglanski (Eds.), *Social psychology: Handbook of basic principles* (pp. 857–913). New York, NY: Guilford Press.

Markus, H. R., Mullally, P. R., & Kitayama, S. (1997). Selfways: Diversity in modes of cultural participation. In U. Neisser, & D. Jopling (Eds.), *The conceptual self in context: Culture, experience, self-understanding* (pp. 13−61). New York, NY: Cambridge University Press.

Marsden, N. (2014). Doing UX: Doing gender. *User Experience Magazine, 14*(1). Retrieved from http://uxpamagazine.org/doing-ux/.

Masuda, T., Ellsworth, P. C., Mesquita, B., Leu, J., Tanida, S., & Van de Veerdonk, E. (2008). Placing the face in context: Cultural differences in the perception of facial emotion. *Journal of Personality and Social Psychology, 94*(3), 365−381.

Masuda, T., Gonzalez, R., Kwan, L., & Nisbett, R. E. (2008). Culture and aesthetic preference: Comparing the attention to context of East Asians and Americans. *Personality and Social Psychology Bulletin, 34*(9), 1260−1275.

Masuda, T., & Nisbett, R. E. (2001). Attending holistically versus analytically: Comparing the context sensitivity of Japanese and Americans. *Journal of Personality and Social Psychology, 81*(5), 922−934.

Matsumoto, D. (1992). American-Japanese cultural differences in the recognition of universal facial expressions. *Journal of Cross-Cultural Psychology, 23*(1), 72−84.

Matsumoto, D. (1999). Culture and self: An empirical assessment of Markus and Kitayama's theory of independent and interdependent self-construals. *Asian Journal of Social Psychology, 2*(3), 289−310.

Matsumoto, D. (2002). Methodological requirements to test a possible in-group advantage in judging emotions across cultures: Comment on Elfenbein and Ambady (2002) and evidence. *Psychological Bulletin, 128*(2), 236−242.

Mazzarella, W. (2003). *Shoveling smoke: Advertising and globalization in contemporary India.* Durham, NC: Duke University Press.

McCarthy, J., & Wright, P. (2004). *Technology as experience.* Cambridge, MA: The MIT Press.

McClure, S. M., Li, J., Tomlin, D., Cypert, K. S., Montague, L. M., & Montague, P. R. (2004). Neural correlates of behavioral preference for culturally familiar drink. *Neuron, 44*(2), 379−387.

McDowell, J. (1994). *Mind and world.* Cambridge, MA: Harvard University Press.

McLaren, M. (2003). *8-Bit Punk.* <http://www.wired.com/wired/archive/11.11/mclaren_pr.html> Accessed 10.03.13.

Medin, D. L., Ross, B. H., & Markman, A. B. (2005). *Cognitive psychology.* (4th ed.). New York, NY: Wiley.

Miller, J. G., & Bersoff, D. M. (1994). Cultural influences on the moral status of reciprocity and the discounting of endogenous motivation. *Personality and Social Psychology Bulletin, 20*(5), 592−602. Available from http://dx.doi.org/10.1177/0146167294205015.

Mitamura, T., & Nyberg, E. (1995). Controlled English for knowledge-based MT: Experience with the KANT system. In *Proceedings of TMI-95.*

Morgan, L. H. (1987). Ethnical periods. In H. Applebaum (Ed.), *Perspectives in cultural anthropology* (pp. 49−60). New York, NY: State University of New York Press.

Morris, M. W., & Peng, K. (1994). Culture and cause: American and Chinese attributions for social and physical events. *Journal of Personality and Social Psychology, 67*(6), 949−971.

Nagashima, A. (1977). A comparative 'made in' product image survey among Japanese businessmen. *Journal of Marketing, 41,* 95−100.

Nico, H. F. (1986). *The emotions.* Cambridge, MA: Cambridge University Press.

Nielsen, J. (1994). Heuristic evaluation. In J. Nielsen, & R. L. Mack (Eds.), *Usability inspection methods.* New York, NY: John Wiley & Sons.

Nielsen, J. (1996). International usability engineering. In E. Del Galdo, & J. Nielsen (Eds.), *International user interfaces.* New York, NY: John Wiley & Sons.

Nielsen, J. (1999). *Designing web usability: The practice of simplicity.* Thousand Oaks, CA: New Riders Publishing.

Nielsen, J., & Pernice, K. (2010). *Eyetracking web usability.* Thousand Oaks, CA: New Riders.

Nielsen, L. (2004). *Engaging personas and narrative scenarios.* Copenhagen: Samfundslitteratur.

Nielsen, L. (2008). Different cultures' perception of personas descriptions. In *Cultural usability and human work interaction design—Techniques that connects. Proceedings from NordiCHI 2008 Workshop Sunday October 19* (pp. 43−46).

Nielsen, L. (2010). *Personas in cross-cultural projects, . Human work interaction design: Usability in social, cultural and organizational contexts* (316, pp. 76−82). Hamburg: Springer.

Nisbett, R. E., & Masuda, T. (2003). Culture and point of view. *Proceedings of the National Academy of Sciences of the United States of America, 100*(19), 11163−11175.

Nisbett, R. E., Peng, K., Choi, I., & Norenzayan, A. (2001). Culture and systems of thought: Holistic versus analytic cognition. *Psychological Review, 108*(2), 291−310.

Norenzayan, A., & Nisbett, R. E. (2000). Culture and causal cognition. *Current Directions in Psychological Science, 9*(4), 132−135.

Norenzayan, A., Smith, E. E., Kim, B. J., & Nisbett, R. E. (2002). Cultural preferences for formal versus intuitive reasoning. *Cognitive Science, 26*(5), 653−684.

Norman, D. A. (2010). Natural user interfaces are not natural. *Interactions, 17*(3), 6−10.

Norman, D. A. (2013). *The design of everyday things.* New York, NY: Basic Books.

Oh, H. J., & Ogawa, K. (2014). A proposal of measurement levels of acculturation among international students in Japan. *Communications in Computer and Information Science, 435*(2), 123−127.

O'Neill, S. (2008). *Interactive media: The semiotics of embodied interaction.* London: Springer.

Open Letter to Malcolm McLaren by gwEm. <http://micromusic.net/public_letter_gwEm.html> Accessed 31.03.13.

Oyserman, D. (2006). High power, low power, and equality: Culture beyond individualism and collectivism. *Journal of Consumer Psychology, 16*(4), 352−356.

Peng, K., & Nisbett, R. E. (1999). Culture, dialectics, and reasoning about contradiction. *American Psychologist, 54*(9), 741−754.

Pettersson, R. (2002). *Information design: An introduction.* Amsterdam: John Benjamins Publishing.

Petty, R. E., & Cacioppo, J. T. (1986). The elaboration likelihood model of persuasion. *Advances in Experimental Social Psychology, 19*(1), 123−205.

Pollay, R. W., Tse, D. K., & Wang, Z. (1990). Advertising, propaganda, and value change in economic development: The new cultural revolution in China and attitudes toward advertising. *Journal of Business Research, 20*(2), 83−95.

Pruitt, J., & Adlin, T. (2006). *The persona lifecycle: Keeping people in mind through-out product design.* San Francisco, CA: Morgan Kaufmann.

Rainie, L., & Wellman, B. (2012). *Networked: The new social operating system.* Cambridge, MA: MIT Press.

Reber, R., Schwarz, N., & Winkielman, P. (2004). Processing fluency and aesthetic pleasure: Is beauty in the perceiver's processing experience? *Personality and Social Psychology Review, 8*(4), 364−382.

Reynolds, S. (2012). *Energy flash a journey through rave music and dance culture.* New York, NY: Soft Skull Press.

Robertson, C. J., & Hoffman, J. J. (2000). How different are we? An investigation of Confucian values in the US. *Journal of Managerial Issues, 12*(1), 34−47.

Rohrer, K. (2012). Symbolism of color: Using *color for meaning.* The Incredible Art Department, Web 24.10.12.

Ross, A. (1991). Strange weather: Culture, science, and technology in the age of limits. *The Haymarket Series.* London; New York, NY: Verso.

Ross, L. (1977). The "false consensus effect": An egocentric bias in social perception and attribution processes. *Journal of Experimental Social Psychology, 13*(3), 279−301.

Ross, M., Xun, W. Q., & Wilson, A. E. (2002). Language and the bicultural self. *Personality and Social Psychology Bulletin, 28*(8), 1040−1050.

Rothenbuhler, E. W. (1998). *Ritual communication: From everyday conversation to mediated ceremony.* Thousand Oaks: Sage Publications.

Roxanne, L., & Paula, A. (2012). Article No. 5, *Proceedings of the 19th conference on Pattern Languages of Programs (PLoP)*.

Rubin, J. (1994). *Handbook of usability testing*. New York, NY: John Wiley & Sons.

Rugman, A. M., & Collinson, S. (2009). *International business*. London: Prentice Hall.

Sanjek, D. (1994). Don't have to DJ no more: Sampling and the autonomous creator. In M. Woodmansee, & P. Jansi (Eds.), The Construction of Authorship: Textual Appropriation in *Law* and Literature. New York, NY: Duke University Press.

Schmitt, D.A., International Programming for Microsoft Windows, Microsoft Press, April 2000.

Schmitt, D. P., & Allik, J. (2005). Simultaneous administration of the Rosenberg Self-Esteem Scale in 53 nations: Exploring the universal and culture-specific features of global. *Journal of Personality and Social Psychology*, 89(4), 623−642.

Schutz, A., & Luckmann, T. (1973). *The structures of the life-world*. DeKalb, IL: Northern University.

Schwartz, S. H. (1992). Universals in the content and structure of values: Theoretical advances and empirical tests in 20 countriesIn M. Zanna (Ed.), *Advances in experimental social psychology* (Vol. 25, pp. 1−65). San Diego, CA: Academic Press.

Sears, A. J., & Jacko, A. (Eds.), (2009). *Human-computer interaction: Design issues, solutions, and applications* Boca Raton, FL: CRC Press, (2012 in text).

Sebastian Deterding, R. Khaled, L. E., & Nacke, D. D. Gamification: Toward a definition. In *CHI 2011, May 7−12, 2011, Vancouver, BC, Canada*. <http://gamification-research.org/wp-content/uploads/2011/04/02-Deterding-Khaled-Nacke-Dixon.pdf> Accessed October 2016.

Sedikides, C., Gaertner, L., & Toguchi, Y. (2003). Pancultural self-enhancement. *Journal of Personality and Social Psychology*, 84(1), 60−79.

Segall, M. H., Campbell, D. T., & Herskovits, M. J. (1963). Cultural differences in the perception of geometric illusions. *Science*, 139(3556), 769−771.

Segall, M. H., Campbell, D. T., & Herskovits, M. J. (1966). *The influence of culture on visual perception*. Oxford: Bobbs-Merrill.

Sen, S., Burmeister, M., & Ghosh, D. (2004). Meta-analysis of the association between a serotonin transporter promoter polymorphism (5-HTTLPR) and anxiety-related personality traits. *American Journal of Medical Genetics Part B: Neuropsychiatric Genetics*, 127(1), 85−89.

Shao, A. T., & Herbig, P. (1994). Marketing implications of China's 'little emperors.' (China's one-child policy). *Review of Business*, 16(1).

Shavitt, S., Lee, A., & Johnson, T. P. (2008). Cross-cultural consumer psychology. In C. Haugtvedt, P. Herr, & F. Kardes (Eds.), *Handbook of consumer psychology* (pp. 1103−1131). Mahwah, NJ: Erlbaum.

Shiraev, E., & Levy, D. (2007). *Cross-cultural psychology* (3rd ed.). Boston, MA: Allen & Bacon.

Shneiderman, B. (1998). *Designing the user interface* (3rd ed.). Addison Wesley Inc.

Shunmuga Krishnan, S., & Sitaraman, R. K. (2012). *Video stream quality impacts viewer behavior: Inferring causality using quasi-experimental designs. Proceedings of the 2012 ACM conference on Internet measurement conference* (pp. 211−224). New York, NY: IMC.

Simonson, I., Carmon, Z., Dhar, R., & Drolet, A. (2001). Consumer research: In search of identity. *Annual Review of Psychology*, 52(1), 249.

Singelis, T. M. (1994). The measurement of independent and interdependent self-construals. *Personality and Social Psychology Bulletin*, 20(5), 580−591.

Smith, A., & Yetim, F. (2004). Editorial: Global human−computer systems: Cultural determinants of usability. *Interacting With Computers*, 16, 1−5.

Smith, A., Dunckley, L., French, T., Minocha, S., & Chang, Y. (2004). Process model for developing usable cross-cultural websites. *Interacting With Computers*, 16, 63−91.

Smith, P. B. (2004). Acquiescent response bias as an aspect of cultural communication style. *Journal of Cross-Cultural Psychology*, 35(1), 50−61.

Smith, P. B., & Fischer, R. (2008). Acquiescence, extreme response bias and culture: A multilevel analysis. In F. J. van de Vijver, D. A. van Hemert, & Y. H. Poortinga (Eds.), *Multilevel analysis of individuals and cultures* (pp. 285−314). London: Erlbaum.

Snygg, D., & Combs, A. (1959). *Individual behavior: A perceptual approach to behavior* (2nd ed.). New York, NY: Harper.

Soares, A. M., Farhangmehr, M., & Shoham, A. (2006). Hofstede's dimensions of culture in international marketing studies. *Journal of Business Research, 60*(3), 277–284.

Sondergaard, M. (1994). Hofstede's consequences: A study of reviews, citations and replications. *Organization Studies, 15*(3), 447–456.

de Souza, C. S. (2005). *The semiotic engineering of human-computer interaction. Acting With Technology.* Cambridge, MA: MIT Press.

Sparke, P. (2013). *An introduction to design and culture: 1900 to the present.* London: Routledge.

Staines, G. M. (2012). *Universal design: A practical guide to creating and recreating interiors of academic libraries for teaching, learning and research. Chandos Information Professional Series.* Oxford: Chandos Publishers.

Steele, C. M. (1988). The psychology of self-affirmation: Sustaining the integrity of the selfIn L. Berkowitz (Ed.), *Advances in experimental social psychology* (Vol. 21, pp. 261–302). San Diego, CA: Academic Press.

Stricker, L. J. (1963). Acquiescence and social desirability response styles, item characteristics, and conformity. *Psychological Reports, 12*(2), 319–341.

Sturrock, J. (1986). *Structuralism* (p. 89). London: Paladin.

Suinn, R. M., Ahuna, C., & Gillian, K. (1992). The Suinn-Lew Asian Self-Identity Acculturation Scale: Concurrent and factorial validation. *Educational and Psychological Measurement, 52*(4), 1041–1046.

Sung, Y., & Tinkham, S. F. (2005). Brand personality structures in the United States and Korea: Common and culture-specific factors. *Journal of Consumer Psychology, 15*(4), 334–350.

Swidler, A. (1986). Culture in action: Symbols and strategies. *American Sociological Review, 51*(2), 273–286.

Takahashi, T. (2010). *Audience studies: A Japanese perspective.* London: Taylor & Francis.

Tang, Y., Zhang, W., Chen, K., Feng, S., Ji, Y., Shen, J., ... Liu, Y. (2006). Arithmetic processing in the brain shaped by cultures. *Proceedings of the National Academy of Sciences of the United States of America, 103*(28), 10775–10780.

Taylor, D. (1992). *Global software: Developing applications for the international market.* New York, NY: Springer-Verlag.

Taylor, S. E., & Brown, J. D. (1988). Illusion and well-being: A social psychological perspective on mental health. *Psychological Bulletin, 103*(2), 193–210.

Tractinsky, N. (1997). Aesthetics and apparent usability: Empirically assessing cultural and methodological issues. In: *Proceedings of the conference on human factors in computing systems* (pp. 115–122).

Triandis, H. C. (1989). The self and social behavior in differing cultural contexts. *Psychological Review, 96*(3), 506–520.

Triandis, H. C. (2001). Individualism-collectivism and personality. *Journal of Personality, 69*(6), 907–924.

Triandis, H. C., & Gelfand, M. J. (1998). Converging measurement of horizontal and vertical individualism and collectivism. *Journal of Personality and Social Psychology, 74*(1), 118–128.

Triandis, H. C., Kashima, Y., Shimada, E., & Villareal, M. (1986). Acculturation indices as a means of confirming cultural differences. *International Journal of Psychology, 21*, 43–70.

Tse, D. K., Belk, R. W., & Zhou, N. (1989). Becoming a consumer society: A longitudinal and cross-cultural content analysis of print ads from Hong Kong, the People's Republic of China, and Taiwan. *Journal of Consumer Research, 15*(4), 457–472.

Tylor, E. B. (1871). *Primitive culture: Researches into the development of mythology, philosophy, religion, art, and custom* (2 VolsLondon: John Murray.

Tylor, E. B. (2010). *Primitive culture: Researches into the development of mythology, philosophy, religion, art, and custom.* Cambridge: Cambridge University Press.

Uren, E., Howard, R., & Preinotti, T. (1993). *Software internationalization and localization: An introduction.* New York, NY: Van Nostrand Reinhold.

UsabilityFirst. *Glossary » screen real estate.* Colorado: Foraker Labs of Boulder. <http://www.usabilityfirst.com/glossary/screen-real-estate/> Viewed 09.06.14.

Varela, F. J., Thompson, E., & Rosch, E. (1999). *The embodied mind: Cognitive science and human experience.* Cambridge, MA: MIT Press.

Vaughn, L. (2010). *Psychology and culture: Thinking, feeling and behaving in a global context*. New York, NY: Psychology Press.

Verdery, K., & Humphrey, C. (2004). *Property in question: Value transformation in the global economy. Wenner-Gren International Symposium Series* (English ed.). Oxford, New York, NY: Berg.

Vohs, K. D., & Heatherton, T. F. (2001). Self-esteem and threats to self: Implications for self-construals and interpersonal perceptions. *Journal of Personality and Social Psychology, 81*(6), 1103–1118.

Wang, J. (2000). *Foreign advertising in China: Becoming global, becoming local* (1st ed.). Ames, IA: Iowa State University Press.

Wang, Y., Burke, M., & Kraut, R. (2013). Gender, topic, and audience response: An analysis of user-generated content on Facebook. In *CHI '13 Proceedings of the SIGCHI conference on human factors in computing systems* (pp. 31–34). Association for Computing Machinery (United States), Special Interest Group on Computer and Human Interaction.

Weiner, I., Healy, A. F., & Proctor, R. W. (2003). *Handbook of psychology: Experimental psychology*. New York, NY: Wiley.

Wenger, E. (1998). *Communities of practice: Learning, meaning, and identity*. New York, NY: Cambridge University Press.

Whorf, B. L. (1956). *Language, thought, and reality*. Cambridge, MA: MIT Press.

Witkin, H. A., & Goodenough, D. R. (1981). *Cognitive styles: Essence and origins*. New York, NY: International Universities Press.

Witkin, H. A., Lewis, H. B., Hertzman, M., Machover, K., Meissner, P. B., & Karp, S. A. (1954). *Personality through perception*. New York, NY: Harper.

Wong, N. Y., & Ahuvia, A. C. (1998). Personal taste and family face: Luxury consumption in Confucian and Western Societies. *Psychology and Marketing, 15*(5), 423–441.

Wright, M. (1998). *Retrospective-Karsten Obarski*. <http://www.textfiles.com/artscene/music/information/karstenobarski.html> Accessed 24.03.13.

Wu, S., & Keysar, B. (2007). The effect of culture on perspective taking. *Psychological Science, 18*(7), 600–606.

Yamaguchi, S. (1994). Empirical evidence on collectivism among the Japanese. In U. Kim, H. C. Triandis, C. Kagitcibasi, S. C. Choi, & G. Yoon (Eds.), *Individualism and collectivism: Theory, method and applications* (pp. 175–188). Newbury Park, CA: Sage.

Yan, Y. (2000). Of Hamburger and social space: Consuming McDonald's in Beijing. In D. S. Davis (Ed.), *The Consumer Revolution in Urban China* (pp. 171–200). Berkeley and Los Angeles, CA: University of California Press.

Yang, K. (1981). Social orientation and individual modernity among Chinese students in Taiwan. *Journal of Social Psychology, 113*(2), 159–170.

Yeo, W. A. (1998). Cultural effects in usability assessment. In *Proceedings of the conference on human factors in computing systems* (pp. 74–75).

Yeo, W. A. (2001). Global-software development life cycle: An exploratory study. In *Proceedings of the conference on human factors in computing systems* (pp. 104–111).

Zajonc, R. B. (1984). On the primacy of affect. *American Psychologist, 39*(2), 117–123.

Zeithaml, V. A., Bitner, M. J., & Gremler, D. D. (2002). *Services marketing*. New York, NY: McGraw-Hill.

Zeldman, J. The puzzle of Japanese Web Design. New York, NY: zeldman.com. <http://www.zeldman.com/2010/07/25/the-puzzle-of-japanese-web-design/> Viewed 09.06.14.

Zhang, J., Beatty, S. E., & Walsh, G. (2008). Review and future directions of cross-cultural consumer services research. *Journal of Business Research, 61*(3), 211–224.

Zhang, Y., & Gelb, B. D. (1996). Matching advertising appeals to culture: The influence of products' use conditions. *Journal of Advertising, 25*(3), 29–46.

Zhang, Y., & Neelankavil, J. P. (1997). The influence of culture on advertising effectiveness in China and the USA: A cross-cultural study. *European Journal of Marketing, 31*(1), 134–149.

Index

Note: Page numbers followed by "*b*," "*f*," and "*t*" refer to boxes, figures, and tables, respectively.

Printed in the United States
By Bookmasters